ENGLISH CULTURE

ENGLISH CULTURE

FROM THE EIGHTEENTH
CENTURY TO THE PRESENT

JEREMY BLACK

AMBERLEY

For Charles Saumarez Smith

First published 2024

Amberley Publishing
The Hill, Stroud
Gloucestershire, GL5 4EP

www.amberley-books.com

Copyright © Jeremy Black, 2024

The right of Jeremy Black to be identified as
the Author of this work has been asserted in
accordance with the Copyright, Designs and
Patents Act 1988.

ISBN 978 1 3981 1849 2 (hardback)
ISBN 978 1 3981 1850 8 (ebook)

All rights reserved. No part of this book may
be reprinted or reproduced or utilised in any
form or by any electronic, mechanical or other
means, now known or hereafter invented,
including photocopying and recording, or in any
information storage or retrieval system, without
the permission in writing from the Publishers.

British Library Cataloguing in Publication Data.
A catalogue record for this book is available
from the British Library.

1 2 3 4 5 6 7 8 9 10

Typesetting by SJmagic DESIGN SERVICES, India.
Printed in the UK.

CONTENTS

Preface: The Importance of Culture	7
1 Background: 1500-1700	17
2 Eighteenth Century: Spheres of Patronage	41
3 Eighteenth Century: Sites and Styles	70
4 Eighteenth Century: Xenophobia versus Cosmopolitanism	101
5 Nineteenth Century: Spheres of Patronage	118
6 Nineteenth Century: Sites and Styles	131
7 Nineteenth Century: The Culture of Empire?	162
8 1900 to the Present: Spheres of Patronage	169
9 1900 to the Present: Sites and Styles	198
10 1900 to the Present: 'National, American, Europe, or What?'	243
Envoi	267
Further Reading	272
Endnotes	274

Preface

THE IMPORTANCE OF CULTURE

Fielding sat back in the pew and peered up at the roof: 'You can still see remnants of the original hammerbeam roof. What an architectural feat that was. Look what the English Medieval carpenter achieved with the tools at his disposal.'

'Yeah, I just see an old roof,' Low said.[1]

Culture. What is it for you? Paintings or television? The National Gallery or Waterstones? There is of course no one answer, no agreement. But what is clear is that culture, however defined, plays a key role as a form and content of identity, while it is affected by changes in the patterns and pressures of identification. Far from being just interesting or enjoyable, individual or communal, bracing or disturbing, culture becomes a means to express value and encode values. As such, it brings together the varied spheres of patronage within and for which artistic works are produced, and by which culture is financed

English Culture

and experienced. These are the sites and styles of cultural activity.

'High' and 'Low' life, however defined, could be brought together in English culture. Indeed, to do so was seen as a classic aspect of the openness on which the English prided themselves; it was a process eased by the extent to which the common people shared the same language with social élites – lay and ecclesiastical – not employing 'foreign' languages, as had been the case earlier and as was the case in many Continental countries. The appearance of the Bible in English, moreover, gave the language moral authority and literary resonance.

Very differently, the use of English was advanced by John Gay's *The Beggar's Opera* (1728), a popular ballad opera that in part was a satire on the dominance of the London musical stage by Italian opera. The productions meshed literature and music, high and low culture, the use of old English tunes, the Classical trope of the choice of Hercules, and satire on the government. This was so powerful a combination of cultural elements that it led to Kurt Weill and Bertolt Brecht's *Threepenny Opera* 200 years later.

And so for humour. Thus, in 1821, Pierre Egan launched *Life in London: Or, The Day and Night Scenes of Jerry Hawthorn, Esq and his elegant friend Corinthian Tom ... in their Rambles and Sprees through the Metropolis*, a shilling monthly that benefited from illustrations by George Cruickshank and to which George IV accepted the dedication. *Life in London* provided alternative scenes of high and low life with lively dialogue, and it inspired imitations as well as prints, decorations on handkerchiefs and tea-trays, and 'Tom and Jerry' fashions. The play *Tom or Jerry: or Life in London* (1821) enjoyed great success. Similarly, songs could span social and aesthetic categories.[2]

The Importance of Culture

Entertainment took a variety of forms, some of which could be presented as patronised by particular social groups. Thus, until the abolition of the processions followed by public hangings at Tyburn in 1783, the gallows there was one of the major public shows in London, while the pillory was a less lethal counterpart. In 1746, Thomas Harris, a lawyer, noted:

> This has been one of the most entertaining weeks for the mob ... yesterday (which was the top of all) Matthew Henderson [a servant who had murdered the wife of his employer] was hanged, at whose execution all the world (I speak of the lowlife division) were got together; and he died to the great satisfaction of the beholders, that is he was dressed and in white with black ribbons, held a prayer book in his hand and, I believe, a nosegay.

In practice, however, there was no such division, for the social élite also found such occasions of great interest, as they did many other activities, such as cockfighting. In particular, male patterns of behaviour could readily span the social range, a process encouraged by the extent to which many men probed the boundaries of legality.

It is all too easy in providing form and notably categorisation to cultural history to draw boundaries and discern trends that might do violence to the experience of individuals and to the forums in which ideas were framed and 'stories' told. There were often continuities. Thus novels, gossip, and historical writings all offered accounts of individuals and thereby means of understanding and representing individuality, notably with regard to engagement (by speaker/writer and recipient) and social norms. Letter-writing joined those who would otherwise be separate, and there was an epistolary culture with epistolary styles, and not only in letter-writing itself: novels could include or

English Culture

even extensively move forward by means of correspondence. The resulting format could inculcate a somewhat stilted expression of moral purpose, as in Samuel Richardson's highly successful *Pamela; or, Virtue Rewarded* (1740), a form of conduct literature. There could also be a more immediate tone. In her *Memoirs of Emma Courtney* (1796), Mary Hays (1759-1843) made use of her own experiences in a novel in which she drew on her love letters written during an unsuccessful romance – and her offer to live together without marriage. Poetry and songs extended the depiction of individuality in a dramatic fashion; and, like plays, could be offered in a domestic or commercial context.

For most readers, culture means high culture, the world of painters and poets that George II allegedly decried, and in particular, what are judged to be the major works of those who are considered the major writers/painters and equivalents. The distorting impact of such an emphasis is obvious;[3] culture can also be understood in a much broader fashion. This is true not only of its products – pop music to opera – but also of the way in which they are produced, and of the contexts of cultural activity in which they reside. Styles are important, but so also is material culture, the consumption of culture and its impact on consumers. This wider approach will be the subject of this book. As far as examples are concerned, emphasis will be on the culture of print, published material, because it is more accessible, throughout England and further afield, than, say, architecture or paintings. A network of school and public libraries holds many of these works, and they are also generally available in inexpensive paperback editions and are searchable online.

A key context and content of culture was criticism, the evaluation of works in terms of existing norms and the establishment of new conventions. The period covered by this form was essentially bound together by a culture of printed criticism that at once took public, literary forms, and operated

The Importance of Culture

in terms of a clear, rules-based system that linked readers, producers and commentators. This developed after the 'Glorious Revolution' of 1688-9, replacing an earlier process in which judgment about quality was developed within coteries and was frequently based on private manuscript circulation of both works and criticism.[4] However, far more was involved in criticism over the last three centuries than public formats and clear norms. The democratisation of format and opinion seen recently with the use of social media and the decline of cultural deference have highlighted the limitations of what might prove a long but transient age in which printed criticism was to the fore.

Material culture overlapped with what is more generally considered high culture, not least through the settings of both in domestic and public spaces, and the roles in both of consumption and leisure. Domestic spaces as well as communal and commercial ones were important talking shops in which culture was considered, reviewed, and kept alive. In many respects, this was far more significant than the formal processes of reviewing, and indeed this remains the case, as in recommendations of films to see and the subsequent fixing of an impression of them.

The use of the term culture exposes its porosity and the extent to which there is no clear definition. Like the Enlightenment, culture starts to be a bit meaningless. Thus culture is both noun and adjective, with a frequent use in such terms as material culture, visual culture, oral culture,[5] political culture, urban culture, military culture, strategic culture, youth culture, manufacturing culture, industrial culture, and multicultural;[6] as well as the concept of subculture, as in Goth subculture. There is a tension between the idea of a specific culture, or subculture – for example, youth culture – and the reality of several cultures.

The extent to which books were reprinted (and plays staged anew) captures the difficulty of arguing about culture

English Culture

in terms of clearly defined periods. Similarly, instead of styles being sequential, there was considerable co-existence and even interaction between them.

'Accessibility' has always been a key issue in national culture. Thus, in 1733, during a period of political contention, Francis Hare, the Bishop of Chichester, wrote to Thomas, Duke of Newcastle, a senior minister:

> I could wish something were writ in the way of dialogue between two farmers or persons of that size, in a natural easy familiar way, so as to be intelligible to the meanest capacities, in which the nature of the excise might be thoroughly explained, and the objections fairly discussed and answered... It would be more read and have a greater effect than the finest writ papers in the way of a continued argument, which is necessarily above vulgar capabilities; for such things must be minced and cut into small pieces, since they can take in but little at a time.[7]

Provincial culture is an important part of the cultural landscape, but there is a tendency to focus on London. Moreover, when the provinces are considered, the emphasis is on provincial culture, not provincial cultures. This approach captures a widespread sense of difference from London, but it underplays the extent to which there was variety outside London. This had a number of contexts without suggesting that they were necessarily corresponding or causative, notably urban/rural, industrial/ agricultural, educated/uneducated, Dissenter/Anglican, and northern/southern. The concept of a public sphere has attracted scholarly attention, indeed become fashionable, but doubts over its scale, coherence and impact direct attention to the need to handle this established concept with care.[8]

The Importance of Culture

There are also the tensions between national themes, such as xenophobia, and cosmopolitanism. In the space available, this work discusses these issues, as well as key historical changes of relevance, such as urbanisation, the rise of literacy, nationalism, and England's wider links. 'Culture' can be regarded as a sort of add-on to more fundamental elements of history, whether political, socio-economic or, increasingly, environmental. That assumption, however, downplays the significance of culture to considerations of identity and value, and the way in which it can be understood as both context and content, production and response.

In reading or looking today at the works of the past, from buildings to plays, it is important to bear in mind that they were often closely bound up with the worlds of local politics, society, and religion. Thus Assembly Rooms might serve not (or not only) as a common place of relaxation and display driven by entrepreneurial energy, but also as an opportunity for a particular group to meet and socialise. Cultural activity, however defined (and the definitions were often politically and/ or socially loaded), could have more to do with political, religious and social issues than with artistic trends. Those who agreed on the ethics of politeness and the morality of moderation in the eighteenth century, or on the values of a moral cultural content in the nineteenth, or on 'accessibility' today, might disagree on much else. Culture could become an expression of conflict rather than a panacea for strife – most obviously in the modern phrase 'culture wars,' a sense that cultural issues are a matter of fundamental ideological strife, an idea imported from America but, nevertheless, one that gained considerable traction in England from the 2010s. Criticism of the concept failed to address the extent to which powerful controversies over novels and much else were linked to political differences.

English Culture

The more general and lasting presentation of the artist as a commentator on the manners and mores of contemporary society, at the very least as an observer, ensured that politics in the widest sense was covered. Indeed, aesthetics, with its interest in harmony, and therefore order, or, conversely, its rejection of the two, was inherently political. The social purpose of the arts was also part of the debate. Visiting the Haymarket Theatre in 1786, Sophie La Roche noted not only a hostile interplay of fashionable spectators with the rest of the audience, but also the actors, after the play, debating the motion 'That it is the duty of the stage to condemn social evils, and to seek improvement through the medium of wit'.[9]

This raises the question of why I am focusing on England, rather than Britain, given the many and important overlaps and relationships between them. In part, this choice is due to the exigencies of space. There is also the extent to which England does have a particular set of cultural identities and trajectories,[10] or, crucially, was believed to do so even when part of a larger political entity. Thus Jack, the hero of *The Englishman from Paris* (1756), declared at the close of the play: 'Plain good sense, honour, honesty, and a regard for our word, are the characteristics of the English nation ... the most ridiculous object you saw in this country is a Frenchified Englishman.'[11]

Jane Austen in her novel *Emma* (1815) repeatedly praised Englishness, referring to the meeting of the Knightley brothers

... in the true English style, burying under a calmness that seemed all but indifference, the real attachment which would have led either of them, if requisite, to do every thing for the good of the other.[12]

In *Emma*, she also praised Shakespeare as a touchstone of Englishness and wrote: 'It was a sweet view – sweet to the eye and

The Importance of Culture

the mind. English verdure, English culture, English comfort, seen under a sun bright, without being oppressive.'[13]

I hope that this will encourage you to reflect on the country and its arts, locating individual works in terms of these contexts and, not least, to consider cultural history in terms of differing spheres of patronage, overlaps and tensions between 'high' and 'low' culture, and the interactions of cosmopolitanism and nationalism. This is particularly necessary because of what we are losing. The literature of the past has become attenuated. Milton and Bunyan are rarely read, with inexpensive reprints now far less frequent than in the twentieth century, let alone the nineteenth. The novels of the eighteenth century live on, if televised or filmed, as with Fielding and Austen; but not otherwise, as with Richardson, Smollett, and Sterne.

The cultural frame of reference changes, and for many the continuation of past cultural achievement is lost or befogged. In the early 2010s, I was asked in a seminar at the University of Exeter how the cultural frame had changed since I began full-time university teaching in Durham in 1980. I replied that in the early 1980s, I had told first-years that my teaching methods were modelled on the great Victorian educationalist Wackford Squeers, and drew a laugh. When the Exeter class, twenty strong, were asked the identity of Squeers, only one voice suggested a Dickens character, and none could identifying the novel *Nicholas Nickleby*.

There have been other such characters since, and a living culture by its nature discards, adapts, adopts and acquires; but it may well be that the process of discarding has been driven too hard of late. A changing frame of reference is scarcely new, and that element is an important part of the cultural history of the country. Indeed, Scottish-born and London-settled, the writer David Hume closed his history of England from 55 BCE

English Culture

to 1689 by reviewing 'Manners and Sciences' under Charles II, attacking the coarseness of the literature and singling out John Dryden (1631-1700), England's first Poet Laureate, for particular obloquy:

> Most of the celebrated writers of this age remain monuments of genius, perverted by indecency and bad taste; and none more than Dryden, both by reason of the greatness of his talents, and the gross abuse which he made of them. His plays, excepting a few scenes, are utterly disfigured by vice or folly, or both.[14]

Now, instead, Dryden's plays are largely ignored.

It has been great fun to research and write this book. I have also benefited from the advice of a number of friends, including Roger Billis, Bill Gibson, Grayson Ditchfield, Thomas Otte, George Robb and Richard Wendorf. They are not responsible for what follows, but the stimulus of informed friendship has helped me greatly. It is a pleasure to dedicate this book to Charles Saumarez Smith, a friend I got to know when lecturing for several years for his V&A course, and who has always been a most agreeable and wise companion, able to see life with a sagacious mind.

1

BACKGROUND: 1500-1700

They say miracles are past.
Lafeu in *All's Well That Ends Well* (II, iii).

That the culture of the Tudor age still echoes today is in large part thanks to William Shakespeare, and his plays written and performed in English. Indeed, the use of English in its standard form was a fourteenth- and fifteenth-century development that was pushed further under the Tudors (r. 1485-1603), when it became both the language of authority and of culture. The rise of the vernacular, always significant for popular culture,[1] diminished the role of Latin and of Anglo-Norman, the French spoken in England. The English language was increasingly identified with an English people and nation in the thirteenth century, and became more important in literature in the fourteenth, not least with William Langland's *Piers Plowman* (different versions, 1362-92) and Geoffrey Chaucer's *Canterbury Tales* (c. 1387-1400).

English Culture

In many respects, the Hundred Years' War with France (1337-1453) offered a cultural precursor to the Protestant Reformation of the sixteenth century, which gathered pace from Henry VIII's break with Papal authority in 1533. At the start of the Hundred Years' War, the aristocracy of England was international in outlook, and French was the language at Court and of anyone with upwardly mobile aspirations. However, as politics drove the two realms into a long war, so it became awkward that high society in England aped French style, manners, and customs. The government also built up patriotic characteristics and, in so doing, deliberately harnessed linguistic awareness. The earliest parliamentary petition in English was in 1386. Henry V himself switched to English in 1417, a significant year given the intensity then of the war with France. From 1420, Chancery clerks were pushing English as the official language of government.

National distinctiveness was also seen in the Perpendicular, a native architectural style of the fourteenth and fifteenth centuries, and in a distinctive style of English music. Thus, pre-Reformation England was part of an international cultural world, and notably intertwined with the Church and Latinity, but it was far less affected by Continental, especially French, influences than hitherto. Moreover, there were elements of Church life that were national in tone, as in the veneration of Henry VI (r. 1422-61, 1470-71) as a saint and martyr; miracles were attributed to him. The extent of church building and renovation indicated the strength of the religious system. Rochester Cathedral added a Perpendicular-style Lady Chapel in 1490 and Fountains Abbey a tall Perpendicular tower soon after. Shrines continued to attract bequests and pilgrims. This activity made the subsequent breach of the Reformation more abrupt, with monasteries, nunneries and other sites devastated.

Background: 1500-1700

England, meanwhile, played a role, albeit not a central one, in the Renaissance. Henry VII's Court was visited by such leading luminaries as Castiglione (1503) and Erasmus (1499), and the latter spent several years at Cambridge. Henry VIII's court also had an international flavour, with the painters Hans Holbein and Vincenzo Volpe working there. In 1519, Henry appointed the Bavarian astronomer, Nikolaus Kratzer, already an academic at Oxford, as Court astronomer and horologist. The Reformation ensured a religious and intellectual, and thus cultural, shift in England's connections from southern to northern Europe, although links with Italy remained significant, not least in the purchase of paintings.

Cultural and intellectual change in, and after, the Reformation saw both the continuation of existing circumstances and practices, such as the cult of St George (although not that of Henry VI),[2] as well as the development of new ones. A different cultural landscape was created as a result of the dissolution of religious sites. Some of the 12,000 tonnes of stone used by the Cecils to cover the large façade of Burghley House came from monastic buildings in Stamford, and so on across the country. Linked to this, there was a rejection of Latinity. Alongside new interest in Anglo-Saxon England,[3] the English language was developed by Tudor playwrights. Written English became homogenized in the age of print, which saw much translation into English and the wholesale borrowing of foreign words. This process provided a context for Shakespeare's plays, which expressed the aspirations and tensions of the emerging nation-state, and their vocabulary had a major effect upon the language.

The Reformation ensured that good and evil became more literary and less oral or visual, but that did not diminish the need for people to understand their world in terms of the struggle between the two. The journey to an earthly perdition and a

English Culture

hellish end was extensively rehearsed by commentators, both the explicitly religious and the 'secular' – for example William Hogarth's mid-eighteenth century morality series of engravings, including *The Rake's Progress*.

The Bible's translation into English under Henry VIII and its mandatory use in churches had a great impact, as can be seen in Shakespeare's use of many Biblical phrases, a practice seen with writers into the twentieth century, for example Agatha Christie, but now far less common. In 1604, James I established the panel that in 1611 produced the King James or 'Authorized Version,' a would-be definitive translation. Like Shakespeare's plays, the 'Authorized Version' was to prove very important to the development of the English language, cited repeatedly by later authors and frequently used for the titles of literary works.

The process of presenting established works in English included the Classics, for example Ovid's *Metamorphoses*.[4] Another major source for Shakespeare was Erasmus's *Adages*, a collection of passages from the Classics that was likewise translated. The English translation by Sir Thomas North of Plutarch's *Lives of the Noble Grecians and Romans* (in fact a translation of a French translation) was published in 1579 and used by Shakespeare, particularly in *Coriolanus* and *Antony and Cleopatra*, and the first part of George Chapman's translation of the *Iliad* in 1598, the complete work appearing in 1611. Chapman also wrote plays, as well as a poem, *De Guiana*, on English transoceanic enterprise.

Translation was seen as a patriotic task.[5] Shakespeare had a great range of sources available in translation, including Classical French and Italian stories. Classical motifs were very important in other aspects of the English culture of the period, including rhetoric, illustrations and motifs.

In his plays, Shakespeare very much engaged with the past, notably of England, but also of Rome and of Scotland. In his lifetime, there was a greater sense of the past as distinctive and separate to the present. This sense was linked to the emergence of a particular awareness of history, derived notably from the Renaissance typology and progression of historical eras (Classical – medieval – modern), and the related Protestant proposal of Early-Church – Medieval Church – Reformed Church, with the Medieval Church (ie Roman Catholicism) as an age of iniquity. In part, this emergence of a particular awareness of history was an aspect of the general impact of Renaissance Humanism. The significance of time, the separation between past and present, came to be more strongly asserted and more readily understood. This contributed to an awareness of stylistic difference and cultural development.

Staging Religion and the Rise of a Different Theatre

Religious change was an abrupt and more transformative element in the growth of a national culture. For example, the Reformation had a direct impact on existing forms of drama, notably with the end of mystery plays. Like wall paintings, they depicted the world of good and evil in a traditional light. The Coopers' pageant in the 1415 York Corpus Christi play showed 'Adam and Eve and a tree between them, a serpent deceiving them with apples, God speaking to them and cursing the serpent, and an angel with a sword casting them out of Paradise'. Religious vitality had been clearly exhibited in pre-Reformation local culture. Linked to the religious and corporate ethos of guilds and enabling guildsmen to take a role in the social and political agenda of their towns,[6] mystery plays developed: the York ones were written down in the 1460s or 1470s, those of Towneley/Wakefield in the 1520s, and the Chester and Coventry plays were reworked in the 1530s.

Under Protestant Elizabeth I (r. 1558-1603), these mystery plays largely came to an end. The last recorded performances

English Culture

at York, Coventry and Chester were in 1569, 1571 and 1575 respectively, and attempts to revive performances at York in 1579 and Chester in 1591 were abortive. There was, however, opposition to this change. In Tewkesbury, plays were still being performed inside the church in 1600, and as late as 1576 the chalice had not been replaced with a communion cup. Mystery plays lasted in Lancaster and Preston into the reign of James I (1603-25).[7]

There were other forms of public theatre, as with annual shows, for example the Lord Mayor's Pageant in London, probably from the 1520s. Royal entries also meant grand pageantry. In 1599, Henry Hardware, the Mayor of Chester, 'caused the giants in the Midsummer-show not to go, the devil in his feathers not to ride for the butchers, but a boy as the others, and the cuppes, and cannes, and dragon, and naked boy to be put away; but caused a man in compleat armour to go before the showe in their stead'.

This Mayor altered many ancient customs, for example the shooting for the Sheriff's breakfast, and would not permit plays, bear-baiting and bull-baiting – only for the next Mayor to restore all the ancient pageants, which included that on St George's Day.[8] Such activity reflected a longstanding tension in society.

As a reminder about the problem of assuming clear chronological and stylistic divides, there were important links between the mystery plays, traditional pageants, the plays performed for the London guilds, and aspects of the theatre of Elizabethan England, including the works of Shakespeare. The links made up the mental universe, for example the role of the Devil, story lines, the staging, the objects available for drama, notably theatrical properties, and the music.[9] Similarly, there was continuity in the case of other arts, including church

Background: 1500-1700

music, with polyphonic singing continuing in many parishes until the 1580s.[10]

By weakening, or at least challenging, patterns of control over expression, however, the Reformation provided new opportunities for the theatre, notably in what could be covered – which was not the intention of the Protestant reformers. Theatre was an indigenous development, with London the prime setting for the changes in drama, although there were playhouses elsewhere, as in Bristol, and they were important to the identity (and leisure) of urban society.[11] The Theatre, the first purpose-built public playhouse in England, was opened in Shoreditch by James Burbage, an actor and master carpenter in 1576, and it was followed by his Curtain in 1577, the Rose in 1587, and the Globe in 1598. Unlike the new public buildings in the city, notably Gresham's Exchange and the Bourse, these theatres were all located outside the City walls, the Theatre and the Curtain being in Shoreditch and the Rose and the Globe in Southwark. This was due to measures taken by the City authorities, measures which had been encouraged by preaching: a ban on public playing in the City was pressed for from the 1570s and was realized in the 1590s. Nevertheless, in 1595 about 15,000 people visited the London theatres weekly, a figure that included many who were not in the higher strata of society. The Globe, with its capacity of 2,800, could take a larger audience than earlier theatres.

All of these theatres were open-air 'amphitheatre'-type places based on the model of galleried innyards. The more expensive places in the theatres were in the galleries, which were covered, while the yards, for which admission was commonly one penny, lacked cover, exposing those there to rain. The theatres represented an institutionalisation of drama similar to that of the economic market in the Exchange and the Bourse.[12] St Paul's Cross and other open-air pulpits were a religious counterpart.

English Culture

As an alternative, there were entirely covered hall playhouses, which had a smaller capacity and cost more to enter, usually sixpence. The first, the Paul's Theatre for the pupils of St Paul's boys' school, opened in 1575, while Burbage's company used another, in Blackfriars, from around 1606, providing new staging opportunities for Shakespeare. In a pattern that can be seen to the present, despite contrasts in cost, there was considerable overlap in the audience of the two types of theatre.[13] Purpose-built premises encouraged specialisation, and that meant a need for more plays in order to bring in audiences.

The private patronage of the wealthy, as seen with court masques and the sponsored musicians and actors in The Earl of Leicester's Men and other theatrical companies, and of prosperous institutions, were important. Alongside them, public patronage – meaning the paying public, not the state and the taxpayer – and the exigencies and opportunities of the commercial marketplace were crucial to the development of culture and notably of the theatre. The numerous plays that were produced ranged widely in their subject matter, but the vitality of contemporary London was a frequent theme, as were the wealth and social pretension of groups in urban society. Londoners, and the English as a whole, could see themselves depicted on the stage. Moreover, the social dynamics of cities such as Athens, Ephesus, Messina, Milan, Mitylene, Rome, Syracuse, Venice, Verona and Vienna, each of which was a setting for action in Shakespeare's plays, followed, at least in the sub-plots, the social dynamics of London. The list makes clear the dependence of the plots on the Mediterranean, both ancient and modern, and thus the significance of the assumption that it was in many respects similar to England, part of the same culture.

The identification with London was also true of other playwrights. Probably born in Westminster and educated at

24

Background: 1500-1700

Westminster School, Ben Jonson (1572-1637) was made City Chronologer in 1628, succeeding Thomas Middleton.[14] Set in London, his vigorous play *Bartholomew Fair* (1614) depicted the outwitting of a country squire, as well as the attraction of the stall selling roast pork.

Although the plight of the poor could be shown, the theatre and its morality were primarily located within a world of affluence, which was an aspect of its escapism. This location was so even if the audience was invited to mock the corrupt and lecherous wealthy, such as Sir Walter Whorehound in Middleton's comedy *A Chaste Maid in Cheapside* (1611). Social distinction was a theme of plays, but there was also a pride and self-identification of communities and nation, both in plays and with other cultural forms. Books played a major role in the development of this communality, as with John Stow's *Survey of London* (1598).

Books were highly significant because the Reformation, with its emphasis on a vernacular, and therefore easier to read, Bible, ensured that alongside the significance of preaching, representations of good and evil became more literary than hitherto. Every parish was required to have an English Bible, so it was the one book everyone saw. This change of course favoured the literate and thus was disorientating to many. It did not diminish the need or desire of people to understand their world in terms of the struggle between good and evil. Indeed, the shock of change may even have encouraged it.

Shakespeare's work reflected not only spiritual themes, such as atonement, resurrection and temptation, but also more specific Biblical stories, episodes and language; and the audience response drew on the collective religious experience. For example, the idea of resurrection is seen with the re-awakening of Juliet in the last scene of *Romeo and Juliet*.[15] As a consequence of this setting in a

English Culture

world of Christian belief, believers, references and controversies, the plays can frequently be read in these terms, as with the roles of contingency and ghosts in *Hamlet*. These roles were linked to differences between Catholicism and Calvinism, notably over free will and transubstantiation.[16] Moral dilemmas were further complicated by the need to reconcile Christian with Classical teachings, images and examples,[17] which was readily apparent in the plays set in the Ancient World.

Care is required in the search for political references and direct social readings.[18] The limited evidence for audience views, and for their understanding of analogies, are such that 'might' and 'maybe' unfortunately become key terms in analysis. Political and religious references were really or potentially troubling, and legally problematic, in a world divided and fearful over both; what specific references meant to contemporaries is unclear. These points also reflect on modern presentations of the plays. For example, the dynamic 2017 production of *Othello* by the Tobacco Factory, a most impressive company, was described in the publicity leaflet as follows:

One of Shakespeare's most startling contemporary plays, *Othello* is a masterful depiction of a life torn apart by racism and the destructive nature of prejudice. Venice, a western colonial power, employs the newly married Othello, a Muslim general, to lead their army against Turkish invasion. The difficulties of assimilating into a society riven by discrimination, fear and mistrust soon began to take their toll on Othello: manipulated by Iago, his life quickly unravels, and he turns on all he holds dear. A truly timeless play, *Othello* speaks afresh to each society that comes to it: a warning weaved within the fabric of the tragedy, more urgent than ever, compelling us to look beyond divisions of race, religion or culture and acknowledging our universal humanity.[19]

Background: 1500-1700

Maybe so for today – but does this tell us much about the audience in 1604? And that question leaves aside the somewhat misleading description in the leaflet of Venice as a Western colonial power, especially in its resisting Ottoman plans for Christian Cyprus; let alone underplaying the extent to which individual betrayal and personal dynamics are to the fore in the play. With regard to Othello, it is arguably that he is Moorish, not Muslim, that is the issue. And so on for other works, and, correspondingly, for modern works of criticism. In the words of Iago, 'For I am nothing, if not critical.'

Similarly, Shakespeare's religious beliefs have been a matter for claims and controversies, not least as he has been moved from being the national hero of a Protestant state to, in some accounts, becoming a Catholic, and even a Counter-Reformation activist; although others contest this interpretation. In practice, as with many other writers of the period and later, the evidence for his views and position is fragmentary, indirect and ambiguous. This is also the case with the plays, which do not provide conclusive evidence of Shakespeare's religious commitment.

Helena observed in *All's Well That Ends Well*:

Our remedies oft in ourselves do lie
Which we ascribe to heaven; the fated sky
Gives us free scope; only doth backward pull
Our slow designs when we ourselves are dull. (I, i)

This tension between free will and determinism extended to the theatre and its audience, notably the extent to which the playwright, the actors, and the setting sought to lead the response, but, at the same time, had to confront the agency of the audience. More centrally, the prologues and afterwords made the free

English Culture

response of the audience a key element. Prospero's epilogue in *The Tempest* even presses for such applause as a major plot enabler:

I must be here confined by you [the audience],
Or sent to Naples. Let me not,
Since I have my dukedom got
And pardoned the deceiver, dwell
In this bare island by your spell,
But release me from my bands [bonds]
With the help of your good hands [applause]:
Gentle breath of yours my sails
Must fill, or else my project fails. (V, i)

In addition to their depiction on the Elizabethan stage, we can see individuals, as we frequently cannot see their fifteenth-century predecessors, thanks to more lifelike and more numerous portraits. Portraits by Hans Holbein (1497-1543) earlier in the sixteenth century are more famous, but it is the production of more numerous portraits later in the century that is more significant. These include not only major figures of state and Court, most dramatically Elizabeth I, but also portraits of those of a humbler position. One of Shakespeare was produced during his life, a portrait that shows him wearing an earring. Male decoration and display were particularly significant in this period, not least colourful clothes, which displayed status and ambition for status, the latter parodied in the pretensions of Malvolio in *Twelfth Night*.

The World of Print

The printing of vernacular Bibles gave ordinary individuals an opportunity to consider God for themselves and to question traditional teachings from the perspective of their own understanding of scriptural authority. Thus, knowledge was not so much freedom as a cause of the demand for freedoms. The populace was not a passive recipient of policies and initiatives from the more powerful. Yet, while the Reformation was heavily dependent on the ability of publications to overcome traditional constraints on discussion and the spread of ideas, it also reflected the power of the state. Protestant worship was introduced by means of the *Book of Common Prayer* (1549), which contained forms of prayer and Church services for every religious event. Parliament passed a Uniformity Act decreeing that the *Book of Common Prayer* alone was to be used for Church services, which were to be in English. After an order of Convocation (the clerical parliament of the Established Church) of 1571, cathedral churches also acquired copies of John Foxe's *Book of Martyrs* (1563), a potent work about the persecution of Protestants,[20] and many parish churches chose to do likewise.

As yet, the impact of popular literacy and the print revolution upon oral culture was, while important, limited. Visual experiences remained highly significant, including in books. Foxe's *Book of Martyrs* was illustrated, and these images were arguably more powerful than the text, something also true of images of witches. While these images fuelled the anxieties of the age, other images could be celebratory and consoling. Pageantry and costume were also important aspects of visual culture.

About eighty per cent of London craftsmen were literate by the 1600s, but literacy rates were lower, much lower, for the poor, for women, and for the rural population. Most people could neither read nor afford books, nor the manuscript (hand-written) pamphlets and newspapers that remained very important and continued so into the eighteenth century,[21] though chapbooks and almanacs were cheaper.

English Culture

Most people lacked formal education. Thus, printing exacerbated social divisions, and gave an extra dimension to the flow of orders, ideas, and models down the social hierarchy. It is frequently claimed that a common cultural pattern can be detected from the late sixteenth century in both Protestant and Catholic Europe in the shape of an assault on popular culture from the new moral didacticism of Protestant and post-Tridentine Catholic ecclesiastical and secular authorities. New intellectual and artistic fashions and codes of behaviour are held to have corroded the loyalty of the upper and middling orders to traditional beliefs and pastimes, marginalising a formerly common culture and pushing it down the social scale. However, the evidence for such a thesis is problematic, not least because alongside social differentiation there was also the linkage of constituent communities to create and sustain wide-ranging networks.[22]

The inability of the poor to express themselves was certainly accentuated by printing. Yet, there were also possibilities for expression, even if it could be mocked. In *A Midsummer Night's Dream*, Bottom awakes from his encounter with the fairy world, proclaims its uniqueness, and seeks to fix it for posterity in a work of poetry that will be recited:

The eye of man hath not heard, the ear of man hath not seen, man's hand is not able to taste, his tongue to conceive, nor his heart to report what my dream was! I will get Peter Quince to write a ballad of this dream; it shall be called 'Bottom's Dream,' because it hath no bottom. (IV, i)

The literate Quince, the carpenter, allocates the parts in 'Pyramus and Thisbe,' the play within a play, and writes and speaks the prologue.

Background: 1500-1700

Education, the world of print, the impact of government, and the very existence of London, all encouraged the gentry increasingly to view politics and society in national terms. London dominated printing, and language was thereby standardised through reducing the impact of regional linguistic differences. Standardisation was related to the interlinked authority of print and (the) capital.

The impact of print was often indirect and subtle, but, significant in establishing assumptions. For example, printing changed the law by easing and encouraging the processes by which injunctions, information and outcomes were recorded and stored. In place of the variations of, and in, the oral transmission of information and custom, came a demand for certainty and precision linked to the written record. With customary law, a largely oral system was transformed into a written one. Such changes enhanced the prestige of text and its capacity to act as a system of validation, and thus of arbitration and settlement. Shakespeare referred to a new world in *All's Well That Ends Well*: 'They say miracles are past; and we have our philosophical persons to make modern [everyday] and familiar, things supernatural and causeless [inexplicable]. Hence is it that we make trifles of terrors, ensconcing ourselves into seeming knowledge when we should submit ourselves to an unknown fear.' (II, iii).

There were textual variations with printing, notably as a result of errors, changes in new editions, and censorship. Printing, nevertheless, represented a way to fix texts in a fashion different from the instability arising from the continual alterations offered by hand-copied texts and, even more, by the oral transmission of information and opinion. Thus, the character of textual memory, and of memory as a whole, changed. The more fixed character of print was linked to the more public response to what was published, a response seen with the development of printed commentary.

Report and Rumour

The culture of print brought new authorities and new processes of authorisation, a matter in part of censorship by bishops as well as ministers, which served a range of goals, from religious and political control to attempts to regulate the book trade as a business activity. Censorship and licensing, however, were not simply means of restriction, but also of legitimation, marking the boundary of what was respectable. Licensing included the granting of privileges to publish.

This was to be important in the development of novel forms of news-reporting. As Shakespeare's plays made clear, much 'news' could be repetitive and cyclical, as with the cycle of days on which parish bells were rung, and the telling and retelling of familiar tales and superstitions. These activities afforded some security in an insecure world. A sense of news as frequent, even daily, did not represent a secular rejection of a religious world view, but instead, with some similarities to a play, was a common theme in society, offering explication in the form of narrative continuity. At the same time, print, drama, and greater interest in recording and 'telling' time, were all aspects of a cultural shift. The development of time-based forms of publishing, such as astrological publications, news pamphlets and newspapers, was part of this shift. As a result, gossip was given new forms and authority.

Government concern with rumours was seen in 1580 when a proclamation was issued against the spreading of rumours that invasion by Philip II and the Pope was imminent, rumours that were indeed inaccurate. Reporting was shaped by government regulation, entrepreneurial activity, and the purchasing, reading,

Background: 1500-1700

and viewing decisions of many, for whom such choices were acts of political and/or religious affirmation, as well as signs of interest. Branches of knowledge fed by (new) information, such as astrology and the journalistic genre of 'strange newes,' could be used as vehicles for articulating topical grievances.

The publication of plays was a way in which the works of playwrights could be fixed, and they could be identified and also criticized. The first appearance of Shakespeare's name on the title pages of his printed plays was in 1598, in the shape of a quarto of *Love's Labour's Lost*. The original authored 'Complete Works', assembled by his fellow actors, appeared after Shakespeare's death in the 'First Folio' text of 1623, *ie* in a large 'Folio' format.

Publication was important, but the plays were of course staged, they were not appreciated primarily as written texts. This staging involved adaptation to the constraints of contemporary productions and theatres, but these constraints offered opportunities – and could be pushed against. Theatricality included display, which could provide an important component. Solemn processions or dances could end plays: tragedies and comedies respectively. Neither solemn processions nor dances were new features of the culture of the period, but their setting in theatres, in which people were paying to see plays written for commercial ends, was new. The context, as well as the content, of national culture were changing.

However expressed, including on the stage, the information and opinion that circulated were not confined to a system of government-directed control, or to hierarchic patterns of deference, and Ben Jonson was to sound a warning about this development in his play *The Staple of News* (1626). Attempts to control the flow and dissemination of unwelcome material stemmed from concern about the political, religious and, to a lesser extent, social effects of print and drama, including their

English Culture

influence on those who could not read, or even afford to go to the theatre, but who might be swayed in their thinking by those who could.

The development of pamphlets, newspapers and theatre was located within a wider cultural shift that focused attention on what could be presented as news: news from elsewhere. This process of engagement with clearly defined news, especially from a distance, was related to institutional developments, such as the growth of public postal links and of mercantile correspondence systems. This information became more prominent in the sixteenth century, not only with the increase of public or semi-public forms, but also as a result of a greater internalisation of news in the larger number of diarists, many of whom recorded public news.

Entrepreneurial activity helped foster a process in which different media joined, overlapped, or separated. The genre of 'strange newes' was used to provide accounts of Providential tales, and this possibility attracted entrepreneurial publishers. Plot devices in plays that may appear far-fetched would scarcely have done so to the readers of such tales. However, although Providential tales remained an important topic for report, news and fact were increasingly differentiated from exemplary prose in which morality was seen as defining accuracy, for example sermons. So also with plays, although they responded to the possibilities of a range of genres. Political information became a valuable commodity that was turned to profit by the writers of newsletters, as well as providing material for satirical works that, in part, dwelt on the contents and implications of morality.[23]

The interest in developments both at home and abroad, the latter notably due to religious conflict, indeed warfare, from the 1520s, ensured that information circulated more widely. This was a process encouraged by governmental and ecclesiastical

Background: 1500-1700

activity, and by translations. Publications like plays contributed to and drew on a heightening, a focusing, and, to a degree, polarisation of public opinion. They brought a new intensity to the political contention already extant, notably in the 1580s, 1590s and 1620s, and they both reflected and sustained the particular issues of specific political moments. The Crown's fiscal expedients and its sale of commercial privileges were unpopular. In John Donne's Elegy XV, *A Tale of a Citizen and his Wife*, the citizen complains that

> Our onely City trades of hope now are
> Bawd, Tavern-keepers, Whores, and Scriveners;
> The much of Privileg'd kinsmen, and the store
> Of fresh protections make the rest all poor.

The Seventeenth Century

The legacy of the Elizabethan age might appear clear and was certainly to be presented as such in the eighteenth century. In this account, an English Protestant culture had been threatened by the Catholicising, Continental tendencies and Baroque style of the Stuarts, who came to the throne of England with the accession of James I in 1603. As a result, the overthrow of James II in 1688-9 was presented as important to the safeguarding of English culture, creating the subsequent context for debates between cosmopolitanism and more national themes. This is an overly simplistic approach. To take Baroque, it could be favoured by Protestants, such as Christopher Wren (and Johann Sebastian Bach in Germany). The relationship between stylistic choice and political developments was not necessarily clear.

There was certainly cultural change under James I. The Banqueting Hall in Whitehall was built by Inigo Jones, who introduced a Classical architectural style to England where

English Culture

Renaissance influence had until then been fairly superficial. The Banqueting House was intended to be the nucleus of a massive new palace at Whitehall. Fearful of assassination, James had disliked the colonnade in the previous hall on the site. The Banqueting House provided a venue for Londoners and others to see the king and royal family eat in public. This was organised so that, under James and his successor Charles I, tickets were issued for admission. The ceiling, commissioned by Charles I and painted in the early 1630s by Rubens, displayed the apotheosis of James, seen being escorted to Heaven and depicted as the heir of King Arthur and the monarch of universal peace. Charles was presented by Rubens as God's representative on Earth.

Alongside the Bible, which had become divisive due to the Reformation, the Classics were a common inheritance for the European élite, and English patrons avidly purchased Continental works and supported foreign artists. The future Charles I was very impressed on his visit to Spain in 1623 in pursuit of his plan for a marriage by the image of monarchy portrayed in the works of Rubens, Titian and Velázquez, and commissioned and purchased accordingly. Charles's cultural vision was very much in line with that of royal patrons of the arts on the Continent, such as Philip IV and Louis XIII.

At the other end of the spectrum, there was Puritanism, the precursor of Low Church Protestantism, with its distinctively sober and pious lifestyle. This lifestyle could be satirised, as with the hypocritical zealot Zeal-of-the-Land Busy in Ben Jonson's play *Bartholomew Fair* (1614), and 'we of the separation' in his play *The Alchemist* (1610), but Puritanism proposed a set of values against which the royal Court seemed corrupt, and these values were popular in London. Opposed to the theatres, both because they were prudish and because they saw the theatre as a public-order question, the Puritans had them closed down in 1642.

Background: 1500-1700

The Puritans were 'differently cultural', not 'anti-cultural' fundamentalists. Little Moreton Hall, with its biblical texts decorating the Chapel and the parlour frieze depicting the story of Susannah and the Elders was a world away from James's tastes. The barrel-vaulted ceiling in the Gallery at Lanhydrock, a Cornish stately home, was commissioned by its owner, John, 2nd Baron Robartes, leader of the county's Parliamentarians.

Charles' opponents deployed an idea of national culture and a language of national identity with which to criticize the king, a process repeated with his sons Charles II (r. 1660-85) and James II (r. 1685-8). Thus, while presented as a consequence and source of unity, the ideas of national identity and culture were inherently politicised. Moreover, they were not only the product of division, notably the politicization linked to the Reformation, but themselves divisive. Indeed, it was as national divisions encompassing large numbers outside the élite became politically important that the language of national culture became politically significant. It was part of a process in which élite and non-élite political groups manoeuvred and were united in a common cause, thereby dividing the country.

The Civil Wars of 1642-6 and 1648 focused cultural division and destructiveness, with the Parliamentarians attacking religious works they considered crypto-Catholic. When Chester surrendered to them in 1646, the Cathedral was vandalized, the stained glass broken and the organ damaged. Under the subsequent Parliamentary and then Cromwellian governments, there was a major cultural breach in continuity, notably with the destruction of the visible remains of 'superstition' in churches. For the sake of continued reformation and godliness, Puritanism proved oppressive, and the Puritan 'Cultural Revolution' was a failure. Steps such as banning the 'Cotswold Olimpicks', games held at Dover's Hill since 1612, were not welcome. Several

English Culture

preachers compared England to Israel, ungrateful for the gifts of God. At the same time, there was nothing inevitable about the return of the Stuarts, and the culture of the Interregnum (1649-60) engaged both with republican themes and with those of the Cromwellian Protectorate.[24]

Charles I's eldest son, Charles II, came to the throne peacefully in 1660. Maypoles destroyed under Oliver Cromwell were re-erected, while a new Bear Garden was built in Southwark after the prohibition of bull and bear baiting was lifted.

There was a separate breach in 1666 when the Great Fire destroyed London's historic core. There were plans for a transformative rebuilding, but, as King's Surveyor of Works, Sir Christopher Wren had to be content with designing the dramatic new St Paul's, much of which was built in the 1700s, becoming the key work of the English Baroque. Wren was also responsible for designing 51 London churches, for long a highpoint of London's architectural heritage, although, through the depredations of Victorian re-development and German bombing, only 23 remain. St Paul's towered over the City and provided a key point in vistas from elsewhere in London and from the suburbs, but the absence of any coherent plan to the overall rebuilding ensured that St Paul's could no more provide a clear centre to the new London than any of the other buildings in the city.

During Charles II's reign, London was not only the site of battle with fire and the elements. To moralists, there was also the challenge from laxity, more specifically a sexual permissiveness that was a reaction to Puritan zeal. Engine, a maid in Edward Ravenscroft's play *The London Cuckolds* (1681), explained:

This employment was formerly named bawding and pimping, but our Age is more civilised and our language much refined. It is now called doing a friend a favour. Whore is now prettily called

Background: 1500-1700

Mistress. Pimp; friend. Cuckold-maker; gallant. Thus the terms being civilised the thing itself becomes more acceptable. What clowns they were in former ages.

Characters like Engine helped explain the attacks on the alleged profanity and immorality of the stage, for example by the non-juror cleric Jeremy Collier, in his pamphlet *A Short View of the Immorality and Profaneness of the English Stage* (1698). Such agitation led to government pressure on the London playhouses the following year. In contrast, in Thomas Southerne's play *The Wives' Excuse* (1691), marriage to a callous husband was depicted as imprisonment. Aphra Behn, the first English professional female playwright, used *The Rover* (1677), her most famous play, to criticise arranged marriages.

The growth of a public, entrepreneurial culture defined by the market continued. Public concerts became more frequent, those organised by John Banister in 1672 being the first such to be advertised. The role of advertising was enhanced by the expansion of the press from the 1690s, and this, in turn, helped create the sense that music performed for, and paid for, by the public was normal. Henry Playford, who succeeded his father as an active publisher of music, founded, to expand his reach in the music market, a tri-weekly concert in 1699 at a coffeehouse where his music could also be sold, and he established a club for music practice. In his preface to the fourth edition of *The Second Book of the Pleasant Musical Companion*, published in 1701, Playford linked improvement and sociability, both key themes in public culture, notably that of London:

The design therefore, as it is for a general diversion, so it is intended for a general instruction, that the persons who give themselves the liberty of an evening's entertainment with their

English Culture

friends, may exchange the expense they shall be at in being sociable, with the knowledge they shall acquire from it.

The century closed with many of the fundamentals of English politics and society relatively fixed and having consequences in the shape of an abandonment of recent Catholicising tendencies, as in sacred music.[25] The country was not to have an autocratic monarchy but rather one constitutionally constrained, with ministries that were accountable to Parliament. The rule of law appeared fixed, as did a Protestant Church settlement in the form of episcopalian governance and a theology that opposed Calvinism as well as Catholicism. Elite as well as popular culture was vernacular, there was a major role for printed works, and there was wide accessibility for those who could pay. Society remained predominantly rural and small-town, but cities were important and significant cultural forums.

And yet, there was also anxiety, notably concern that the Protestant Succession might be overthrown by a French-supported Jacobite rebellion on behalf of the exiled Stuarts, which indeed appeared a prospect in 1745. There were French invasion attempts in 1759, 1779, and 1805. There was also concern about disruptive political, social and cultural tendencies within the country. Scarcely new, this situation of concern, unease and criticism underlined the extent to which there was no serene backdrop to English culture.

2

EIGHTEENTH CENTURY: SPHERES OF PATRONAGE

Every seat in Covent Garden Theatre was taken last night, in expectation of the new Opera's being performed... Mrs Billington's performance of Rosetta in *Love in a Village* was everything that the Cognoscenti could wish ... concerts and Italian Operas have hitherto been the nurseries of musical genius.
Morning Post and Daily Advertiser, 17 March 1786

Thomas Arne's ballad opera, first performed in 1762, was refreshed by a triumphant performance by Elizabeth Billington, whose salary went up greatly as a result.

Fighting boredom and asserting their polite gentility, the patronage of the middling orders was of growing importance. Unable individually to provide the sustained direct patronage offered by many of the élite, they participated through public performances of works and public markets for the arts. Culture had to be financed. The major expansion of the middling orders helped to provide a public culture that saw itself in terms of openness and reasoned argument. This formed an equivalent to the English self-image of their own religious culture in the shape of the unique Church of England. This idea was significant for the more general ethos of English culture, reinforcing the idea of a distinctive national culture, one of moderation and restraint.

Patronage by the middling orders did not always take place in a public context. There was also a major domestic aspect of cultural patronage and consumption. This was especially important for women, and notably so with reading. Within the domestic sphere, women were able to assert independence and self-control, for example in music-making; although this assertiveness as cultural producers and recipients was far from limited to the domestic sphere.

Similarly, religion could be 'consumed' privately by reading the Bible and sermons, and by individual prayer. Yet it was also fundamental to the cultural understanding, for a key context was the moral economy of a divinely ordained world. Thus, contingencies were not solely a matter of chance, but also reflected this moral economy. Characters in fiction and fact were tested and responded to in terms of acceptance, fortitude, and redemption. Due to divine purpose and the role of Providence, the contingencies of life and fiction were to play out in a context of true fixedness and fairness, as seen for example in Defoe's novels and Handel's oratorios. A struggle against vice linked moralists across the range of culture, and it was also embraced by new literary forms, from the newspaper to the novel. Clerical consumption was an important part of the economy, but it operated with a religious sense of the moral constraints of Biblical injunctions as to what was acceptable and unacceptable consumption.

Eighteenth Century: Spheres of Patronage

In contrast, the nature and role of the commercial market could lead to concern, which was generally related to perceptions of the political and social situation. An entrepreneurship in which values were allegedly dissolved in money was seen as an unworthy corruption of quality and morality. Indeed, the rise of a modern, commercial, urban and increasingly meritocratic culture, at least in terms of the market and its values, was represented critically by those commentators who were under the influence of traditional civic humanist ideas. It was seen as a growth in luxury and effeminacy. The theme of the enervating threat of luxury and indulgence to taste and, more seriously, to morality – indeed to civilisation – was a weighty motif of anxiety. This theme contributed to caricatures of consumerism, fashionability, fashions in prints and prose, and was reflected in much of the literature of the period, whether or not fictional. This process was seen in the ridicule, notably from the 1770s, of the fashionable, affected men termed 'macaronis'. They were concentrated in London, and, for some, the ridicule was a way to strike at the capital.

Musical activity, like much else, was centred in London, but it also showed how culture was by no means confined to the capital. As in the world of the theatre, some provincial towns which nowadays enjoy no live music (other than karaoke in the local pub, a highly derivative process) had regular instrumental concerts and could boast their own amateur musical societies, many of which bought, or subscribed to, all the latest productions of the London music publishers. It was relatively easy for amateurs to participate in instrumental and vocal music, collectively or singly. Choral music flourished in the wake of the Three Choirs Festival held in Gloucester, Hereford, and Worcester from the early eighteenth century. The popularity of glee-singing testified to the widespread enthusiasm for performing vocal

English Culture

music. Families, friends and neighbours all took part in sociable singing, frequently accompanied by other aspects of conviviality, food and drink. In 1793, John Ley reported to his mother that he had visited relatives in suburban Blackheath: 'Monstrous good fun it was, every person in the highest spirits and very much pleased, we danced the most riotous dances we could, Sir Roger de Coverley, Country Bumpkin etc, which on account of the party's being select were very pleasant, we had nine couples.'[1]

Although they were important to her plots, Austen could be sceptical about private performances. Of 'a small musical party at her house' in London held by Mrs John Dashwood, Austen noted:

> The party, like other musical parties, comprehended a great many people who had real taste for the performance, and a great many more who had none at all; and the performers themselves were, as usual, in their own estimation, and that of their immediate friends, the first private performers in England.[2]

Such comments were based on experience and would have resonated, in their own experience or imagination, with many readers.

Chamber and solo works intended for amateurs enjoyed considerable popularity, and instruments, music and manuals were produced accordingly. In 1785, a French visitor commented that music was cultivated 'universally, in London as it is throughout the kingdom'. Music teachers came to play a major role, while women were often depicted in paintings and fiction playing music, as Charlotte Raikes was in her luminous portrait by George Romney. Austen, who sang for her family,[3] in her parody 'Plan of a Novel,' has the heroine, 'particularly excelling in Music – her favourite pursuit – and playing equally well on the Piano Forte and Harp'.

Eighteenth Century: Spheres of Patronage

The private world of music provided the demand for an expansion in the publication of music. This benefited the large numbers who played themselves and connected them. More generally, self-improvement was important across culture, from devotional literature and printed musical instruction to devices to improve artistic skills. Newspaper advertisements offered tuition in a range of subjects, including foreign languages. Reading itself was regarded as improving, which made any suggestions that it was not contentious.

Self-improvement was also highly significant to the matrimonial game. In *Pride and Prejudice*, Miss Bingley pointed out how much young women are expected to achieve to make themselves attractive, only for Darcy to trump this with reading.[4] This was clearly a conversation held in Austen's circle, and one in which Darcy can be assumed to express her view.

Musical instruments were displayed and played in the fine rooms constructed in so many houses during the major rehousing of much of the better-off in both town and countryside that occurred during the century. These instruments also helped to structure family space and activity. New houses had more furniture, chairs, tables, dressers, clocks and looking glasses, as well as plastered ceilings, curtains and fireplaces. Many individuals reflected on the presence, quality or cost of such items. All provided employment for craftsmen, as well as a conversation piece for hosts – and guests, such as the affected and materialistic Mr Collins in *Pride and Prejudice*. Economic expansion, consumerism and material culture were interrelated.

Middle-class patronage was also crucial in the theatre, which had shed its immoral and blasphemous reputation and had developed in London and elsewhere. In response to the use of the stage by opposition writers, not least Henry Fielding, the Licensing Act of 1737 gave the Lord Chamberlain the power to censor plays and

English Culture

made unlicensed theatres illegal. However, although this legislation restricted the permission to stage spoken drama in London to two theatres, in practice the situation, both there and even more so outside London, was more liberal. This was a characteristic aspect of governance in this period. For example, the death penalty was applied far less than its extension to cover more crimes might suggest. London theatre audiences could be undeferential and rowdy.

By 1800, there were nearly 300 theatres in the British Isles, including one in Richmond, Yorkshire, opened in 1788, that can still be visited and that illustrates the close relationship between the actors and the audience.[5] Theatres continued to open, including the New Theatre Royal in Bath in 1805. The Enabling Act of 1788 allowed Justices of the Peace to issue licences for performances. Regional circuits were created out of the routes of strolling players, and they increasingly acted in purpose-built playhouses, just as sermons of course were delivered in purpose-built churches and chapels.

Aside from Parliament and the courts viewed as theatre, tragedy's service to morality was presented on the stage against a variety of backgrounds, both historical and contemporary. Morality was matched by comedy. Whether on the stage, on canvas, or on the printed page, the middling orders watched both themselves and caricatures that reflected the anxieties and drives being depicted and the personality traits debated. The comedies of the transplanted Irish playwright Richard Brinsley Sheridan (1751-1816), *The Rivals* (1775), *A Trip to Scarborough* (1777), *The School for Scandal* (1777), and *The Critic* (1779), were satires on manners that in part explored anxieties over social standing. Mistaken identities played a major role in Sheridan's plays, as they did in Oliver Goldsmith's successful comedy *She Stoops to Conquer* (1773), a play set more closely than those of Sheridan in the social milieu of rural England.

Eighteenth Century: Spheres of Patronage

Although, on a longstanding pattern, mistaken identities were exploited to comic effect in the plays of Sheridan, Goldsmith and others, and provided much of the dynamic of the plots, they also captured a concern about identity, and the worries arising from dangers to which misidentification could lead. The latter focused on the ability to deceive as to character. In the frequently produced *The School for Scandal*, Joseph Surface is menacing in his deceitful self-interest and unctuous hypocrisy, and part of the pleasure of this excellent play derives from seeing him thwarted. Misidentification in this sense is very much the case in Austen's plots, as with George Wickham in *Pride and Prejudice*. Falling in love with the wrong person is a continual danger. Somewhat differently, misperception, of circumstances and/or intentions, is a repeated feature of other novels. This is a repeated theme in fiction, and one that registered stylistic changes.

In comedies, tensions could be defused, and social role-playing could be presented with humorous consequences and no long-term difficulties, thanks to the plot deployment of a benign fortune. Reversals as plot devices captured a sense of social fluidity and yet displayed an underlying set of social rules. However, the sense of fluidity remained disconcerting to many: being an 'actress' was seen by some as next door to prostitution.

Novels

Far from conforming to a common tone, form, intention or characterization, novels, like other cultural forms, varied greatly in content and approach, a trend encouraged by the size and diversity of the reading public. The rise of the novel was for a long time discussed in terms of the works of Daniel Defoe (1660-1731), Samuel Richardson (1689-1761) and Henry Fielding (1707-54), but this approach neglected what was a far greater range of early novels, many written by women, and in doing so misleadingly simplified the origins, character and development of the genre. Although English writers played the key role in the eighteenth-century development of novels and, indeed, the idea of the novel, there were important seventeenth-century precursors, notably Cervantes's *Don Quixote* (1605-15). This greatly influenced Fielding and others. The debt is acknowledged in Charlotte Lennox's *The Female Quixote* (1752), Richard Graves' *The Spiritual Quixote, or The Summer's Ramble of Mr Geoffrey Wildgoose* (1774) and in Fielding's play *Don Quixote in England, a Comedy* (1733). Scenes from *Don Quixote* and Samuel Butler's mock-heroic narrative poem *Hudibras* (1663) in Littlecote House, Berkshire, have recently been attributed to Hogarth in the 1720s.

More generally, the novel looked to a range of literary types, including picaresque tales, travel, books, and romances. In turn, novels took a number of forms, including tales for children: the *Worcester Journal* of 23 March 1749 advertised *The Amusement of Little Master Tommy, and Pretty Miss Polly*. Romances were particularly important in the early eighteenth century, when a novel was often a short story of romantic love, for example Eliza Haywood's successful *Love in Excess* (1719-20). The growing popularity of novels was referred to in *Tom Jones*:

> This young fellow lay in bed reading one of Mrs Behn's novels; for he had been instructed by a friend that he would find no more effective method of recommending himself to the ladies than the improving his understanding, and filling his mind with good literature.' (X, ii)

The common feature of the early novels of these decades was their claim to realism, if not non-fiction, as can be seen in Defoe's *Robinson Crusoe* (1719), *Colonel Jack* (1721), *Moll Flanders* (1722), *A Journal of the Plague Year* (1722), and *Roxana* (1724).

Eighteenth Century: Spheres of Patronage

The subjects of these novels were very different and they looked back to varied influences, *Robinson Crusoe* to travel literature and spiritual autobiography, *Colonel Jack*, *Moll Flanders* and *Roxana* to picaresque tales, with female protagonists ready to use their sexual attraction to help their voyage through life. The common theme in these alleged autobiographies was authenticity, and they had affinities with criminal biographies, a very popular and longstanding genre. The romantic tales, such as those of Haywood, claimed to be accounts of real life and manners, and even Swift's *Gulliver's Travels* (1726) was stated to be a true account.

Novels were not alone in devoting positive attention to the lowly, generally in pursuit of a morality tale. 'Philo-Pater,' in a piece on filial piety in the *London Journal* of 15 October 1726, ended:

Since therefore the lower rank, and more contemptible part of mankind, are not altogether so destitute of virtue and greatness of mind, as some people may imagine; these instances of heroical virtue and magnanimity of spirit, whenever they offer themselves to our view, ought to excite and stimulate the superior class of men, effectually to maintain a real dignity of character, and an essential superiority of the vulgar (whom they hold in the lowest contempt) in the exercise of exemplary virtues, as much as they exceed them in estates and titles.

Gulliver's Travels' combination of traveller's tale, picaresque novella, and satire, proved inimitable, and there was only limited development in prose fiction until Richardson's first novel, *Pamela* (1740), a very popular book on the prudence of virtue and the virtue of prudence. Its success encouraged the publication of more novels in the 1740s, an especially productive period. By 1769, booksellers were advertising nearly 100 self-proclaimed 'novels'.[6] although fewer were published annually. The growth in novels meant new literary criticism.

The appeal of *Pamela* was in part its ability to provide sexual frisson with clear morality, to move from page-turning perils for Pamela to a happy ending, and its epistolary form, which provided a sympathetic insight into the heroine. Pamela, a young maidservant, resists the lascivious advances of Mr B, thwarting attempted rapes by fainting at opportune moments. In the end, a realisation of Pamela's virtues and an appreciation of her virtue leads him to propose marriage, thus fulfilling the fantasy of social aspiration: Pamela marries her employer. The importance of the written word to the structure and form of the novel is indicated not only by the letters but also by the plot device of the theft of Pamela's journal leading Mr B to this appreciation.

Pamela's content and success invited skits and parody, notably Fielding's satirical *An Apology for the Life of Mrs Shamela Andrews* (1741),[7] in which self-interest is to the fore, and his *Joseph Andrews* (1742), Joseph being Pamela's brother; as well as James Dance's comedy *Pamela; or Virtue Triumphant* (1742). John Kelly offered an epistolary novel in *Pamela's Conduct in High Life* (1741), which, as with Richardson's continuation and *Joseph Andrews*, depicted her life as a wife. John Cleland's pornographic novel *Memoirs of a Woman of Pleasure* (1749), otherwise known as *Fanny Hill*, was in the form of a letter, but not a series of individual letters, which was the way to exploit the opportunities of the epistolary form. Although initially suppressed and the printer heavily fined, Cleland's novel became a popular work.

The novels of the 1740s displayed considerable diversity in content, with a number of subgenres significant, notably criminal lives, spiritual autobiographies, and secret histories. With

Jonathan Wild, Fielding produced a major instance of the first. In his novels, he took the comic confusions of his plays and put them into novelistic form, such confusion accompanied by bawdy and chaos.

A common theme in Richardson and Fielding was psychological authenticity. Richardson's use of letters allowed him to vary the tone by using different styles for his writers and helped give *Pamela* an impetus and an urgency. In turn, Fielding insisted that his novels were 'true histories' in that they revealed the truth of behaviour, an approach especially suited to the ironic voice he adopted as narrator, comparable to that he had taken in his plays. Thus, in the last chapter of *Joseph Andrews*, 'this true history is brought to a happy conclusion.' History frequently appeared in the title of novels. The role of historian enabled Fielding to explain his chosen part as narrator, not only as commentator, moralist and humorous reflector, but also as stage director, arranging the depiction, shaping the narrative, and encouraging the reader to appreciate more than surface meanings and unidirectional plots.

The different styles of Richardson and Fielding helped energise novel-writing as they encouraged debate as to best practice. Each had their imitators. With its emphasis on the female plight and perspective, Richardson looked forward to the sentimental novel, as did his stress on the role of the novel as instructional. In *Shamela*, in contrast, Fielding presents Pamela as self-interested, rather than moral, and with her virtue very differently used as a consequence in order to obtain her advantageous marriage with Mr B. There were many different responses to their novels: Dr Johnson despised *Tom Jones* and admired Richardson.

The popularity of novels exemplified the degree to which the expansion of the middling orders ensured that élite activity was less central than hitherto to the dominant cultural world.

English Culture

Élite values and models remained important across society, but others were also of consequence, while considerable play was made of contrasts between these values and the actual conduct of members of the élite. This served not to deny the values or models, but to suggest a measure of hypocrisy on the part of members of the élite, as well as the extent to which appropriate values were not solely displayed by its members. In 'Names of the Principal Persons' in the novel *Sir Charles Grandison* (1753-54), Richardson listed the men and women by their moral worth rather than their rank. In *Joseph Andrews* (1742), the contrast was important to the plot and explicitly mentioned by Fielding, who entered a caveat about judging groups, at the same time indicating the true quality of patronage, before continuing to deadly effect:

> ... as in most of our particular characters we mean not to lash individuals, but all of the like sort, so, in our general descriptions we mean not universals, but would be understood with many exceptions: for instance, in our description of high people we cannot be intended to include such as, whilst they are an honour to their high rank, by a well-guided condescension make their superiority as easy as possible to those whom fortune chiefly hath placed below them. Of this number I could name a peer no less elevated by nature than by fortune who, whilst he wears the noblest ensigns of honour on his person, bears the truest stamp of dignity on his mind, adorned with greatness, enriched with knowledge, and embellished with genius. I have seen this man relieve with generosity while he hath conversed with freedom, and be to the same person a patron and a companion... By those high people, therefore, whom I have described, I mean a set of wretches, who, while they are a disgrace to their ancestors, whose honours and fortunes they inherit (or perhaps a greater to their mother, for

Eighteenth Century: Spheres of Patronage

such degeneracy is scarce credible), have the insolence to treat those with disregard who are at least equal to the founders of their own splendour. It is, I fancy, impossible to conceive a spectacle more worthy of our indignation than that of a fellow who is not only a blot in the escutcheon of a great family but a scandal to the human species, maintaining a supercilious behaviour to men who are an honour to their nature and a disgrace to their fortune.

Fielding was contrasting Ralph Allen with Philip, 4th Earl of Chesterfield, both friends of his, both patrons. Patronage issues brought the mismatch of rank and nobility home to many writers. This encouraged a critique of the values of polite society, as when Fielding wrote that the lascivious Lady Booby was 'perfectly polite, nor had any vice inconsistent with good breeding'. His plots, like those of many other works, frequently revolved around issues of inheritance, a device appropriate for both comedy and tragedy that resonated across society and indeed genres, playing a major role in the first Gothic novel, Horace Walpole's *The Castle of Otranto* (1764). The travails of inheritance, however much depicted in landed society, also echoed at all levels. In the leading work of Fielding's younger sister, Sarah, her novel *The Adventures of David Simple* (1744), David has been disinherited by his younger brother's use of a forged will, while the friends he makes, Cynthia, Camilla and Valentine, have also been harshly treated, the last two by a dishonest stepmother. Henry wrote the preface. In Tobias Smollett's *The Adventures of Roderick Random* (1748), Roderick's father has been disinherited.

Fielding's condemnation of false values was directed across the range of society. In his vigorous mock-heroic novel *The History of the Life of the Late Mr Jonathan Wild the Great* (1743), which was possibly based on earlier writings back to the 1730s, Fielding offered a harshly ironic account of false greatness aimed not only

English Culture

at the criminal but, for example, at great conquerors, Alexander the Great being among those condemned:

> When I consider whole nations extirpated only to bring tears into the eyes of a GREAT MAN, that he hath no more nations to extirpate, then indeed I am almost inclined to wish that nature had spared us this her MASTER-PIECE, and that no GREAT MAN had ever been born into the world. (I, xiv).

The parallel of false greatness and crime had been drawn by St Augustine, in the *City of God*, which appeared in 426: 'Without justice, what are kingdoms but gangs of criminals on a very large scale? What are criminal gangs but petty kingdoms?' Alexander converses with a pirate:

> The king asked the fellow, 'What is your idea, in infesting the sea?' And the pirate answered, with uninhibited insolence, 'The same as yours, in infesting the earth! But because I do it with a tiny craft, I'm called a pirate; because you have a mighty navy, you're called an emperor.' (IV, iv).

Fielding in his *A Dialogue between Alexander the Great and Diogenes the Cynic* (1743) also took aim at the conqueror, very much one of the Ancients of note.

In *Jonathan Wild*, Fielding considered the subject of greatness, proclaiming his moral concerns and his ironic, but deeply felt, hostility to human evil. Social division was part of it: 'The plowman, the shepherd, the weaver, the builder, and the soldier, work not for themselves but others; they are contented with a poor pittance (the labourer's hire).' In contrast, 'the GREAT' enjoyed 'the fruits of their labours' (I,viii). Fielding's approach enabled him to range widely, using a very different authorial voice

Eighteenth Century: Spheres of Patronage

and method to that of the 1725 approach toward Wild by Defoe, which was more focused on the protagonist. *Jonathan Wild* was a novel as well as a morality tale and, as a result, Wild was not only depicted as dangerously harsh but also, on the pattern of John Gay's *The Beggar's Opera* (1728), as charismatic. As such, he deserved attention rather than just castigation.

The twentieth-century films of Fielding's novels *Tom Jones* (1963) and *Joseph Andrews* (1977), each directed by Tony Richardson, present them as jolly romps, much more sexualized than in the original, and notably so in the latter, with the many twists of the plots being contrivances to move the stories along and to obtain comic effect. Missing from them is Fielding's attempt to show the follies of self-serving human searches for control. He emphasised the role of Providence, not as an excuse for an inactive contemplation of divine grace but rather as a counterpart to good human activity that reflects the divine plan. Parson Adams was presented in *Joseph Andrews* as an exemplary individual, not least when, oblivious to his own safety, he hastened to the aid of Fanny Adams who is resisting rape. Fanny declares that she had 'put her whole trust in Providence', and Adams sees himself as the means of Providential deliverance.

This is at once humorous and deadly serious: the vehicle of divine judgement might be comic, but it alone could save the innocent from unhappy coincidence and the wretched designs of the sinful. This was a variation of the great instability of human affairs readily discerned by those who considered international and domestic politics.[8] Furthermore, the role of Providence, alongside the explicit interventions of Fielding as author-narrator, demonstrated the need for readers to be cautious in anticipating events, passing judgement and determining the plot, thus instructing them in a humility to match that of the benign characters who are depicted.

English Culture

In *Tom Jones*, returning home and going to his chamber, Allworthy 'spent some minutes on his knees, a custom which he never broke through on any account' (I, 3). Life, however, was far from orderly, through accident but also as a result of human misperception, indeed misplacing, due to vice and foibles, notably hypocrisy. Accident provides much of the drama for Fielding's novels, but the characterization often focused on aspects of hypocrisy. Central to *Joseph Andrews* and *Tom Jones*, Fielding attacked hypocrisy in other works.

The sense of social distinction in traditional classification was captured by Fielding in his preface to *Joseph Andrew*. He showed his knowledge of Classical literature and the classification to which it had given rise when he distinguished comic from tragic romances in terms of characters, manner and language:

A comic romance is a comic epic poem in prose, differing from comedy as the serious epic from tragedy; its action being more extended and comprehensive, containing a much larger circle of incidents, and introducing a greater variety of characters. It differs from the serious romance in its fable and action in this, that as in the one these are grave and solemn, so in the other they are light and ridiculous; it differs in its characters by introducing persons of inferior rank and consequently of inferior manners, whereas the grave romance sets the highest before us; lastly, in its sentiments and diction by preserving the ludicrous instead of the sublime.

Homer's lost *Margites* served Fielding as an alleged model for his novels, which he claimed were 'comic epics in prose'. He thereby outlined the background to this novel and, more generally, to his writing. Fielding was careful to distinguish his comedy from burlesque, arguing that the latter is unnatural, offering a parallel

Eighteenth Century: Spheres of Patronage

between painting and *caricatura*, placing Hogarth with the former and therefore as a comparison for him.

In social terms, the rise of the novel can best be seen as an important instance of the embourgeoisement of culture, notably in terms of patronage – though until about 1800, sermons still outsold novels. There was an emphasis on seeking the support of individual patrons, who were presented as crucial protectors, responsible for the cultural health of the nation. In practice, support from such patrons could make it easier for authors to deal with publishers and could provide some funds. Yet, prefiguring Dr Johnson's point about his *Dictionary* and Philip, 4th Earl of Chesterfield, there was a wider social positioning, underlined by Fielding in the preface to his *Historical Register for the Year 1736*, which was dedicated to the public. His publisher, he pretends, had something to say about such a dedication:

> 'What,' says he, 'does more service to a book or raises curiosity in a reader equal with "dedicated to his Grace the Duke of __", or "the Right Honourable the Earl of__" in an advertisement? I think the patron here may properly be said to give a name to the book.'[9]

Novels created and responded to a large readership and were not dependent on a distinguished list of subscribers, or on political patronage. Fielding's *Joseph Andrews* sold 6,500 copies in three editions in thirteen months, and he received £183 from his energetic publisher, Andrew Millar. In the opening chapter of *Tom Jones*, Fielding compares an author to 'one who keeps a public ordinary, at which all persons are welcome for their money,' with, as a consequence, a need to satisfy them, and better than many of the innkeepers he described. The patronage of the public created an additional reason to emphasise reviews. The more rarified

English Culture

appeal of epics was not compatible with the commercial literary climate.

Following on from a theme in his plays, the opening chapter of *Joseph Andrews* offered a determined preference for the modern. Fielding referred to 'those ancient writers which of late days are little read, being written in obsolete, and, as they are generally thought, unintelligible languages, such as Plutarch, Nepos, and others which I heard of in my youth.' Instead, he expressed a preference for the vernacular: 'Our own language affords many examples of excellent use and instruction, finely calculated to sow the seeds of virtue in youth, and very easy to be comprehended by persons of moderate capacity.'

Fielding sought to use satire to lead readers away from folly or vice through comedy, enabling them to detect the gap between proclaimed values and conduct and thus provide humour, but also an affirmation of those values. Thus, satire was fun and moral at the same time, the fun part of the process of controlling the passions.[10] The satire was given greater depth by Fielding's authorial commentary, making himself into another, but very different, character, with a separate narrative. This intervention was infrequent but ensured that the idea of the novel as reality was both interrupted and confirmed, and in an ironic fashion. Writing as a topic in itself was brought further to the fore in frequent reflections on Classical writers.

Alongside the moral critique of affectation in much of the writing of the period, and the preference for honesty as an aesthetic as well as a moral choice, is the sense of flux and uncertainty that led to a lack of clarity over identity and classification, or, at least, a challenge to them. In this situation of flux, performance was the condition of mankind, certainly in the social maelstrom of London and the viewing gallery of Bath. Performance was also a challenge to appropriate conduct and to the social categorisation that it was supposed to reflect and sustain. In terms of the affirmation, testing or breaking of norms, the representation of men and women in fiction threw light on the situation in the public sphere. Moreover, looked at differently, this fluidity provided plots and satisfied public interest.

Social and Gender Positioning

The role of the middling orders was important in the definition of taste, and, by means of this definition, both conduct and the imagination were organised and encouraged, and culture was developed. Yet, a focus on 'politeness,' consumerism and the public sphere, the well-established analysis, can lead to an underplaying of the continual role of élite culture and also an exaggeration of secularization. There was in practice a 'trickle-down' effect from the élite, in both form and content. Emulation was crucial, as the plots of novels revealed. This emulation was seen more widely, in both material culture and manners. Thus, Josiah Wedgwood's pottery was an important instance of emulation: he made élite objects, for example for Queen Charlotte, and then cheaper copies for the middling orders. Engravings are another instance of the same process.

Difference, even divisions, affected every aspect of life, from style to politics, and that theme is not adequately worked out if the stress is solely on polite consumerism or on a 'trickle-down'. Working-class culture, that of the streets, was less to the fore, although, very movingly, Austen has William Price recall to Fanny their Portsmouth childhood: 'We used to jump about together many a time, did we not? When the hand-organ was in the street?'[11] The internal experience of that culture can be difficult to recover as opposed to external spectating upon it.

While sharing the same cultural world as men, women had different access and presentation. In conversation pieces, the

English Culture

group portraiture that presented relationships, men took the more prominent roles and also commissioned the paintings. Performance, moreover, was dominated by men. Orchestras were male, and in London instrumental music was largely an all-male profession, although there were women pianists.

In addition to theatres, private productions of plays, as in the Austen household, provided women with opportunities. These could involve the socially prominent. John O'Keeffe's *The Agreable Surprise* (1781), a comic opera about confused identities and the triumph of love, was performed at Brandenburg House in 1795, with Albinia, Countess of Buckinghamshire, the wife of the third Earl, among the cast.

Women in particular benefited greatly from the expansion of public libraries, but assertive women outside their 'proper' roles aroused concern. There was certainly a degree of typecasting and condescension toward them, as in Tobias Smollett's popular novel *The Adventure of Roderick Random* (1748), in which Narcissa is presented as an unsuccessful writer 'without consistency or capacity' to bring her work to completion, but also, extraordinarily, writing not of love, but rather tragedies that did not cover it. There were differences in plots between male and female writers: a rather crude generalisation, but duty or love was the choice posed by many male writers, while female authors were apt to unite the two.

Female writers prominent in their day, such as Jane West (1758-1852), have frequently slipped from attention. In part, this is simply because the canon of major works emphasises male writers. Although West, an industrious writer who was typical, with novels, plays and poems, in producing across different genres, had a somewhat leaden style. More significantly in terms of tastes, West was an insistent moralist who was opposed to what she saw as the troubling radicalism of writers such as Mary

Eighteenth Century: Spheres of Patronage

Wollstonecraft. West's conservative politics were illustrated by her *Elegy on Edmund Burke* (1793), and her moralism by her novel *The Advantages of Education: or The History of Maria Williams* (1793). Male writers writing like West also tend to be forgotten.

The canon was, is, and will continue to be, fluid, and possibly more so than over the last century. Hannah More, another critic of Wollstonecraft, wrote *Percy* (1777), one of the most successful plays of the period, as well as books that at the time greatly outsold Austen's. She was then long overlooked but has recently made a return to the spotlight with the first modern biography. More saw herself as a conservative, and (*not* but) also envisaged women playing a prominent role. The implication of her call for female patriotism was that politics in its broadest sense had to involve women, who were responsible for protecting the morality of the country. Morality was presented as a patriotic guarantee of the nation. Novels were very much associated with female writers and readers, not least due to the epistolary form that was so important in many novels and to much female socializing, as marriage or other factors led female friends to live apart. Letters were definitely a form of conversation, and that was an important aspect of the leisure of the period, and notably so for women.[12] In Austen's circle, commenting on novels was prominent in correspondence. Novels could be, like letter-writing, an important part of the world of women's activity. Of course, many epistolary novels were written by men, notably the genre-setter *Pamela*.[13]

Less instrumental than correspondence, and personal rather than social, novels could also be presented as a drug, as was done satirically in Sheridan's play *The Rivals*: 'Madam, a circulating library in a town is an evergreen tree of diabolical knowledge! It blossoms through the year! And depend on it, Mrs Malaprop, that they who are so fond of handling the leaves, will long for the fruit at last.'[14]

English Culture

At the same time, novels dealt with issues of concern. Most were about courtship, or used it as an important plot device. They therefore offered women models of desirable partners, and of wooing, that were different from whatever might be sanctioned by parents. This was troubling to the latter, but proved particularly attractive to many female readers, and thus sustained the feminisation of the genre. On the whole, marriage for love was very much endorsed in fiction. However, in accordance with conventions of sensibility and practicality, marriage for love was constrained by an emphasis on propriety and on filial duty, notably to fathers.

Such marriage was often the concluding episode of a story that was essentially about growing up into society, with a young woman, frequently very young, as with Fanny Price in *Mansfield Park*, usually serving as the protagonist, and her trajectory as the dynamic course and chronology of the plot. Adaptation to others and to social conventions was a key theme. In Fanny Burney's first novel, *Evelina: Or, A Young Lady's Entrance into the World* (1778), a novel written in the form of letters, Evelina is shown being brought into the world at the age of seventeen, a course which closes when she marries one of her guides, the sage Lord Orville. This process of maturation provided opportunity for exciting, but predictable, sensibility. In the preface, Burney explains her plan 'to draw characters from nature, though not from life, and to mark the manners of the times'. A far less benign upbringing, with malevolent guardians, a melodramatic descent to insanity, and a touch of the Gothic, was offered in Burney's second novel, *Cecilia, or an Heiress* (1782).

The third novel, *Camilla, A Picture of Youth* (1796), was less unsettling and more conventional. Burney presented it to George III and Queen Charlotte, and Austen, who greatly admired Burney's work, was on the subscription list for the novel. The

Eighteenth Century: Spheres of Patronage

challenges in *Camilla* were more marked than those in *Evelina*. Several of the characters have faults. Edgar Mandlebert, the wealthy hero, is judgemental, difficult and overly concerned about appearances. Eugenia, the heroine's younger sister, is crippled as a result of an accident, having already suffered from smallpox, but her personality is a demonstration of true beauty. The heroine's older brother, Lionel, is highly mischievous and selfish, while another instance of selfishness is provided by her beautiful, flirtatious cousin, Indiana. Her brother Clermont is harsh to the servants and a bully. Camilla's father, a positive figure, is a cleric. The plot includes the kidnapping, by Alphonso Bellamy, a fortune-hunter, of Eugenia, who is forced into marriage, which provides a Gothic dimension.

While not a successful dramatist,[15] Burney was an important and recognised female novelist. Alongside the theme of adaptation in Burney's work, there was also that of the pressures, including violence, to which women were subject. As a result, Burney has been depicted as a writer of contradictions, sometimes fired by anger, but she, like many authors, eludes ideological fixing.[16] Moreover, the character of Burney's writing varied in each novel.

Men were also of course readers of novels, and Austen's father George bought them, which helped ensure their availability to his daughters. In *Northanger Abbey*, Henry Tilney, who was not opposed to fiction, responded to the suggestion that 'young men despised novels amazingly': 'It is *amazingly*; it may well suggest *amazement* if they do – for they read nearly as many as women. I myself have read hundreds and hundreds. Do not imagine that you can cope with me in a knowledge of Julias and Louisas.'

In *Northanger Abbey*, Catherine Morland herself was 'left to the luxury of a raised, restless, and frightened imagination over the pages of *Udolpho* [Ann Radcliffe's *The Mysteries of Udolpho*], lost from all worldly concerns of dressing and dinner'.

English Culture

She discovers that the abbey of the title is not a setting from the pages of Gothic fiction. Yet, ironically, in *Northanger Abbey*, real life turns out unpleasant, as Catherine is exposed to the ire of the avaricious General Tilney. He bullies his children, creating an atmosphere at Northanger Abbey that is differently unpleasant, and more real and emotionally menacing, than the imagined perils of Gothic fiction.

The tendency of women in sentimental novels to lack self-restraint, or what was depicted as self-restraint, was presented as a sign of heightened nerves and emotions, or as a lack of maturity. Heightened nerves were also a commonplace in sentimental plays. The audience was given unmissable clues. This process was mocked in Sheridan's *The Critic*: 'When a heroine goes mad she always goes into white satin.' Novelists could work with these conventions, or question them in order to make points, or both. Often, in characterisation or plotting, concerns were raised about female sensibility, and they were sometimes, as in conduct literature, treated as if they were minors. More positively, women were also presented as they were, as the key figures in family life and the culture of sociability.

Increasingly, children were treated as a distinctive part of society, with products being designed particularly for them. These included children's literature, a massive publishing phenomenon, and a genre in which women writers played an important role. Much of this literature was didactic. Thomas Day's best-selling *History of Sandford and Merton* (1783-89), an exemplary tale for children, presented the meritorious Harry Sandford, the son of a farmer, and Tommy Merton, the lazy son of an affluent gentleman. Morality through comparison, the theme in most novels, a theme that looks back to sermons and to secular equivalents such as Hogarth's 1747 series of engravings 'Industry and Idleness' was to the fore in this novel and in the genre as a

Eighteenth Century: Spheres of Patronage

whole. Yet, the depiction of children also became more informal. As in other respects, the conventions were far from unchanging.

This was also the age of the Enlightenment. Reason was a goal, as well as a method and a system.[17] Contemporaries believed it necessary to use reason in order to appreciate mankind, society and the universe, and thus to improve human circumstances, an objective in which religious faith, utilitarianism, and the search for human happiness could combine, for the English Enlightenment was religious in both context and content. Reason and moderation were believed to be the distinguishing marks of mankind, and, correspondingly, the insane were usually regarded as monstrous. Reason was presented as the characteristic of human development and social organisation, while the savage mind was held to be obsessed by a world of terror in which monstrous anxieties were projected onto nature. In *Emma*, Mr Knightley provides an account of maturity in terms of fighting off fears: 'I can allow for the fears of the child, but not of the man. As he became rational, he ought to have roused himself and shaken off all that was unworthy in their authority.'[18]

As part of the Enlightenment, notions of causation changed greatly, at least for some. In this context, a displacing of Providence was particularly apparent in the case of the weather. Instead of demonstrating immediate divine purpose, the weather was increasingly understood as a natural process. Equipment to aid that understanding was offered in the form of barometers and thermometers. Knowledge was displayed and enjoyed in the furnishing of houses with cased barometers, globes and maps, part of a more general desire to assert social and intellectual status.[19]

The Scientific Revolution was an aspect of public culture as well as personal interest. People became members of literary and philosophical societies, attended scientific lessons, and observed

English Culture

the movement of an orrery, a clockwork machine that showed the workings of the solar system. The topic of one of the best paintings of Joseph Wright of Derby (1734-97), *A Philosopher Lecturing on the Orrery* (1766), displayed Enlightenment values and knowledge, although another, his painting of *An Experiment on a Bird in the Air Pump* (1768), shows a girl distressed at the death of the bird as a result of the experiment. This highlighted an Enlightenment dilemma: how could medical knowledge be reconciled with sentimental feelings for animals? Wright was not simply a scientific artist but a deeply religious painter.

The vogue for geology was linked to an interest in the workings of Providence, in history, in the underpinning of physical geography, and with tourism. The work of James Hutton (1726-97), the key figure in the development of geology, was made more readable by John Playfair (1748-1819), notably with his *Illustrations of the Huttonian Theory of the Earth* (1802). Geology was displayed in William Smith's *Delineation of the Strata of England and Wales with Part of Scotland* (1815). This depiction was linked to the evolution of minerology, another aspect of accessible and useful knowledge.

There was a parallel in the developing appreciation of landscape. Daniel Defoe had referred in his *Tour* to the frightful character of mountains, the Lake District was 'all barren and wild'. By the end of the eighteenth century, the situation was very different. The romantic landscape came to the fore as William Cumberland had called for in his *Ode to the Sun* (1776) when he sought an engagement with the English 'sublime.' Geological debate influenced the contemporary aesthetic of poetry and art by revealing the majesty and antiquity of the Earth, exploring slow but profound processes and imagining great catastrophes and vast subterranean depths.

The Enlightenment was not only about science, knowledge and discovery. It also drew on, but reconceptualised, a general

Eighteenth Century: Spheres of Patronage

worthiness. Religion was a major (but today often under-appreciated) influence on this worthiness, as in the campaign against the slave trade.

In *Pride and Prejudice*, the arrogant, foolish and selfish Caroline Bingley suggests that balls were 'insufferably tedious... It would surely be much more rational if conversation instead of dancing were made the order of the day.'[20] What is being satirized here are not Enlightened views, but her ridiculous attempt to manipulate her way into Darcy's notice by throwing words like 'rational' around. She imagines that opposing balls in the name of rationality is going to attract Darcy, who has a big library and does not like dancing. Indeed, in contrast to Caroline's intentions and methods, really Enlightened attitudes are promoted by the novel. Elizabeth has to learn to judge Darcy and Wickham on the evidence, instead of going by her initial, irrational, impressions.

Tensions within intellectual and cultural tendencies affected socialising, as with contrasting ideas in *Emma* of how to enjoy the visit to Mr Knightley's organised around strawberry collecting. Mrs Elton proposes

> ... a sort of gipsy party. – We are to walk about your gardens, and gather the strawberries ourselves, and under trees, – and whatever else you may like to provide, it is to be all out of door – a table spread in the shade, you know. Every thing as natural and simple as possible. Is not that your idea?

This proposal earns a rejoinder from a more practical Knightley, one that acts as a clear qualification to enthusiasm:

> My idea of the simple and natural will be to have the table spread in the dining-room. The nature and the simplicity of gentlemen and ladies, with their servants and furniture, I think is best observed by

English Culture

meals within doors. When you are tired of eating strawberries in the garden, there shall be cold meat in the house.[21]

Like sentiment, reason and the natural could look in different directions. Knightley is also proposing English moderation.

A more pointed critique of the Enlightenment, and of false values in general, comes in another Austen novel, *Sanditon*, when Mr Parker, disparaging a rival bathing resort, remarks: 'We may apply to Brinshore, the line of the poet William Cowper in his description of the religious cottager, as opposed to Voltaire – "*She*, never heard of half a mile from home."' Parker misunderstands Cowper's *Truth* (1782) in which the pious cottager is contrasted with Voltaire – 'His the mere tinsel, hers the rich rewards'. Austen, the daughter of a cleric, praised Cowper (1731-1800), the son of another. Cowper became an Evangelical, and was also a prominent hymnodist and an opponent of slavery. Austen had characters approve of him.[22] The cottager understands true value as far as Austen was concerned. Morality throughout was important to culture, although it led in different artistic directions.

Seduction by men was a frequent danger in novels, with the misleading attraction and false promises of men a common theme, the result often being betrayal and the dangers of abandonment and pregnancy, as in Hannah Foster's *The Coquette* (1797) and Susan Rowson's *Charlotte: A Tale of Truth* (1794). In pursuit of morality, politeness and gentility were emphasised, as in Anna Maria Porter's novel *Walsh Colville: or, A Young Man's First Entrance into Life* (1797), alongside faith and reason. However, the reality of exploitation was captured in William Blake's bleak poem 'London' (1794) which included not only 'In every voice ... the mind-forged manacles I hear,' but also a comment on venereal disease:

Eighteenth Century: Spheres of Patronage

But most, through midnight streets I hear
How the youthful harlot's curse
Blasts the new-born infant's tear,
And blights with plagues the marriage-hearse.

The pain stemming from iniquity played a key role in William Godwin's *Things As They Are; or The Adventures of Caleb Williams* (1794), one of a number of radical political and social novels that included Charlotte Smith's *Desmond* (1792), Mary Hays' *Memoirs of Emma Courtney* (1796) and *The Victim of Prejudice* (1799), and Mary Wollstonecraft's *The Wrongs of Woman: or Maria* (1798), which dealt with the heroine's detention in a madhouse at the behest of a dishonest husband.

Aspects of radicalism included the reaction against the corruption and decadence of cities seen in the *Lyrical Ballads* (1798) by William Wordsworth and Samuel Taylor Coleridge and their effort to display a 'prosaic poetry' to show how far the language used by the bulk of the population, however poor, could serve the ends of poetry. This effort had only limited influence, but reflected the sense of cultural and political flux that was strong at the close of the century.

3

EIGHTEENTH CENTURY: SITES AND STYLES

... a company of comedians, that were going to make a summer campaign in the country. The company seemed not much to disapprove of me for an associate. They all, however, apprized me ... that the public was a many headed monster, and that only such as had very good heads could please it: that acting was not to be learnt in a day; and that without some traditional shrugs, which had been on the stage, and only on the stage, these hundred years, I could never pretend to please.

Oliver Goldsmith, *The Vicar of Wakefield* (1766) (chapter 20).

Eighteenth-century satirists, such as Alexander Pope and Jonathan Swift, might have been much amused by the vocabulary, tone and content of modern academic debates about cultural trends and causes. Such amusement is not without reason, but at the same time, it is necessary to appreciate that great works do not exist in a vacuum.

Eighteenth Century: Sites and Styles

The most familiar approach today is to focus on developments in style and artistic movements, which for this period takes us eventually from the Baroque to Romanticism, a Whiggish approach that emphasises 'progress' and modernity. There are many problems in describing changes in style, particularly since these developments can be perceived fully only through an appreciation of specific texts, objects and performances. The appropriateness of the accepted stylistic vocabulary is also open to question: a description, vocabulary or chronology of change that might suit portraiture is not necessarily applicable to opera, or poetry, or architecture. There can be a risk of reducing the past to an organised system of apposite items, ideas and styles.[1]

Although stylistic labels do serve purposes, they are unable to capture the full picture. For example, movements such as the English Baroque, associated in particular with Christopher Wren and John Vanbrugh, and with a Grand Style or manner across the arts, are open to very different definitions. Even in the important but restricted case of architecture, there was a difference in Baroque terms between the work of Wren and William Talman and that of Vanbrugh and Nicholas Hawksmoor. The East Front of Dyrham Park, designed by Talman, was very different to Easton Neston, a contemporary seat where Hawksmoor boldly used giant Classical orders. The arbitrary character of some definitions extends from styles to periodisation.

While common themes can be discerned in some fields of cultural activity, it is generally more appropriate to write in terms of stylistic tendencies, rather than to suggest that distinct uniformities can be discerned. We cannot assume that different styles and influences clashed and competed. Public criticisms of existing styles were indeed part of the establishment of an identity for newer styles, but there was coexistence and often overlap of apparently competing styles and influences, and,

English Culture

indeed, considerable mutual influence. Thus, alongside criticism of Baroque architecture on behalf of the Palladian style came a melding of elements of both styles, as in the work of James Gibbs.

These different styles can in part be related to the disparate goals sought by both patrons and artists. If some art was seen as a public medium that could improve society, rather than as a private luxury, the latter was also important and goals could coexist. Similarly, a stylistic device could be used to different ends. Thus, the letter was used as the form for Samuel Richardson's serious and influential novel *Pamela* (1740), as well as in Christopher Anstey's comic depiction of the Blunderhead family in his *New Bath Guide* (1766), both successful works, although the latter is now forgotten.

Nevertheless, whatever the goals of their creators, forms and styles had certain connotations. This was seen with the Grand Style in literature. Whereas Shakespeare had used prose alongside iambic pentameters, there had been a major shift in the seventeenth century, associated in particular with Milton and Dryden, to an emphasis on epic poetry with a consistent pentameter rhythm, and the use of polysyllables, rather than monosyllables. Couplets were preferred to blank verse.

When Pope died he was planning an epic entitled *Brutus*, who Geoffrey of Monmouth believed was the founder of Britain. Pope's interest reflected not simply a strong Latinity in literary culture, seen with writers very much perceived as English, such as Samuel Johnson, but also a striving for significance in themes, similes and characterisation, not least an association of exalted characters with Classical gods and heroes. Pope's translations of Homer were great commercial successes and contain some of the high points of eighteenth-century rhymed couplets.

Uplifting language appeared appropriate for uplifted characters. The Grand Style did not lend itself to comedy, which was handled differently, not least with a strong reliance on wordplay. The

Eighteenth Century: Sites and Styles

declamatory acting style that went with such uplift was associated in particular with James Quin (1693-1766), who was noted for playing the roles of Brutus and Cato. The equivalent on canvas was a preference for the noble, and for nobles, for heroic behaviour and elevated stances. This was an art that was statuesque, not intimate, and its corollary was the emphasis on passion and grand gestures in the Italian operas popular in London. Commemorative art took a number of forms, from monumental sculpture to the depiction of the battlefield. This art attracted much attention and was typical of other genres in that established conventions were adapted to changing artistic and social norms.[2]

At the same time, the ready availability of periodicals, the presence of a range of artistic bodies and learned societies, and the forcing hand of entrepreneurial activity, helped create a cultural climate that was receptive to new ideas and works. This was seen across the arts. Music provides a good instance. For example, in Norwich, where there was a very active musical life, both public and performers were ready to respond to quite rapid change. At the end of the century, concert-goers were able to hear the latest British and German works. Itinerant Italian bands of musicians performed in genteel places in the market towns of Norfolk.[3] Foreign musicians more generally played a significant role: Albinoni's *concerti grossi* were the role model for many English composers, notably Capel Bond, Charles Avison and later John Garth. Pieter Hellendaal ended up as an organist in Cambridge. Carl Friedrich Abel and Johann Christian Bach were prominent, Bach becoming music master to Queen Charlotte.

The foundation and growth of provincial festivals was a feature of the century. The provinces also provided new sites for sociability, leisure and domestic culture. Gloucestershire exemplified the wider tendency of the gentry to build houses that were counterparts to the more lavish edifices of magnates.[4]

English Culture

So also with the development of leisure activities that could be celebrated in the arts, as with paintings of racehorses and racing, for example Thomas Spencer's *Sir Edward Marshall Riding a Chestnut Horse* (1752) and Richard Roper's *Driver and Aaron Running the first heat at Maidenhead* (1754).

The willingness to accept frequent revisions of taste was also recorded in individual buildings. Powderham Castle, the seat of the Earls of Devon, gained impressive bookcases by John Channon with a continental-style decoration (1740) and a grand staircase supported by exuberant Baroque decoration (1754-56), but also a large Neo-Gothic apsidal-ended music room added by James Wyatt in 1794-96.

The desire to be fashionable was mocked by satirists. In her novel *Camilla* (1796), Fanny Burney presented Mr. Dubster showing guests around his grounds, which included the decoration of an island in a pool in front of his house:

> Mr Dubster then displayed the ingenious intermixture of circles and diamonds projected for the embellishment of his grotto; the first of which were to be formed with cockle-shells, which he meant to colour with blue paint; and the second he proposed shaping with bits of shining black coal.

As England was part of European culture, both affected by and influencing it, so all the major stylistic and thematic changes occurred on a continent-wide scale. Nevertheless, there were significant national variations and differences in chronology, while individual writers and artists could also make an important contribution. Thus, as an aspect of artisan culture, the poet and artist William Blake (1757-1827) developed a distinctive way to engrave both text and illustrations on the same plate.

At the beginning of the eighteenth century, the most important European architectural style was Baroque. Although to varying

Eighteenth Century: Sites and Styles

degrees emanating from Rome and associated with Catholicism, Baroque was also a style, or even ethos, seen in England in particular with the architecture of Wren and Vanbrugh, the music of Purcell, the drama of Dryden, and the formulaic structure of performances of Italian *opera seria*. Thanks to the extensive use of paint, moulding and sculpture, Baroque architecture made great play of painterly and sculptural qualities, so that decorated ceilings and walls contributed to a grandeur that overpowered the spectator, taking him or her into a world that was above and beyond them. This could be further accentuated by devices such as *trompe l'oeil* and mirrors. This emphasis on spectacle and scale – the great domes at St Paul's Cathedral and Greenwich Hospital being the first large domes and lanterns in England – was particularly suited to the grandeur of position, especially of monarchy, aristocracy and the established church. It offered less to the middling orders who desired to participate in cultural life other than as audience. Visitors to Castle Howard, a stately home that Vanbrugh designed for the Earl of Carlisle, were reminded of their status by approaching through a substantial arch crowned with a pyramid above heavy machicolations. Nobility was a key theme. All the viewer was expected to do was spectate, for example in response to Kneller's *The Triumph of Marlborough* (c. 1706), a sketch for a Rubenesque work of martial glory joining Earth to Heavens in a fantasy that would have seemed incongruous later in the century.

A highpoint of the Baroque was the Painted Hall at Greenwich, part of Christopher Wren's Royal Hospital for Seamen, which indicated the staged quality of its architecture and decorative theme. In 1708, James Thornhill was commissioned to paint the Great Hall. His rich painting of the ceiling (1708-12), an explicitly grand state painting, was a triumphant work proclaiming national power. The painting represents William III and Mary bringing Peace and Liberty to Britain and Europe.

English Culture

Oxford was also a centre of the Baroque, with buildings such as the Sheldonian Theatre, the Radcliffe Camera and the interiors of Queen's and Trinity College chapels. Thornhill was also responsible for the 'Apotheosis of Archbishop Chichele', a fresco at the east end of the chapel of All Souls College, Oxford, which, with its sky-lit character, painted architectural details, massed angels and ascending layout would not have been out of place in Rome.[5] A less grandiose Baroque can be seen at Beningbrough Hall, built under the supervision of William Thornton, who had worked under Vanbrugh at Castle Howard. Beningbrough has a two-storey hall of architectural quality and fine plasterwork, characteristics associated with the Baroque.

For those who worshipped, the sheer assertive bulk of Nicholas Hawksmoor's work, as in his St George-in-the-East, London (1714-29), encapsulated Baroque values of scale. Interior decorating was greatly influenced by Italian artists who came over to work at houses such as Burghley. Italian *stuccatori* applying stucco helped spread the fashion across provincial networks. For example, from the Hall and High Saloon at Castle Howard, they went on to tackle the interior of merchants' houses in Leeds, and the opera house at the Queen's/King's Theatre in London.

The phrase English Baroque can encompass a variety of tones and one has to consider contemporary criticisms of these works, not least from the cheerleaders for Palladianism, who rejected what was seen as the impure Classicism of the Baroque in favour of a return to true Classical forms. This had a politico-cultural dimension, as the Baroque could be associated with Papism, Italianism and even the Frenchification of these forms, with Palladianism, in contrast, a return to a purity comparable to that of the Primitive Church and of virtuous, public, non-authoritarian politics.

The Rococo style followed the Baroque, though it is sometimes described as Late Baroque. There was also a critical response to

Eighteenth Century: Sites and Styles

the Rococo, one located in a different social and moral resonance: the Rococo aesthetic, with its emphasis on pleasure, was different to the ethos and ambience of sentimentality which was most popular in mid-century, and found its expression in novels. Rococo is a term commonly associated in England with painting and interior decoration, characterised by mirrors and wall panels in carved wood, asymmetry, flowing curves, and shell and leaf patterns, rather than architecture. Very labour-intensive and therefore expensive, whole decorative schemes in Rococo style are rare and limited to the homes of the very rich. The Master's Chair of the Fruiterer's Company produced in 1748 was light, swirling, sinuous and decorated, with the cabriole legs rising from lion-paw feet and headed by men-of-the-woods masks. Rococo embellished the rich ornamentation of Baroque, but without its apparent solidity or at least grandeur; it was freer in shape and suggestion, and lacked the rigidity of the ordered rules of Classical architectural detail.

The Baroque was also replaced by an emphasis on a more refined and less demonstrative feeling that from the 1740s has been described in terms of a sensibility that was as much moral as aesthetic, and that did not necessarily correspond to the realities of behaviour. The rise of sentimentality represented a different impulse from that of the Rococo. According to the adage 'scratch a cynic and you find a romantic', sentimentality was the counterpoint to political and social cynicism. Its manifestations were varied, including an ostentatious moderating of the amorality and bawdy of much late-seventeenth-century comedy, which had already been diminished by the religious criticism of commentators such as Jeremy Collier, the Societies for the Reformation of Manners being joined in a more positive fashion by essayists in periodicals urging restraint and an awareness of social value, an argument pushed in particular by the *Spectator*.

English Culture

Many plays now encouraged a restrained consciousness opposed to indulgence, whether decadent aristocratic mores or popular ignorance and vice. Colley Cibber, the dire actor, playwright, and Poet Laureate from 1730 until 1757, made his name with *Loves Last Shift* (1696), a sentimental comedy of marital reconciliation (husband brought back from rakish lifestyle by his disguised wife), and this was followed by a series of such comedies, including Cibber's *The Careless Husband* (1704) and *The Provoked Husband* (1728). In Richard Steele's *The Conscious Lovers* (1722), virtue and sensitivity are rewarded.

Earlier playwrights were tidied up for modern tastes, as with Cibber's version of Shakespeare's *Richard III* (1700). Alexander Pope was not impressed by Cibber's laureateship:

In merry old England it once was the rule
The King had his poet and also his fool
But now we're so frugal I have you to know it
That Cibber can serve both for fool and for poet!

In 1771, when Aphra Behn's *Oroonoko: or The Royal Slave* (1688) was performed in Exeter, the proprietor in the playbill noted that the original script had been altered, so that what he saw as the pernicious immorality of the comic scenes could be replaced by more acceptable sentiments of fidelity, generosity and affection.[6]

Similarly, a number of painters moved from a grandiloquent style in portraiture toward a focus more on private character. This is evident in the work of Joseph Highmore (1692-1780), for example in his portrait of William Fellowes of Shotesham Park commissioned in 1748 as a present for his friend Robert Marsham. Rather than making an heroic statement, portraitists increasingly sought to bring out individual personality, consciously seeing themselves as akin to biographers.[7] Biography

Eighteenth Century: Sites and Styles

in fact developed in this period, with, for example, Oliver Goldsmith's lives of Bolingbroke, Richard Nash and Thomas Tarnell, and Samuel Johnson's *Poets*. Such works were an aspect of an evolving culture of individualism.

The cult of 'sensibility', of sentiment and fine emotion, at once individual and formulaic, had a considerable influence on the theatre and the newly emerging novels of the period, helping, as a result of the interacting development of fashion and psychological receptivity, to shift the focus from tragedy and epic to more domestic genres and themes, particularly the sentimental play and the novel.[8]

By calling forward a response, the depiction of distress in novels and on the stage gave the audience an opportunity to show their goodness and morality. A poised compassion towards virtue in distress made it possible to show a refined feeling that was artistically meritorious. By the 1780s, this was increasingly to be seen as affectation, although a comic ambivalence can already be noted with Yorick, the protagonist in Laurence Sterne's *Sentimental Journey through France and Italy* (1768). Despite the portrayal of bogus sensibility or, indeed, criticism of sensibility itself, it went on being important in both published work and private reflection.

Sensibility and sentimentalism were associated with a greater emphasis on the display of feelings in the shape of emotionalism. Samuel Richardson's popular novels *Pamela* (1740) and *Clarissa* (1747-48) were seen as displaying admirable sentiment in terms of moral lessons and emotional honesty, and many other sentimental novels followed, including Henry Brooke's *The Fool of Quality* (1766-72). Sentimental comedies, such as Hugh Kelly's *False Delicacy* (1768), also benefited from the vogue for the display of feelings, although this was a matter of benevolent gentility, not raw emotion. In the 1740s, although the leading actor and theatrical entrepreneur David Garrick acted in Benjamin Hoadly the younger's successful comedy *The Suspicious*

English Culture

Husband (1747), the taste of which was to be regarded as questionable, he also sought to raise the moral tone of the theatre, as others, such as John Dennis, Aaron Hill and James Thomson, had earlier sought to do. The sentimental comedy that resulted generally lacked bite, and theatre did not greatly flourish in the second half of the century, but its morality reflected audience wishes; although these are not easy to recover, and surviving comments indicate a variety of responses. Samuel Johnson, not the famous one but the young son of William Johnson of Torrington, wrote from London to his sister Elizabeth in 1774:

> I have been at one play since I writ you my journal. *The Beggar's Opera* with *The Druids*: my inducement for going was to hear Signor Rossignol's most amusing imitations of singing birds, which he does to that perfection that it is impossible to distinguish them from the finest notes of the nightingale, canary bird, goldfinch, linnet, etc; for all appearance of the human voice is entirely lost; the sound is produced with a very great effort and exertion of the lungs, and he is obliged to stop for breath and drink a glass of water in the middle of his performance.

He was not much of a theatregoer, but his letters home indicated that going there was expected. The following January, the young Samuel

> ... went to the play with cousin John, which is the only time since I have been here, which is owing to two reasons, want of time, and an indifference for new plays, which have swarmed this winter. *Matilda* is the play which I saw; but I would rather read two plays to you, than see such a one again, though they say this is the queen of the hive. I thought it a drone.

Going to see prominent actors was clearly a plus. February 1775:

Eighteenth Century: Sites and Styles

... went to see Garrick act Leon in *Rule a Wife and have a Wife*; we got very good seats, and I was for the only time since I have been here very much entertained with the play, and indeed as much at King and Mrs Abingdon as at Garrick, for I hardly think that Garrick exceeded either of them; the farce was a pantomime.

Two days later, because his aunt had taken twelve seats, his cousin and he saw *The Rivals*, 'though very much against our inclination', and four days after that went to Robert Jephson's new tragedy *Braganza*:

This play had been so exceedingly cried up that the boxes were all taken for fifteen nights before the play came out; this was the first night... I suppose Garrick appeared to support the great encomium which he had bestowed ... it met with great applause, but people's expectations were by no means satisfied; there is no one epithet will express my opinion of it better than insipid.

Johnson's uncle intended 'to see Garrick in the *Wonder*, and their Majesties who were at the play'.[9] The royal presence stamped plays as respectable. Actors were immortalised for élite audiences not simply in portraits and the whole genre of theatrical paintings but also porcelain. At Belton House the porcelain collection includes a pair of Bow white figures of Henry Woodward as the Fine Gentleman and Kitty Clive as the Fine Lady in Garrick's face *Lethe*, first performed at Drury Lane in 1740.

The focus was on established forms, a civilised tone, comedies of manners, and the testing but affirmation of emotional and family stability. If lovers were apart due to mischance or parental disapproval, these were overcome. In *The Clandestine Marriage* (1766) by George Colman the Elder and Garrick, the secret marriage of Fanny, the daughter of a wealthy merchant,

English Culture

and Lovewell, his clerk, is forgiven at the magnanimous request of Lord Ogleby; Fanny herself confesses to self-reproach and says she 'must be miserable for ever' if she does not receive her father's forgiveness. At the close of the popular *The West Indian* (1771), by Richard Cumberland (satirised as Sir Fretful Plagiary in Sheridan's *The Critic*), there was a typically contrived denouement, at once dramatic and sentimental. Belcour discovers that he is the son of Stockwell, who declares:

> How happily has this evening concluded, and yet how threatening was its approach!... Belcour, I have watched you with a patient, but inquiring eye, and I have discovered through the veil of some irregularities, a heart beaming with benevolence, an animated nature, fallible indeed, but not incorrigible; and your election of this excellent young lady makes me glory in acknowledging you to be my son.

In Thomas Holcroft's very successful comedy *The Road to Ruin* (1792), the discovery of a new will and the surprising salvation of the failing family bank sets the scenario to rights. Oliver Goldsmith's sole novel, *The Vicar of Wakefield* (1766), was also reliant on an improbable happy ending which required the actions of a benign knight, the revelation that neither a fake marriage nor a death from grief had occurred (the marriage was in fact real), and the change of heart of a swindler. Alongside villains came those capable of showing sensibility. If Squire Thornhill in *The Vicar of Wakefield* proves a malevolent force, his uncle, Sir William, acts as restorer. In Thomas Morton's successful musical melodrama *The Children in the Wood* (1793), the murderous villain out to have the children killed is the wicked Sir Rowland:

> Soon their silence shall be eternal. My brother being concluded dead, that lustrous orb being set in night, shall these pygmy

Eighteenth Century: Sites and Styles

satellites eclipse me? No. That fellow I am sure of. From his eye remorse is banished, and unmasked murder lowers upon his brow.

Social harmony, however, is restored, Lord Alford and Lady Helen regaining their children, while Walter proves an honest yokel.

Hogarth criticised aristocratic mores, but most painters depicted aristocrats in an exemplary light. Instead of seeing the commercialisation of leisure as a triumph of bourgeois culture, the role of the middling orders was largely to patronise both new and traditional artistic forms, rather than developing or demanding distinct styles. A desire for sensibility meant approval for the acting style associated with Garrick that was seen as more measured and less demonstrative than the earlier declamatory style. The comparable music was the easy (but carefully contrived) elegance of Johann Christian Bach's sonatas and concertos of the 1760s and 1770s, and the music written for Vauxhall Gardens by James Horn, who was composer and organist there from 1774 to 1820. In poetry, there was a shift in emphasis from satire to sensibility.

The art to which the pressure for a moral culture gave rise is generally described as Neo-Classical, although that was not a term used in the period, the 'true style' being the favoured description. The idea that culture should be exemplary had never been lost. Once a public debate about the purpose of art and the artist developed, it was likely that it would have taken the attitude critical of the Rococo and of cultural borrowings that was adopted in mid-century. Criticisms focused not so much on the quality of the work as on its purpose, or apparent lack of it, for artist and patron.

Although there was an increasing sense of the happiness of the individual (and of society) as an important goal of human society, critics found art for what they saw as mere pleasure inadequate. Instead, they sought a didactic art capable of arousing sentiment and morality. In his 'Discourses' as the first President of the Royal

English Culture

Academy, founded in 1768, a position he held until his death, Joshua Reynolds (1723-92) propounded a purposeful view of art. In 1770, he claimed that a true painter 'instead of endeavouring to amuse mankind with the minute neatness of his imitation ... must endeavour to improve them by the grandeur of his ideas'. He offered an exemplary portrayal, but this did not have to mean grandiloquence. His portrait of the surgeon William Hunter, who in 1768 became the first Professor of Anatomy to the Royal Academy, depicted a man of simple dress, the focus being on his face, hands and work, rather than on the trappings of power. This was not matched by the portrait of Dr John Ash in begowned finery. Ash, a physician, was a gentleman, socially superior to a mere surgeon.

Improvement was not simply a matter of rules. Indeed, in 1769, in his second Discourse, Reynolds suggested that once thoroughly grounded in the discipline, the painter might 'try the power of his imagination... The mind that has been thus disciplined, may be indulged in the warmest enthusiasm, and venture to play on the borders of the wildest extravagance.' Nevertheless, truth had to be the basis and in 1774 Reynolds criticised the French-born Philip James de Loutherbourg for not basing his paintings on observation: 'There are many good landscapes of Loutherbourg, but they are very much *manierata*. They seem to be the works of a man who has taken his ideas at second hand, from other pictures instead of nature.'[10] Loutherbourg was to go on to have a distinguished career as the painter of theatrical sets.

The exclusive court and aristocratic circles that patronised the Rococo and favoured cosmopolitan styles were not especially interested in public debate, but they were not totally insulated from it and were affected by the Neo-Classical current by the 1760s. This had a number of manifestations including, most simply, the depiction of characters, in fiction, on stage or on canvas, in Classical poses. George Romney painted Elizabeth, Viscountess Bulkeley as

Eighteenth Century: Sites and Styles

Hebe, the wife of Hercules and daughter of Jupiter, who appears behind her in the portrait in the guise of an eagle. Her plain dress with its draperies is reminiscent of those in Classical reliefs. Classical plans and motifs dominated buildings, not only secular works but also, increasingly, ecclesiastical ones. Begun in 1760, although not completed and consecrated until 1812, Gibside Chapel, the work of the architect James Paine, was based on the buildings of Roman antiquity and churches of Palladio which Paine had seen on a visit to Italy. A Classical building on the plan of a Greek cross, with a double portico closing the vista along the avenue, its six Ionic columns line the entrance façade. Above the portico is a pediment in front of a parapet carrying urns. The work on the estate was funded by the coal wealth of George Bowes, MP for Durham County, who died leaving a fortune estimated at £600,000.

Neo-Classical architecture was characterised by an absence of Baroque ornamentation and Rococo exuberance. Instead, the emphasis was on a geometry of clarity, with clean straight lines and plain surface. Simplicity was a key Neo-Classical value, being associated with integrity, both individual and collective.

Neo-Classical themes were also seen in interior decoration, especially in the work of Robert and James Adam in the 1770s, as well as in the pottery designs used by Josiah Wedgwood. The influential, light, elegant style introduced by Robert Adam, when he returned from Italy in 1757, included ornamental motifs from Classical antiquity, especially after the discoveries at Pompeii. At Kedleston Hall, in the 1760s, he designed twelve painted benches for the Marble Hall, the design inspired by a sarcophagus in the Pantheon. The design by William Ivory for the plasterwork on the ceiling in the Peter the Great Room in Blickling Hall derived from ceilings discovered in Pompeii and Herculaneum.

Sculptures appeared particularly apt for Neo-Classical buildings. The first gold medal for sculpture awarded by the Royal Academy

English Culture

was given to John Bacon in 1769 for a bas-relief representing Aeneas escaping from Troy. Thomas Banks, who was in Rome from 1772 until 1779, initially thanks to support from the Royal Academy, produced relief sculptures, including *The Death of Germanicus* for Thomas Coke of Holkham and *Caractacus* for George Grenville. Classical models (and remains) had an air of reborn integrity, and Neo-Classicism possessed a quality of statuesque drama seen not only in architecture and sculpture but also in painting, particularly with the popular Classical manner of Reynolds. This also affected other painters. Joseph Wright of Derby abandoned his 'Flemish' style in favour of Reynolds's manner, as the Italian school of painting was considered superior to the Dutch school.

The term Neo-Classicism refers to Classical influences in the second half of the century. This was certainly true of Greek models, but, in practice these influences could be found throughout the period. Augustan is a term applied to the writers of the first half of the century, especially Pope and Swift; and Goldsmith wrote *An Account of the Augustan Age in England* (1759). The writers of this period were much impressed by Virgil, Horace and Ovid, Latin poets of the reign of Augustus, especially by Virgil's *Eclogues* and *Georgics*, both of which greatly influenced Pope. The heroic pentameter couplets that dominated poetry provided a structure that offered much to satire, but that also lent itself to the poetry of sensibility.

Goldsmith's *Account* implied that by 1759 there had been a falling off in quality. There had certainly been a shift in mood. The preference for satire over sensibility seen earlier had been reversed, although neither approach was absent in either period. The more reflective and intimate and less 'public' poetry of the period of sensibility, famously represented in Thomas Gray's *Elegy Written in a Country Churchyard* (1751), was not without important Classical roots, as the notion of withdrawal from the corruption of the city was a powerful one among the influential

Eighteenth Century: Sites and Styles

Roman models of the period. Nor were poets alone in looking back to Classical roots and models.

The emphasis on elegant clarity in sentiment and expression seen in the English Augustan writers had equivalents in Neo-Classical activity in other art forms later in the century, but there were also differences. In both periods, however, there was an assumption that the educated public would understand Classical references and be interested in Classical themes. Thus, playwrights produced works such as Colley Cibber's *Perolla and Izadora* (1706), set during the Second Punic War, as well as Charles Beckingham's *Scipio Africanus* (1718) and Philip Frowde's *The Fall of Saguntum* (1727), on topics that would attract no attention today. Addison's *Cato* (1713) was a greatly influential play recalling a heroic Roman at a time when the Whigs were confronting the prospect of a dangerous future once Queen Anne died. Richard Glover (1712-1785) made his name as a writer for the 'Patriots' against Sir Robert Walpole, with his lengthy and much reprinted epic poem *Leonidas* (1737), and later wrote a series of tragedies on Classical themes – *Boadicea* (1753), *Medea* (1761) and *Jason* (1799), as well as another lengthy epic poem, *The Athenaid* (1787). Some of this Classical history was fundamental to the Italian opera produced in London.

The range of Classical influence is indicated by the use of Roman dress in portraiture and funeral statuary. For the aristocracy in particular, the oligarchic system of republican Rome appeared an apt model, but it was not only the aristocracy that was attracted to the comparison. The potency of the Classical inheritance helps explain concern about corruptions of it, and therefore the philological emphasis on producing (and reading) accurate texts. More generally, this offered one way in which the Moderns could add to the contribution of the Ancients, and ensured that controversy could develop over works judged

English Culture

problematic, such as Pope's edition of Shakespeare (1725) and Conyers Middleton's *Life of Cicero* (1741): the former was criticised in Theobald's *Shakespeare Restored* (1726), while the authenticity of documents cited by Middleton was questioned by James Tunstall in works published in 1741 and 1744.

The Classical influence did not prevent a debate over the respective merits of Ancients and Moderns, which led to such works as Swift's *The Battle of the Books* (1704) and *A Tale of a Tub* (1704), mock-heroic satires that supported the Ancients, and to Pope's attack on the Moderns in *The Dunciad* (1728). This debate testified to the role of the Classics as a standard for judgement.[11]

The debate between Ancients and Moderns became less potent, certainly in the literary world, in the second half of the century, as the rise of the novel put the emphasis very much on Modern forms, while Classical themes were more generally reshaped. Nevertheless, the Ancients and Moderns debate became central to music in the 1770s and 1780s, with the foundation of the Concerts of Ancient Music, while the role of the Classical world in shaping aesthetic judgements continued to be reiterated. In 1786, the fifth edition of Nicholas Tindal's *A Guide to Classical Learning: or Polymetis Abridged* (1st edition 1764) was advertised as 'absolutely necessary, not only for the right understanding of the Classics, but also for forming in young minds a true taste for the beauties of poetry, sculpture and painting'.[12]

In 1766, Louis Dutens, a Huguenot immigrant patronised by the Duke of Northumberland, published a work translated three years later as *An Inquiry into the Origin of the Discoveries attributed to the Moderns: Wherein it is Demonstrated, that our Most Celebrated Philosophers have, for the Most Part, Taken What they Advance from ... the Antients; and that Many Important Truths in Religion were Known to the Pagan Sages.* Advertising, however, tended to benefit the Moderns because the idea of novelty was seen as an important seller.

Eighteenth Century: Sites and Styles

The mid-century cultural tensions continued into the second half of the century. No one category is adequate to cover the variety of artistic developments from then until its close. Neo-Classicism and pre-Romanticism vied for attention, but so also did the Neo-Gothic and *Chinoiserie*.[13] Romanticism, itself a retrospective concept, has been variously defined, with an increased emphasis since the early 1980s on social and political elements, not least a greater awareness of the political and social interests of nearly all the major writers.[14] Yet, there is still value in an older view of what would be seen as the Romanticism of the 1790s in which it is associated with the individual emotions of the artist, often at variance with social and cultural conventions, and inspired by the intoxicating power and wildness of elemental natural forces.

There were certainly harbingers of this emphasis, and in them a changing appreciation of nature was important. James Thomson in his preface to *Winter* (1726) presented nature in reflective terms rather than with the emotional intensity seen toward the close of the century:

> I know no subject more elevating, more amusing; more ready to awake the poetical enthusiasm, the philosophical reflection, and the moral sentiment, than the *Works of Nature*. Where can we meet with such variety, such beauty, such magnificence? All that enlarges, and transports, the soul? What more inspiring than a calm, wide, survey of them? In every dress *Nature* is greatly charming!

In the second half of the century, in contrast, there was an interest in landscape painting with a new appreciation of the 'sublime' qualities of savage landscape, which contrasted with earlier formal gardens. Nature was increasingly seen as an elemental creative force, not as a pleasing and inconsequential landscape, and, correspondingly, the human soul as a seat of passion, rather than

English Culture

harmony. The changing nature of the emphasis on sensibility, and its growing linkage with the notion of spiritual awareness, were very important in forming proto-Romantic taste. What can be seen as an early anticipation of this was provided by the poet Mark Akenside in *The Pleasures of Imagination* (1744), a didactic poem that stressed the value of a well-formed imagination. The equivalent in portraiture was the attempt to give subjects natural and open expressions, as in Reynolds's *Mrs Levina Luther* (1763-66).

Towards the close of the century, a taste for picturesque landscape was widely diffused and it served to direct popular tastes towards what would later be seen as Romantic values. Linked to this came an interest that was pronounced from mid-century, sometimes pseudo-melancholic, in ruins, which were increasingly presented as an innate part of the landscape.[15] William Mason closed his paean to 'Landscape' in *The English Garden* (1772): 'most happy, if thy vale below/Wash, with the crystal coolness of its rills,/Some mouldring abbey's ivy-vested wall.' Similarly, from Thomas Warton's 'The Solemn Noon of Night' in *The Pleasures of Melancholy* (1747) we have the appeal of 'yon ruin'd Abbey's moss-grown piles'. 'Berry Pomeroy Castle' by the Exeter-based landscape painter Francis Towne (1739-1816) showed trees growing up among the ruins. Thomas Whately captured what was seen as the suggestible nature of the human imagination, and therefore its openness to the arts:

At the sight of a ruin, reflections on the change, the decay, and the desolation before us, naturally occur; and they introduce a long succession of others, all tinctured with that melancholy which these have inspired.[16]

An interest in ruins was related to the focus on mortality by those later termed the 'graveyard poets'. Locating their meditations in nocturnal churchyards, writers such as Robert Blair and Edward Young sought sublime effects that meshed religious thoughts and fine sensibility, moving beyond melancholia to find a more active reflection. Although not addicted to churchyards, the same was true of William Bowles's popular *Fourteen Sonnets Written Chiefly on Picturesque Spots during a Journey* (1789). Bowles, like Gray and Young, was a cleric. Aside from poetry on mortality, there was also prose fiction, although that was less common. 'J.S.' in *Swinney's Birmingham and Stafford Chronicle* of 11 January 1776 published an allusive dream essay on time, pleasure and death, with time's inexorable triumph the major theme.

More prominently, Edmund Burke's *Philosophical Enquiry into the Origin of our Ideas of the Sublime and the Beautiful* (1759) put an emphasis on the extent to which the sublime could transform the reader and spectator. Sublime was a word used of Handel's music at the time, but it was defined by Burke as whatever led to ideas of danger, pain or terror: he suggested obscurity, vastness, privation and infinity. Burke argued that if the source of these ideas was imaginary, they could cause delight. Emotions and potent sensory experiences, rather than nobility, reason and dignity, were crucial for Burke.[17]

This argument was important in the Gothic impulse that owed much to the publicity surrounding Horace Walpole's novel *The Castle of Otranto* (1764). Walpole, who had the time to do so, did not write another Gothic novel after *The Castle of Otranto*, but followed in 1768 with *The Mysterious Mother*, a Gothic tragedy set in the Middle Ages. Incest plays a key role in the plot, with the manipulative French countess committing suicide when her tormenting guilt is revealed. The Catholic clergy featured are dishonest and, for Walpole, she has reason to defy them and their attempts to make her achieve religious repentance. Guilt is a key theme in the play. The topic and outcome made the play

English Culture

inappropriate for the stage, but there were private readings and several editions. *The Castle of Otranto* was cited as 'a very spirited modern attempt' upon the plan of the *Arabian Nights* 'adapted to the model of Gothic romance' by Anna Aikin (later Anna Bartauld) in her 'On the Pleasure Derived From Objects of Terror' which appeared in her *Miscellaneous Pieces in Prose* (1773). She provided in this piece an explanation of the sublime dimension of surprise that included 'the agency of invisible beings... Passion and fancy co-operating elevate the soul to its highest pitch ... the more wild, fanciful, and extraordinary are the circumstances of a scene of horror, the more pleasure we receive from it.'

Anna Aikin also observed the consumerism of public interest: 'The Greediness with which the tales of ghosts and goblins, of murders, earthquakes, fires, shipwrecks, and all the most terrible disasters attending human life, are devoured by every ear'. She gave Shakespeare as an instance of the process. The preface to *Miscellaneous Pieces* came with 'Sir Bertrand, a Fragment' (1773) by John Aikin (although often attributed wrongly to his sister Anna), an unfinished piece which provided a sinister, apparently deserted, Gothic castle with a mysterious moving flame, and a dead hand grasping the protagonist, both, notably the former, devices that were to be used frequently. The lid of a coffin flies open:

A lady in a shroud and black veil rose up in it, and stretched out her arms towards him... Sir Bertrand flew to the lady and clasped her in his arms – she threw up her veil and kissed his lips; and instantly the whole building shook as with an earthquake, and fell asunder with a horrible crash.

This passage offered an early instance of the themes and images of illicit and dangerous sexuality, a veil, and earthquakes as both

Eighteenth Century: Sites and Styles

plot and an indicator of fundamental disruption. This sexuality was to lead to the nineteenth-century strand of Gothic vampirism. Anna Aikin (1743-1825) was a successful 'woman of letters,' particularly as a writer of children's literature. She was also a literary critic and a supporter of political reform. Her brother John was a doctor who became a writer, notably a biographer.

There was no preface to the next significant work, Clara Reeve's *The Champion of Virtue* (1777), but when it was published the following year as *The Old English Baron: A Gothic Story*, it had a preface that paid full attention to Walpole's novel, which was the defining point until Radcliffe's novels changed the paradigm in the 1790s. In this preface, Reeve presented her work as

> ... of a species which, though not new, is out of the common track, the literary offspring of the Castle of Otranto, written upon the same plan, with a design to unite the most attractive and interesting circumstances of the ancient Romans and modern Novel, at the same time it assumes a character and manner of its own, that differs from both; it is distinguished by the appellation of a Gothic Story, being a picture of Gothic times and manners.

Reeve argued that to attain the uniting aim, it was necessary to have 'a sufficient degree of the marvellous, to excite the attention; enough of the manners of real life, to give an air of probability to the work; and enough of the pathetic, to engage the heart in its behalf'.

Bringing the past under scrutiny was a feature of much cultural activity, in fiction, plays, painting and building. Rosetta Ballin's *The Statue Room; An Historical Tale* (1790), for example, a melodramatic historical novel in which Elizabeth I was a villain due to her (in practice fictionalised) treatment of Mary, Queen of Scots. John Wesley's *Concise History of England* has the heroine

English Culture

search for her imprisoned lover. Ballin offered an alternative history that was in accordance with the dynastic inheritance puzzles of so many Gothic novels. Catherine of Aragon is (falsely) described as pregnant when rejected by Henry VIII, and her suppositious child, who is given the Saxon name of Adelfrida, secretly marries the Duke of Alençon, only to be poisoned on the instructions of Elizabeth, while Adelfrida's daughter, Romelia, is also the target of the Queen. A vision leads her to seek to murder Elizabeth, only to fail and then commit suicide.

There were also developments in tone within this process of scrutinising the past, the change in the depiction of Shakespearean scenes being instructive. The first known painting of a Shakespearean scene, William Hogarth's *Falstaff Examining his Recruits* (1730), which may also have been the depiction of an actual performance, was essentially comic and non-suggestive. The situation, however, subsequently changed, with a probing of more mysterious aspects.

In the painting of the period, there was a strong interest in mystery. Thus, focusing on the magical *Tempest*, Francis Hayman, George Romney and Thomas Jones all painted Prospero and Miranda spying the shipwrecked Ferdinand. Romney (1734-1802) was particularly interested in Shakespeare, offering a nightmare scene, *King Lear in the Tempest Tearing off his Robes* (1760-1), as one of his first major paintings.

As a reminder of the problematic nature of separating styles for analysis, the neo-Gothic had many links with Romanticism. Thus, Ann Radcliffe in her very successful novels offered a popular Romanticism. In *The Italian* (1797), the captured Ellena provides an appropriate response to the darkening forcefulness of the landscape that she was thrust into with all the attention of an enraptured spectator of an awesome painting, and, indeed, there are references to illustrations:

Eighteenth Century: Sites and Styles

It was when the heat and the light were declining that the carriage entered a rocky defile, which shewed, as through a telescope reversed, distant plains, and mountains opening beyond, lighted up with all the purple splendor of the setting sun. Along this deep and shadowy perspective a river, which was seen descending among the cliffs of a mountain, rolled with impetuous force, fretting and foaming amidst the dark rocks in its descent, and then flowing in a limpid lapse to the brink of other precipices, whence again it fell with thundering strength to the abyss, throwing its misty clouds of spray high in the air, and seeming to claim the sole empire of this solitary wild. Its bed took up the whole breadth of the chasm, which some strong convulsion of the earth seemed to have formed, not leaving space even for a road along its margin. The road, therefore, was carried high among the cliffs, that impended over the river, and seemed as if suspended in air; while the gloom and vastness of the precipices, which towered above and sunk below it, together with the amazing force and uproar of the falling waters, combined to render the pass more terrific than the pencil could describe, or language can express. Ellena ascended it, not with indifference but with calmness; she experienced somewhat of a dreadful pleasure in looking down upon the irresistible flood; but this emotion was heightened into awe, when she perceived that the road led to a slight bridge, which, thrown across the chasm at an immense height, united two opposite cliffs, between which the whole cataract of the river descended. The bridge, which was defended only by a slender railing, appeared as if hung amidst the clouds. Ellena, while she was crossing it, almost forgot her misfortunes.

The sublime could be seen across a host of activities, for example the acting of Garrick, particularly his re-creation of Shakespeare's Macbeth from 1744 and his depiction of Hamlet faced with the

English Culture

ghost of his father.[18] This matched the presentation of moments of strong emotion by painters, a presentation that could link sensibility to Romanticism.

The idea of the soul as a seat of passion, and passion often as the cause of anguish, was most luridly expressed by the Swiss painter Johann Heinrich Füssli (he anglicised his name as Henry Fuseli) (1741-1825), who spent most of the period from 1764 in England, becoming a member of the Royal Academy in 1790. He offered visions of horrific fantasy, comparable to some of the contemporary Gothic novels. A precursor of Romanticism, Fuseli argued that the individual and society, art and morality, were in conflict, and that the arts were a divine gift which elevated man by their force, impact and terror. Praised by George III and William Blake, his most famous painting was *Nightmare* (1781; exhibited 1782), a Gothic fantasy that offered a powerful vision of the mysterious and the subconscious. Producing work designed to arouse the imagination, Fuseli painted visions that exposed the limited sway of social order and psychological balance and harmony, and depths in human experience which reason could not explain. His paintings looked toward the unfixed, metaphorical quality that was to be so important to much Romantic work, and that was also pronounced in Gothic literature, such as Radcliffe's novels, although, at the end of each, she provides a rational explanation to what had seemed supernatural.

Reynolds's massive *Macbeth and the Witches*, painted in the late 1780s, echoed aspects of Fuseli's work. The grip of *Macbeth* on the imagination reflected interest in the supernatural and in fantastical stories but was also in accord with the instinctive response by audiences then increasingly fashionable, in contrast to the earlier intellectual response. This was an aspect of a shift from text to a theatrical experience in which emotional atmosphere

Eighteenth Century: Sites and Styles

created by other means, such as the scene-painting, was more important than hitherto.

Drama that tested contemporary boundaries was provided in a different way by William Beckford's *Vathek: An Arabian Tale* (1786), a novel about the quest for deadly knowledge and legendary power in which the explicit defiance of established morality was in part expressed by a sexual adventurousness seen as part of its subject's desire to fulfil his sensuality. This looked to the exoticism of some Gothic fiction, and to troubled villains, such as Ambrosio, the protagonist of Matthew Lewis's novel *The Monk* (1796). Ambrosio is presented as a victim of his own irrational impulses, specifically lustful self-destructive drives, which are at the end of the novel unconvincingly attributed to diabolical forces. He was more frightening than the earlier Gothic novel creations of Horace Walpole and Ann Radcliffe. Like the paintings of Füssli, the plots of Gothic literature tested conventional notions of probability, not least the established patterns of expressing and moulding experience with reference to the interior and natural world.

Gothic fiction reworked many of the images of landscape poetry. Monastic stonework and trees became ruined abbeys and sinister woods that served as malign settings for the plot and also represented the psychological strains of the psyche. This was very different to the metropolitan settings that had dominated the culture of print at the start of the century.

The emphasis on the wilful protagonist was located in the Romantic fascination with the ego. To be heroic, however, the Romantic hero required a brooding quality, a dignified melancholy and mysterious introspection, that separated him from the more easily driven and readily explained villains of Gothic novels, although Schedoni, the complex, troubled, austere

English Culture

monkish villain of Radcliffe's *The Italian* (1797) showed signs of being such a hero.

Dramatic accounts of character were offered by painters, as with Reynolds' 1784 portrait of *Mrs Siddons as the Tragic Muse* (1784). Siddons (Sarah Kemble, 1755-1831), the leading tragic actress of the age, was successful in showing that the Gothic could be theatrical and that the potent psychology of the paranormal that Gothic had come to express could be channelled to dramatic effect.[19] Reynolds's rich, dark painting with its figures of Pity and Terror looked forward to Romanticism. The painting was a great success, praised by James Barry as 'The finest picture of the kind, perhaps in the world, indeed it is something more than a portrait.' The last point reflects the shift in Reynolds's later portraits away from conversation pieces and towards a style that is more otherworldly, with more clouds and smoke.[20]

Pictorial representation in turn influenced the theatre, while the theatre frequently provided material for painters. Hogarth was commissioned to depict a scene from John Gay's *The Beggar's Opera* and produced a frontispiece for the published version of Henry Fielding's play *Tom Thumb the Great*. Sarah Siddons was held up for praise by Frances Crewe because she relied on 'feelings' not 'attitudes'. Vital simplicity was applauded:

Action is the Language of Nature... Mrs Siddons would make us weep, or rage, in short just as she chose to affect us... There must, I know, be *Machinery* in everything, but ought we see it? ... What Sir Joshua Reynolds somewhere says of drapery, is exactly what I think of imitation, 'It should be woollen, or silk, or linen, it should be *drapery*, it should be nothing more.' An actress should not be Italian, or French, or English, she should be a woman and nothing more.[21]

Eighteenth Century: Sites and Styles

Literary criticism flourished, as well as to a more widespread process of criticism in which attempts were made to improve the quality of individual works. The publication of critical works in book, pamphlet and periodical form reflected the contentious nature of the public sphere and the level of reader interest. Much of the criticism was didactic. Yet, alongside a belief that the arts were of more general social and cultural importance, it was frequently felt necessary to add a humorous tone in order to attract readers, as in *The Dramatic Censor, or Critical Companion. Being an instructive and entertaining preceptor for the playhouse* (1776). Some writers made their name as critics, seeking to regulate literature and other forms, John Dennis produced *The Advancement and Reformation of Modern Poetry* (1701) and *The Grounds of Criticism in Poetry* (1704). Joseph Addison's popular play *Cato* (1713) led to the publication of several commentaries that discussed whether the rules of drama had been observed in the play. Most were praiseworthy, although in Dennis' *Remarks upon Cato* (1713) there was criticism of a dearth of appropriate moralising. More prominent writers and artists also tried their hand at criticism, Pope producing an *Essay on Criticism* (1711) in heroic couplets. Critics became figures of fun in satires, Dennis appearing as Sir Tremendous in the farce *Three Hours After Marriage* (1717) and, alongside Lewis Theobald, in Thomas Parnell's book *Homer's Battle of the Frogs and Mice, with the Remarks of Zoilus, to which is prefixed the Life of the said Zoilus* (1717).

Revisions to, and criticism about, particular works, interacted with more general issues about style and also reflected the specific needs of individual genres. This can be seen in a letter from William Pitt the Elder, not a figure generally associated with the arts, who wrote in 1751 to James Oswald, a fellow MP, about a

English Culture

manuscript play the latter had sent him to read. Pitt had read it with George Lyttelton, a politician-author and patron of Fielding,

> ... with much pleasure. We both found great spirit and imagery in it, as well as much deep and strong sense; there is likewise character. We think the business had better open between Agis and the mother, and leave out an unnecessary preceding scene. The great situation of the judgement is well kept up, in part: towards the end of it, something more of dignity and greatness might be thrown in to hold it up to the last. With all this merit no one can answer for the success of the play.[22]

Pitt's sentiments contain a Classical stress on dignity and greatness.

The critical debate was more public for printed and displayed works, while institutional formats aided debate: the commencement in 1769 of annual exhibitions by the recently established Royal Academy of Arts encouraged art criticism.

As serious works lent themselves to serious discussion more than comedy, let alone on what might be seen as low comedy, buffoonery or farce, so they enjoyed more critical attention, but this does not equate to popularity. In contrast, the comedies of Thomas Morton (1764-1838), especially, but not only, *The Way to Get Married* (1796), *A Cure for the Heart-Ache* (1797) and *Speed the Plough* (1800), were staged at Covent Garden, popular and frequently revived, but he rates few mentions today. Whereas this might be an appropriate literary response to the stock characters and scenarios of the plays, it is but part of the general critical problem of addressing the variety of the period.

4

EIGHTEENTH CENTURY: XENOPHOBIA VERSUS COSMOPOLITANISM

Eloping with the daughter of a Duke is not par for the course for Regius Professors, no more than grudgingly accepting the post from a Prime Ministerial chum after failing to get a Headship of House. It may be far more normal if you are a Regius not to give one's expected lectures, but I would not recommend anybody to try to pursue a career today with the affirmation 'he prides himself upon being an Englishman, an English Protestant, a Church of England man, a Divine.'

It is of course easy to make fun of Edward Nares, the Regius Professor of Modern History in Oxford from 1813 until his death in 1841, but he represented both a late flourish of a particular eighteenth-century world in which history was seen as of great public purpose, and a continuance of that world into different waters in the nineteenth. Nares nicely bridges the divides, as a Georgian Fellow of Merton who eloped with Lady Charlotte

English Culture

Spencer in 1797, a cleric who reassured the public that national victories proved divine support in a struggle that included that against those who seek 'to discard all ancient opinions as prejudices', and a Regius who owed the favour to a friend from Blenheim theatricals, the 2nd Earl of Liverpool, and in 1832 was to be investigated for failing to give his lectures. He was also a very active writer, including in 1828, a major, scholarly three-volume life of Elizabeth I's leading minister, William Cecil, Lord Burghley.

As a youth, Nares had benefited from his father's library, including reading Goldsmith's *History of England* (1771). Another who benefited from a paternal library, Jane Austen wrote a *History of England, from the reign of Henry 4th to the Death of Charles 1st. By a partial, prejudiced, and ignorant Historian,* which was a parody of Goldsmith's *History* adding Austen's personal views. Austen also wrote over one hundred marginal comments in her brother James's copy of Goldsmith, marginalia that very much reflected the Tory view of history. Family members recalled Austen's strong support for Charles (r. 1625-49), and her *History* praised him and his loyal supporters. Referred to as 'villains', his opponents were blamed for the civil wars of the 1640s.

Much of the emphasis in work on the eighteenth century is on modernity, with a plethora of revolutions, a veritable line 'to the crack of doom' jostling for attention (and academic self-aggrandisement). Thus, the Industrial has been followed by the Agricultural, Transport, Financial, Commercial, Consumer, Demographic, Emotional, Sexual, and whatever else fertile keyboards can fire up. New ideas, new techniques, new technologies, new sciences, new cultural forms, are thrust to the fore as part of the pursuit of a world-changing Enlightenment of Modernity, or Modernity of Enlightenment; at any rate the capitalisation is always apparent.

Eighteenth Century: Xenophobia versus Cosmopolitanism

Now clearly turnpikes, steam engines, canals, novels, landscape gardens, Adam Smith, patents et al are scarcely indicators of an unchanging world; but two elements are apt to be underplayed in all this. First, is the extent to which this was also a profoundly historical culture. Second is the extent to which, far from competing 'opposites', an approach that has launched many lectures stronger on rhetoric than reason, these elements interacted.

The historical bent of the years from the Glorious Revolution to the Great Reform Act can be found in thought, religion, politics, law, society, literature, art, architecture, music, sculpture, and much else, and was true at all levels of society. History was also present-centred, and to a degree that made it the focus of national debate in a way that much modern university history fails to manage. Major topics, such as the Christian faith, the character of civil and religious liberties, the nature and legitimacy of the state, the engagement with interests overseas, and the nature of society and civilisation, were opportunities for historical writers to connect the past with the present.

There is a standard cast for modern attention presided over by Edward Gibbon and William Robertson, but this cast can underplay the range of writing, from newspaper accounts to John Wesley's far from short *A Concise History of England from the Earliest Times, to the Death of George II* (1776), a successful work, that, alongside similar histories by Smollett, Hume, Goldsmith and Catharine Macaulay, and (today) less prominent writers such as John Lockman and Richard Rolt, indicated the buoyancy of that market. Indeed, serviced by entrepreneurial publishers and writers, the public demand, as also for example with cartography, acted as an important spur and a source of contemporary coherence, and that irrespective of whether historians of the period are treated as high or low, philosophical

English Culture

or hack, impartial or partial, belle-lettrists or miscellarians. The similarities arose not only from common conventions and a shared audience, but also from the extent to which the subsequent separating tendencies of university and popular were not to the fore.

Although they had important strengths, Oxford and Cambridge were not prominent in their postclassical history. It was the public forum that was crucial, and history writing was a branch of 'Grub Street' as much as of the 'Republic of Letters'. Many of the historians of the period have dropped from attention, for example John Campbell and the Salmon brothers, Nathanael and Thomas, but their works reflected the range of the market. Other writers, such as Godwin, Hume and Smollett, are prominent now for books other than their histories.

An emphasis on individual motivation characterised not only novels and biographies but also much of the historical work of the period. A stress on individual free will and not determinism brought a rejection of Calvinist predestination and, instead, legal and political engagements with the role of choice; plus a relative lack of interest in later themes of revolutionary adaptation and historical materialism. This emphasis encouraged an overlap with fiction, with history a term deployed there to suggest truth. History to contemporaries meant narrative. While novels sought to be true histories, historical writing was supposed to capture character.

Like novels, histories tried to capture the secret nature of the truth, as in David Jones's *The Secret History of White Hall from the Restoration of Charles II down to the Abdication of the late King James* (1697). Such secret histories teased the reader that they were being let into a hidden past and looked toward and drew on accounts of contemporary politics; for example, the belief that, having resigned, John, 3rd Earl of Bute was secretly

Eighteenth Century: Xenophobia versus Cosmopolitanism

directing court politics, or Edmund Burke's concern about conspiratorial support for pernicious ideologies both in Britain and France.

Bringing history, journalism, novels, theatre, paintings and sculpture together was the presentation of the past as a morally exemplary tale, a key element in narrative drive, exposition, and explanation. Whether the stress tended toward individual free will or a providential intervention linked to behaviour, the emphasis was on a world best understood in moral terms, as with the presentation of Oliver Cromwell as having made a pact with the devil, a claim repeated in the second volume of Laurence Echard's *History of England* (1718). Moralism lent itself to the use of history in political contention; and this use helped ensure that the coverage of history was not only extensive but also very much brought into the present.

At the same time, the frame of historical reference, whether in books, newspapers, the arts, or private correspondence went back to the Classical period of British and Continental history; contrasting with the situation for most today. British writers in the 'long eighteenth century' maintained the earlier seventeenth-century interest in the 'Ancient Constitution', whether found in Saxon forests or not. Thus, in William Hutchinson's *The History of the County of Cumberland* (1794), pre-Roman culture was greatly praised, with the Druids described as learned, moral and in harmony with the universe. Hutchinson was highly critical of the Romans, presenting them as bringing in 'nothing but articles of luxury and magnificence'.

Newspaper history came from a range of talented pens, both well-known, such as Bolingbroke and Smollett, and less familiar historical writers, such as John Banks. Newspapers ranged widely. The *Monitor* happily found lessons in the reigns of Edward III, Henry V, and Elizabeth I. The frame of historical reference was very different to the present day.

English Culture

History recorded the rivalries and links in England's relationship with the wider world. And so with the 'Glorious Revolution' of 1688-9 which was at once both cosmopolitan and xenophobic. It was cosmopolitan in that England was invaded by William III of Orange and a Dutch army and, once he had become king, brought into a war against France, which, with an interruption in 1697-1702, lasted until 1713. It was xenophobic in that the overthrow of James II was very much presented as a defeat for a foreign monarchy and religion. Moreover, conflict with Jacobitism increased the English dominance of the British Isles, and war with France helped in the definition of a clear and bellicose nationalism.

Crucial to the creation of the Whig Ascendancy in England was what was termed the Whig approach, which emphasised a Protestant identity for the nation, respect for property, the rule of law, and parliamentary sovereignty as a means to secure liberty. This approach combined a patriotic sense of national uniqueness with a frequently xenophobic contempt for foreigners. History was presented as moving in an inevitable direction, one of steady improvement, a teleological progressivism.

English national consciousness, and thus patriotism, were given a tremendous boost and fresh definition by the Glorious Revolution, but this consciousness was politically defined and partisan. It was directed against Jacobites and those thought likely to support the exiled Stuarts, especially Catholics in England and, to a lesser extent, Episcopalians in Scotland; and of course against Louis XIV, the principal patron of the exiled James II (and VII of Scotland). Louis established himself as the national enemy from 1689, more by his real and apparent backing for the Stuarts and their British supporters than by his aggressive activities on the Continent against Britain's allies. The brutal treatment of the Huguenots (French Protestants) in the 1680s was also important.

Eighteenth Century: Xenophobia versus Cosmopolitanism

After the overthrow of James II in 1688, English patriotism was necessarily divisive, and derived much of its drive from this partisan character. The Glorious Revolution led to the development of two competing theses of patriotism, one of which triumphed, and was able therefore to define patriotism accordingly. Such a process was not new. Indeed, it was a key aspect of the lengthy Reformation crisis. A national culture was defined accordingly. Handel's oratorios joined the authority of the Biblical story in rallying patriotic enthusiasm.[1] In Fielding's *Joseph Andrews*, the squire who hunted Adams and wants to seduce Fanny, is a middle-aged bachelor whose mother had spoiled him before sending him on the Grand Tour. He returns

> ... well furnished with French clothes, phrases, and servants, with a hearty contempt for his own country, especially which had any savour of the plain spirit and honesty of our ancestors ... he soon procured himself a seat in Parliament and was in the common opinion one of the finest gentlemen of his age; but what distinguished him chiefly was a strange delight which he took in everything which is ridiculous, odious, and absurd in his own species. (III, vii).

This chimed with a commonplace critique of tourists.

In the dedication of 1760 to the fourteenth edition of his *A New History of England*, the prolific writer John Lockman 'endeavoured to set the whole in such a light as may inspire the readers with an ardent love for our pure religion, and its darling attendant, liberty; and, on the other hand, with a just abhorrence of popery [Catholicism], and its companion, slavery'. By slavery, English commentators, as in 'Rule Britannia,' referred to the situation at home, and not that across the empire, in short to political control and not the use of labour for economic purposes.

English Culture

This was Englishness defined by being different to Frenchness. And different to a feudal past that had seemed all-too-present in the shape of support for Jacobitism among Highland Scots and among Englishmen living in marginal political communities: marginal because reactionary and reactionary because marginal.

Lockman's remarks captured the clear ideological framing of a sense of distinctive nationhood. This framing took place in large part in opposition to apparent threats; responses to challenges were significant both to national identity and to government policy, foreign and military. This proved an effective mechanism for unity and identity, unity in identity and identity in unity, until recent decades when it appears to have broken down.

This Whiggish account did not satisfy all, and in opposition there was a vibrant Tory critique that sought to focus on a more defined Englishness. This critique was one in which the preservation of the Church of England, supposedly in danger from ministers and senior clerics opposed to orthodoxy, played a greater role, although from the 1720s there was a reconciliation between the Whig and Church élites. The Englishness offered by the Tories was anti-cosmopolitan, if not xenophobic. This was clearly displayed in 1753 by the crisis over Jewish naturalisation. A Parliamentary Act to that end was reversed due to public agitation. There was also hostility to Protestant immigrants, notably 'poor Palatines' from Germany and Huguenots from France, although Church briefs raised funds for Protestants in Europe in large quantities. The position of the Church appeared to many Tories to be under threat from Whig attitudes and policies, but this became less pronounced. Earlier, a dilution of the Englishness of the Church of England was an important aspect of this apparent threat. The Huguenots were presented as allies of the Whigs. Nationalism was cumulative, but also open to a variety of interpretations.

Eighteenth Century: Xenophobia versus Cosmopolitanism

The role of religion was crucial because it differentiated England (and Wales) from Scotland and Ireland. Much of the politics, ideology and political culture of the seventeenth century was a matter of the 'processing' of the union of the crowns in 1603, and this process continued until the crushing defeat of Jacobitism at the battle of Culloden in 1746. The key decision on the political level might be that of a loss of separate identity as a result of the union of the London and Edinburgh parliaments in 1707 and with it a clearer creation of a British political identity. Yet, from the religious perspective, this was not the case. Both England and Scotland were anti-Catholic, but they had rival Protestant establishments, and the contrast between the Church of England and the Church of Scotland was highly significant to the continued separateness of the two. Had there been a union at the religious level, in the sense of a common Church structure, liturgy and much else, then this would have encouraged a joining of national histories. Instead, the Scots in part defined themselves by successfully pursuing and defending a distinctive religious settlement, one in which the episcopalian church in Scotland was in a weak position.

As a result, much that focused on the Church was in effect a pursuit of English nationalism. Popular accounts of the culture of the period tend to have a secular slant, especially television and film treatments. This is a prelude to a similar tendency for succeeding centuries and is an aspect of a separation of 'modernity' from an earlier period of religious zeal and feudal behaviour. It is a questionable account because it separates modernity from religion and the role of religion in cultural history is inaccurately downplayed. Indeed, there was a strong engagement with religious faith, both at the personal level as a communal activity, and as a national creed of belief and commitment, thought and action.

English Culture

Religious works could sell extremely well. *The Church Catechism Explained by Way of Question and Answer, and Confirm'd by Scripture Proofs* (1700) by the Kent cleric John Lewis, a keen defender of the Church of England, went through 42 editions by 1812. It was not alone. 10,000 copies of Robert Nelson's *A Companion for Festivals and Fasts of the Church of England* (1704) were printed in four and a half years, and a 30th edition appeared in 1826. Anti-Catholicism was part of the equation. The SPCK (Society for the Propagation of Christian Knowledge) aimed to ensure that every household owned a copy of *The Whole Duty of Man* (1658). It was so widely known that Hume, Franklin and Sheridan (in *The Rivals*) referred to it. *The Preservative Against Popery* tracts of the 1680s were enormously popular and influential in the eighteenth century.

Most of the English viewed events in their own age as directly driven by God, including the Jacobite defeats of 1715 and 1745, the growth of empire, military victories, and even the London earthquakes of 1692 and 1750. Nationhood was held to reflect the intervention and support of Providence. The idea of Britain (in practice England) as an 'elect nation' and a second Israel, chosen by God, contributed to contemporary views of national exceptionalism and also to a sense of historical distinctiveness. This was seen in the popularity of Handel's oratorios. His *Samson* (1743) was performed eight times in its first season, a considerable triumph. The Handel celebrations of 1784-91 showed the continuing popularity of his approach.

In these and other works, elect status was seen to develop from a long sequence of events that justified God's endorsement. This approach could be traced back not only to the Reformation, but further into a distant past that included Edward the Confessor (r. 1042-66), who was first claimed to have the power to cure the 'King's Evil' (a practice only discontinued in 1714), and even

Eighteenth Century: Xenophobia versus Cosmopolitanism

to more mythological but powerful figures like King Arthur, as well as to King Alfred, a real figure. The ambient identification of nationalism with divine support meant that the recording of Providential sanction was of great significance for the idea of nationhood. Religious perspectives remained important to this idea into the late twentieth century, and current issues about Islamic identity and loyalty indicate the continued salience of these issues.

The significance of religion also rested on its ability, despite serious divisions over belief, to be socially inclusive, unlike the culture of print, which excluded the illiterate. Religious belief and practice interacted with a popular folk culture in which the past was very much a living presence. This was brilliantly satirised by Laurence Sterne in his novel *Tristam Shandy* (1759-67).

Historical works found Providence the key defender of nationhood and they were thus an appropriate way to assert nationalism. In his dedication of volume two of his history of England to George I, Laurence Echard, a clergyman, described the Glorious Revolution as 'wonderful and providential.'

> England in an especial manner has been such a mighty and distinct scene of action, in the latter ages of the world, that during the compass of this History, there appears a greater variety of changes, governments and establishments; and there seems to have been more visible and signal instances of judgements and punishments, mercies and deliverances from above, then perhaps can be paralleled in any other part of the Western world.

The text was very clear that 'Divine Providence' played a key role, not least due to the lapsed nature of mankind as a consequence of Adam's Fall.[2] This lapsed nature made divine support even more necessary, a point valid for nations as well as individuals, now

English Culture

and for all time. The Restoration of Stuart monarchy in 1660 was described accordingly as 'the most free and exalted expression of a delivered and overjoyed nation, triumphantly restored, without one drop of blood, by the All-merciful and powerful Hand of Heaven'.[3] National history and identity, the two mutually dependent, could not be separated from Providence.

Echard was a moderate Tory. The Whigs added a powerful theme of human intervention in the shape of the balance of power. This interpretation permitted a representation of England in terms of moderation, which was to be a standard trope in the self-presentation of English distinctiveness and culture, one that lasted for many foreign commentators until the public grief in 1997 following the death of Diana, Princess of Wales. Key sources of the idea of moderation were the supposed middle way or *via media* in Church matters between radical Protestantism and Catholicism, and also Classical ideas of moderation: μηδὲν ἄ´γαν. nothing to excess. In political terms, there was a standard Aristotelian tension between royal prerogatives and popular privileges, a tension that, at its best, produced a balance that guaranteed liberty. The Saxon *witan* and the post-1688 Parliament were presented as the prime instances of this balance. The dedication in 1744 to Frederick, Prince of Wales by Nicholas Tindal, an Anglican clergyman, of a translation of Paul de Rapin-Thoyras's influential Whiggish history of England, set out this theme:

You will see here the origin and nature of our excellent constitution, where the prerogatives of the Crown, and Privileges of the subject are so heavily proportioned, that the King and the People are inseparably united in the same interests and views. You will observe that this union, though talked of by even the most arbitrary princes with respect to their subjects, is peculiar to the

Eighteenth Century: Xenophobia versus Cosmopolitanism

English monarchy, and the most solid foundation of the sovereign's glory, and the people's happiness.

Accordingly, you will constantly find, that in the reigns where this union was cultivated, the kingdom flourished, and the prince was glorious, powerful, trusted, beloved. On the contrary, when, by an arbitrary disposition, of evil counsels, it was interrupted, the constitution languished, mutual confidence vanished, distrust, jealousy, discord arose; and when entirely broken ... confusion and civil wars ensued.

Similar views were found in the writings of George Lyttelton, a Whig MP and writer, who saw a longstanding English identity which he traced back to the Saxon system of limited royal power. This was then presented as surviving the Norman Conquest, only for a division to open up between the 'nobles' and 'the People,' with the former a burden to the latter. Lyttelton praised the reign of Elizabeth as coming 'to an equal balance, which is the true perfection of it', only to degenerate under the Stuarts, before revival as a result of the Glorious Revolution: 'The government was settled on a new foundation, agreeable to the ancient Saxon principles from which it had declined.'[4]

This understanding of a revolution as a return to past circumstances, and, ideally, to a past golden age that had been lost as a consequence of usurpations of some type, was a significant variant on the progressivism or improvability with which Whig thought is associated. The account of 1688-9 as a Glorious Revolution made it possible to reconcile both views and sets of images, and this helped Whiggism act as a potent and resonant ideology. Moreover, the continuing importance of the Glorious Revolution as a later version of Magna Carta, the totemic limitation of royal authority in 1215, was readily apparent. Multiple interpretations and echoes, like identities, are significant.

English Culture

The construction of nationalism in these terms was challenged by the accession of the Dutch William of Orange as William III (r. 1689-1702), and then by the accession of the Elector of Hanover as George I (r. 1714-27), which began a dynastic link with Hanover that lasted until 1837. The foreignness of the monarch helped accentuate the role of Parliament, while showing that nationalism had to be understood in terms of demonstrated Protestantism. That William III, George I, and George II (r. 1727-60), were clearly identified with the Whigs helped make their origins and interests vulnerable to attack by the Tories and further complicated understanding nationalism.

Nationalism was however to be redefined as a result of the integration of Toryism into a national political culture and language in mid-century. This integration reflected sweeping victory over France and Spain in the Seven Years' War (1756-63), and the accession of George III (r. 1760-1820), a king who had conspicuously broken with the Hanoverian identity of his two predecessors, George I and George II, even though he continued to care about Hanover.

The 1760s saw a strong focus on national cultural interests, notably with the Shakespeare Jubilee in 1769 and the foundation of the Royal Academy in 1768. The Academy was the realisation of long-held ideas for an institution that would combine artistic education with national glory. In 1772, Joshua Reynolds, the President of the Academy, could depict England as more dynamic than France. At the same time, Samuel Johnson attempted to fix the English language with his massive *Dictionary*. William Blackstone, appointed in 1758, the first Vinerian Professor of English Law at Oxford, published the *Commentaries on the Laws of England* (1765-9), in part to acclaim Common Law against Roman Law. In combination, these cultural elements were a powerful endorsement of a sense of distinctiveness, one, in particular, that was defined in terms of ideas of Englishness.

Eighteenth Century: Xenophobia versus Cosmopolitanism

There was no comparable Britishness involved, although in part a lack of precision in England provided such a Britishness. For example, 'An old-fashioned Englishman,' in a letter printed in the *St James's Chronicle* of 13 May 1769, claimed:

> We are a people that should be often roused to a sense of our blessings, and to the means of securing them. French clothes, French cookery, French literature, French plays, French shoes, and French hats, have so possessed us from top to toe, that if we do not guard against these encroaching refinements, we shall have even our immortal Shakespeare plucked from his eminence by French critics, and degraded to the character of buffoon and drunken savage, which the spirit of envy and ignorance has been pleased to call him by the pen of Monsieur de Voltaire ... while we can think and feel like Britons, we shall ever glory in the immortal productions of the greatest poet which any age or country has produced.

Culture was essentially defined in comparison with and against France and Italy, the former notably in art and the latter in music, although other elements played a part. There had long been pressure for changing the language of the law from (old) French and Latin to English, and this was achieved in 1731, although in 1752 Britain was brought into line with the Continental calendar. There was an emphasis on the supposed truthfulness of English culture and on the alleged artfulness and artificiality of others. Cultures were presented as rivals. Key issues included the language used in opera, specifically the preference for Italian rather than English, the patronage of foreign as opposed to native performers, resistance to the presence of Catholic images, and the engagement with the past.[5] Popular images and stereotypes included John Bull.

English Culture

A sense of cultural tension was bound up with food, the *London Magazine* commenting in January 1773:

> Times are changed... Here stood the large, plump juicy buttocks of English roast beef, and there smiled the frothy tankards of English beer... Now... Our tables groan with the luxuries of France and India. Here a lean fricassee rises in the room of our majestic ribs.

Consumerism was a key context and means, John Roach observing about taverns in *Roach's London Pocket Pilot: or, Stranger's Guide Through the Metropolis* (1796): 'The fortuned voluptuary may indulge his appetite, not only with all the natural dainties of every season, but with delicacies produced by means of preternatural ingenuity.'

In the eighteenth century, the public market for an explicitly English engagement with English culture and history became far stronger, creating models for the future. The past was interpreted to emphasise Englishness. The shared Classical heritage could reflect differences in literary and political culture. Thus, in England, the metropolitan French were seen as fawning followers of Horace, civilised, urbane, sophisticated, fashionable servants or slaves, but the English as rugged, no-nonsense, plain-speaking followers of Juvenal, and hence free. Augustan Rome had room for both Horace and Juvenal, but in England there was an emphasis on Classical republican virtue that looked back to republican Rome.

The model of a progressive society, although it owed much to the Scottish Enlightenment, was perceived abroad as English. For example, French and German historians and lawyers talked about England, not Britain. Foreign travellers focused on England, and, indeed, as with Montesquieu and Voltaire, London.

English culture was spread with the rapid expansion of the empire and of commerce, one celebrated in many works, notably

Eighteenth Century: Xenophobia versus Cosmopolitanism

in the celebration of ships, which was close in some respects to a sub-genre of the developing landscape school, a major departure from the emphasis on portraits. A number of painters became famed for their shore and river scenes, with Samuel Scott (1702-72) called 'the English Canaletto'.[6] Edward Young's *Ocean: An Ode* (1728) connected the grandeur and power of the sea to Britain's maritime dominance. This process produced sites for transition, as the transoceanic English cultures saw more admixture with other British forms (*ie* Scottish) than was the general case for English culture across the British Isles. There was also in the transoceanic English cultures the influence of colonial drives, transitions and influences, including responses to non-British influences. The future culture of the United States, at once English, British and different, was a key consequence.

5

NINETEENTH CENTURY: SPHERES OF PATRONAGE

The opening scenes of the would-be great story may, in a rash moment, have been printed in some popular magazine before the remainder is written; as it advances month by month the situations develop, and the writer asks himself, what will his characters do next? What would probably happen to them, given such beginnings? On his life and conscience, though he had not foreseen the thing, only one event could possibly happen, and that therefore he should narrate, as he calls himself a faithful artist. But, though pointing a fine moral, it is just one of those issues which are not to be mentioned in respectable magazines and select libraries. The dilemma than confronts him, he must either whip and scourge those characters into doing something contrary to their natures, to produce the spurious effect of their being in harmony with social forms and ordinances, or, by leaving them alone to act as they will, he must bring down the thunders

Nineteenth Century: Spheres of Patronage

of respectability upon his head, not to say ruin his editor, his publisher, and himself.

Thomas Hardy on the problems of being a novelist, 1890.[1]

The State and Culture

In all periods, government provides a context for cultural activity, from specific patronage to the roles of taxation, public order and regulation. The nineteenth century, sometimes described as a 'nightwatchman state' of limited governance, is not generally seen as a period of centralised cultural control. This is not least in contrast to the more regulatory twentieth century, a period in which the state became both larger and a more significant source of patronage for the arts.

Yet, in the nineteenth century, the state was significant, and not simply in greatly expanding the empire, providing a multiplicity of themes and contexts for artistic activity. There was also a determined engagement in England, notably London, with providing a cultural competition to Napoleonic France (1799-1815) and subsequently with celebrating victory and affirming imperial strength. Thus, the Prince Regent (r. 1811-20), later George IV (r. 1820-30), supported the development of the West End, St Paul's Cathedral became the nation's pantheon, its monuments and Trafalgar Square commemorating heroism, and the National Gallery affirming national artistic centrality, both in a public context, being intended to educate the public.[2]

Parliamentarians became interested in the education of public taste from the 1830s, with a Select Committee on Arts and Manufactures established in 1835, the Royal Commission of the Promotion of the Fine Arts following in 1841 and the Museums Act in 1845. Utilitarian philosophy and German examples were important factors. Subsequently, Prince Albert played a major role in the utilitarian cultural assertion and activity that focused on the Great Exhibition of 1851, but was not limited to it.[3]

This state action varied in content, tone and prominence, reflecting in part cross-currents also seen abroad,[4] but remained significant throughout the century. It was linked to a cult of progress, as proclaimed in the *Western Luminary*, a newspaper, on 2 January 1855: 'Progress is the great animating principle of being. The world, time, our country have advanced and are advancing.'

Triumphant Marketplace

At the same time, the triumph of the market is the major theme in nineteenth-century English cultural history. By the market, we mean the role of consumers in determining the success of particular art forms and artists. Such a situation was scarcely new. The cultural marketplace had come to the fore in the eighteenth century, as patronage by individual wealthy patrons was largely replaced by the anonymous patronage of the growing market of the world's leading economy. This 'patronage' meant producing works for sale to individuals the artist had not met. It led to a new series of cultural meeting points and places of cultural consumption: art galleries and auctions, concert halls and choral festivals. The crucial links were provided by entrepreneurs: concert organisers, art auctioneers and, most significantly, publishers. Publishers of course financed book production and arranged the sale of the finished product.[5] These entrepreneurs treated culture as a commodity whose value was set by the market. This was a particularly fluid market, one in which style and novelty were crucial in enhancing value and attracting recognition and sales and, from the 1740s, in the context of a continually and rapidly rising population.

This remained the case during the nineteenth century, but the scale of the cultural marketplace was greater and its nature

Nineteenth Century: Spheres of Patronage

greatly changed. This was largely due to the movement of the bulk of the population into a market that had been hitherto patronised essentially (although not exclusively) by the middling orders. In the Victorian period, in addition, the working class, especially the skilled artisans, gained time and money for leisure, building on the already well-laid foundations by which many had a degree of self-schooling at least. Diaries and letters attest to the influence of a range of cultural forms.[6]

Much of this new time and money was expended on leisure. Association football emerged as a very popular spectator sport, while other sports, such as horse racing, also attracted a large working-class following. (Greyhound racing was not introduced until 1926.) As with sport, so with holidays.[7] The large music halls were built in this period. They offered both spectator entertainment and an opportunity to participate, by singing along or engaging in repartee with the performers.

The major increase in printed material, in part due to the development of publication technology linked to steam power, was important. There was a determined and persistent attempt to make publications more accessible, and thus to serve and expand the popular market. William Cobbett, who launched the *Political Register* in 1802, wrote in a readily accessible style, without the complicated sentence structure and opaque meanings that had characterised so many earlier essays. The anti-Catholic Evangelical periodical *The Record* appeared in 1828, unusually twice-weekly, promising to exclude from its pages anything that would be objectionable to 'that sanctuary of modesty and refined feeling – the bosom of a well-regulated *English* Family'.

Sunday newspapers, which expanded greatly from the 1840s after the lowering of Stamp Duties, proved particularly successful in melding the news and fiction. They offered crimes and titillation, the sensational and the salacious. Many of their

English Culture

articles proved particularly appropriate for large typeface advertising. Crime in particular offered a way to link excitement and morality and encouraged the exaggeration of crime and law-breaking. There was a parallel with the religious newspapers and tracts that were an important and usually underrated aspect of individual, family and national culture, their explicit moralisation part of a moralised culture. With their confessions, lurid tales of sin, redemption and retribution, pious deaths, and elements of the supernatural, many religious publications provided readily grasped content in an exciting series of individual morality tales that paralleled crime literature and newspaper reporting. Such accessibility and variety meant the sale of publications was increasing at a greater rate than that of the rapidly rising population. The weekly *Penny Magazine* (1832-45) was lavishly illustrated and inexpensive.

The abolition of the newspaper duties in 1853-61 expanded the press, as did the introduction of web rotary presses able to print directly onto continuous rolls from the late 1860s. Trains distributed publications, leading to a major change in the nature and purpose of local newspapers. Purchasers were served by railway bookstalls. By the time William Henry Smith died in 1891, he had opened 150 station shops, the first in 1848.

During the same period, *organised* middle-class cultural activity also greatly expanded. This owed much to the expansion of the middle class in cities. They pursued culture not only for pleasure, as in the rise of restaurants,[8] but also as a way of defining their purpose and leadership. The middle class patronised a great upsurge in art, poetry, and the performance or production of music, leading to popular art movements such as the Pre-Raphaelites – William Holman Hunt, John Millais and Dante Gabriel Rossetti – who enjoyed considerable popularity from the mid-1850s. Birmingham, Glasgow, Leeds,

Nineteenth Century: Spheres of Patronage

Liverpool, Manchester and Newcastle founded major art collections and musical institutions, such as the Halle Orchestra in Manchester in 1857. Although these cities were individually dwarfed by London, collectively they became more significant as well as having more disposable wealth than in the past and a greater sense of their own significance. An awareness of this transformation was noted, as with the 1859 description of Manchester by John McCulloch, a Scotsman who had become the first Professor of Political Economy at University College London in 1828:

> Great improvements have been made within the last 30 years; narrow lanes have been pulled down to make way for broad avenues; noble public buildings, which would be ornamental to any capital in the world.

Yet, there was also a warning of separation between capital and labour, one that challenged the idea of cultural cohesion: 'The whole tendency of society, in modern times, is to make interest, taking the term in its most literal and sordid sense, the link by which all classes are held together.'[9]

Natural history, astronomy and geology provided an opportunity for individual commitment and self-improvement. Such activities were in part institutionalised with, for example, numerous natural history societies and observatories around the country. This process extended to include the study of history itself, especially local history. Societies for local history were founded and their journals publicised their proceedings. Research had a public voice.

There was also a boom in middle-class sports, such as golf and lawn tennis, the rules of which were systematised in 1874. Sporting institutions and facilities were created across Britain,

English Culture

creating foci for local sociability. Northumberland Cricket Club, for example, had a ground in Newcastle by the 1850s, while Newcastle Golf Club expanded its activities in the 1890s. Civic organisations played a major role in such expansion, but the essential dynamo was commercial. This was even more obviously the case with individual activity, whether the expansion of private music-making (by individuals and by families) or the great expansion of reading.

The triumphant marketplace, however, met with resistance. The idea of cultural values as under threat from middle-class and popular mores and taste was an established one, not least in response to suburbia and to the way in which it provided an alternative locus for activity and socialising to established, élite ones. In part, this was a matter of hostility to female assertiveness.[10]

Other Sources of Patronage

Established forms of patronage were maintained. The range of personal and institutional commissions remained significant. In many respects, these were important to the triumphant marketplace, with which they overlapped. Individual commissions were seen across the arts. Portrait painting was supplemented by portrait photography.

Traditional sources of patronage – the aristocracy, the churches, the Crown and town councils – all remained significant. Furthermore, for much of the period they had more money available for expenditure, notably as a result of rising rentals from urban and rural property, and due to mineral exploitation rights. The situation became less positive for some from the 1870s as a consequence of the sustained agricultural depression that began with large-scale imports of grain and meat in steamships. However, even then there were still funds available in parts of rural society earned from urban expansion, shooting rights

Nineteenth Century: Spheres of Patronage

and public service. The continuation of institutional patronage, notably by the churches and by town councils, kept many in work, from organists to librarians. It is all too easy to forget the persistence, indeed dynamism, of established sources and methods of artistic patronage when focusing on the developing demand of the mass market. Religious works such as John Robert Seeley's *Ecce Homo* (1867), which sought to employ scholarship to present a positive view of Jesus as a human incarnation, created massive attention, not least as this was a period of religious response to Charles Darwin's ideas about evolution.[11] At the same time, as so often, such attention was a matter of range and continuum, rather than simply sharp contrasts with those of differing views.

These sources of patronage became relatively less significant compared to the expansion in the purchasing power of the bulk of the population, both middle and working class. Nevertheless, they remained important and highly dynamic in some areas. Thus, the Victorian age was a great one for church building, with anxieties about a lack of faith in the expanding cities fuelling an activity that drew in funds from a range of sources, including wealthy individual donors. Church building and other aspects of ecclesiastical activity reflected a diverse religious culture, open to lay influences and engaging with broader artistic and intellectual developments.[12]

The opening of the Great Exhibition, a dramatic and totemic celebration of the potential of technology, included a prominent benediction from John Bird Sumner, Archbishop of Canterbury, and a display of Bibles. The openness of the Church to talent and the ability of clerics to contribute to culture was impressively demonstrated in the life of William Whewell (1794-1864), the son of a Lancaster master carpenter who became a prominent academic and also wrote poetry. In his influential *Bridgewater*

Treatise (1833), Whewell found evidence of divine design in the laws of nature.

Individual patronage remained significant in architecture. For example, a magnificent, decorated chapel of High Victorian Gothic Revival type was built at Clumber Park in 1886-9 by G. F. Bodley for the 7th Duke of Newcastle, a prominent Anglo-Catholic. The stained glass and other contents were in the same style. A similar church was built at Studley Royal by William Burges in 1871-8 for another Anglo-Catholic, the 1st Marquess of Ripon.

Given the extraordinary social transformation during the nineteenth century, it is not surprising that cultural assumptions and patterns were put under pressure. The most acute was that to religiosity, and the Anglican character of England in 1800, not least its legal position, was shattered by the rise of religious pluralism and by concern about the increase of irreligion. The two developments were very different in their content, but they combined to encourage a sense of crisis. This had varied consequences, from the missions to the cities in a drive for religious renewal, to a despair that became more pronounced among commentators later in the century. Church-building was inherently political. The 1818 Church Building Act, which granted public money to a new Church Building Commission, led to an increase in the pace of building, but one that was opposed by Dissenters as well as by ratepayers.

The debate over Anglican practice and devotion, between what might be regarded as 'High' and liberal 'Broad' tendencies, became more strident but also different in the nineteenth century, notably with the Oxford Movement and Evangelicalism; although the two agreed on important doctrines, including baptismal regeneration. The arts provided many opportunities for playing out this cultural division, from architecture and church decoration

Nineteenth Century: Spheres of Patronage

to church music and sermonising. Sermons had an impact in the literary world. William Enfield's (1741-97) entry in the 1815 *Encyclopaedia Britannica* ended:

> His posthumous sermons, in 3 volumes, had a very numerous list of subscribers, a strong proof of the estimation in which he was held by all who knew him, either personally or by report. In these discourses he treats chiefly on moral topics, which he discusses with the nicest discrimination, and in a train of the most pleasing and manly eloquence. (VIII, 43)

Most prominently in Antony Trollope's Barchester novels (1855-67), the Church became a setting for fiction.[13] High Church and Evangelical were not discrete cultural and artistic categories, but contexts within which there was a range of views and practices, including millenarianism. This has remained the case to the present, and such a strand of cultural activity should not be underestimated. For many, this world provided a context within which to respond to other cultural and artistic developments. It is striking, for example, that examination of youth culture or urban culture in the nineteenth and twentieth centuries tends often to minimise the significance of religious institutions and views. This reflects an excessive secularisation of viewpoint. It is more helpful to note that the right to private judgement in religious matters was increasingly stressed by Protestants.

There could also be a social complexion to cultural experience and artistic preference, as in the audience for Italian opera in London, an expensive pastime. The privileged socio-economic context was maintained by subscription boxes, which were generally subscribed by aristocrats, notably women. As with church pews, this form of ownership displayed rank and encouraged a sense of distinction which in the opera led to gossiping, networking and a lack of aesthetic interest, about which Fanny Burney complained in *Evelina* (1778). It encouraged an audience culture of inappropriate applause, booing, or more serious forms of intervention such as the Tamburini riots at the Haymarket Theatre in 1840. In turn, opera became a less raucous experience, with quieter audience responses increasingly trumping earlier patterns of social behaviour from the 1850s.[14]

The Regional Theme

Alongside national trends, there were also regional forums for cultural activity, the survival of traditional forms and significant variation in the settings for new involvement. In the first case, it is instructive to consider the continuation of dialect writers. A good instance was Robert Anderson of Carlisle (1770-1833) who captured local speech patterns and produced verses for reading aloud. His *Ballads in the Cumberland Dialect* (1828) captured the vitality of local vernacular literature and folk traditions, a vitality preserved by the world of print, which was not in this respect its antithesis.[15] William Barnes (1801-86), a cleric, did the same in Dorset. The growth of economic activity in the eighteenth century had facilitated similar processes, albeit on a smaller scale

The variation in the settings for new activity arose in large part from the consequences of industrialisation, which included the accumulation of capital and the presence of relatively well-paid jobs that encouraged both internal migration and more expenditure on leisure.

A very different aspect of the regional theme was provided by the buildings that met the new demands of the economy and society. Architects and artists combined to provide the new railway stations, as in John Dobson's painting of the final design for the porticoed Newcastle Central Station.

Nineteenth Century: Spheres of Patronage

Criticisms of Forms

In May 1887, in the magazine *Nineteenth Century*, Matthew Arnold, a prominent literary figure, attacked publications for their sensationalism and lack of accuracy. Earlier, in 1868, the novelist Anthony Trollope had criticised the fictional Quintus Slide, the editor of *The People's Banner*. This criticism, and Arnold's phrase, 'The New Journalism', expressed unease with some of the leading press figures of the age, such as W. (William) T. Stead, who ran the *Pall Mall Gazette* from 1883 to 1889, a prominent press campaigner, notably against the prostitution of minors. Stead was a muckraker with confidence in his own rectitude and the consequent justification for twisting facts. He was also highly talented and understandably frustrated by the condescension that he experienced, often on social grounds.

Stead was also an example of the press as moral arbiter that was an aspect of the changing society. There were periodic moral panics, often provided by or linked to crimes, which definred what were seen as social problems. These encouraged the novelistic features of the press, a congruence seen in particular in works such as the *Illustrated Police News*.

Many writers had for long moved between journalism and fiction, including Defoe, Fielding and Smollett. Dickens continued this tradition, and social questions, the 'Condition of England' issues, were addressed in both fiction and the press, each helping to shape the other. Moreover, the growth of the readership of each created contexts within which the other was approached and understood. Overlaps included the syndication of fiction in newspapers.

In George Gissing's novel *New Grub Street* (1891), Whelpdale, the newspaper entrepreneur, aims to serve 'the quarter-educated [with] chit chatting information' and does so to great profit to himself, if not to his authors. The work reflected the more general

English Culture

fascination that the press held for authors, a fascination that owed much to their experience as journalists, as with J.M. Barrie's novel *When a Man's Single* (1888) and Jerome K. Jerome's *Tommy and Co* (1904).

Alfred Harmsworth launched the *Daily Mail* in 1896 and pressed his staff to simplify, the circulation rising to over a million in 1901. The Prime Minister was disparaging: 'a paper for those who could read but not think.' But more read the paper than the accounts of his speeches, or the *Times*, which Harmsworth, now Lord Northcliffe, purchased in 1908.

The 'Condition of England' also addressed the environment, from railways to cities. The human impact on the natural world was captured by Henry James, an American settler who, in 1888, praised the 'magnificent mystifications' of London's fog, which

> ... flatters and superfuses, makes everything brown, rich, dim, vague, magnifies distances and minimises details, confirms the inference of vastness by suggesting that, as the great city makes everything, it makes its own optical laws.

Somewhat differently to those who presented moonlit scenes, such as the Leeds painter Atkinson Grimshaw (1836-93), London fog was brilliantly captured by painters such as Claude Monet and writers like Dickens and Arthur Conan Doyle. It was a suffusing instance of the more general extent to which the established parameters of life, experience and perception were changing greatly. The direct impact of this on culture and the arts are worthy of consideration.

6

NINETEENTH CENTURY: SITES AND STYLES

The Novelists' Britain

The nineteenth century was less 'visual' than the modern age but, in part due to the spread of illustrated publications, more so than the eighteenth. There was reproduction of paintings and other visual material, as well as the potent institutionalisation seen, for example, with the National Gallery. Founded in 1824, it moved into its new building on Trafalgar Square in 1838.

Yet there was no equivalent to the stimulus and excitement of widespread advertising, cinema and television, all of which have made visual appeal normative in modern culture and thus helped set the content for social media, despite the scale of the image that could be displayed. Instead, it was the written word that took precedence in the nineteenth century. This reflected the traditional prestige of print: the medium of the Bible and the classics, as well as its power as the language of authority, and the impact of rising literacy. More people were able to enjoy the printed

English Culture

word than ever before and print culture itself became more normative. So also with the provision of facilities accordingly, and the development of cultural industries. For example, whereas Birmingham had 12 printers in 1799, it had 33 in 1828. Aside from their number, their scale increased greatly.

Much of our image of Victorian Britain comes from the famous novels of the period, especially those of Charles Dickens (1812-70). Whereas Austen (1775-1817), now the best-known novelist of Regency England, is noted for her acute observation of provincial propertied society, and Sir Walter Scott (1771-1832), the leading Scottish novelist of the period, for his historical works, Dickens deliberately addressed social conditions and urban society. In his childhood, Dickens had experience of hardship, with his father going to the Marshalsea Debtors' Prison and, at the age of twelve, Dickens beginning menial work in London in Warren's blacking factory, a shocking experience for him. Later, after work as an office boy, a court reporter and a journalist, Dickens began as a writer, the successful serialisation of his *Pickwick Papers* starting in 1836.

Dickens was a committed reformer, especially over capital punishment, housing and prostitution, and his novels presented the inadequacies of existing institutions, which therefore made a case for reform, although its mode of implementation was unclear. In *Nicholas Nickleby*, published in monthly parts in 1838-9, Nicholas, sent to teach at Dotheboys Hall in Yorkshire, is horrified by the headmaster, Wackford Squeers, who, knowing their uncaring parents will not intervene, mistreats and starves the pupils and doses them with brimstone and treacle. Nicholas rebels and thrashes Squeers unconscious. The story also featured Ralph Nickleby as a dishonest and callous financier, and Sir Mulberry Hawk as a selfish and sinister member of society.

Nineteenth Century: Sites and Styles

Bleak House (1852-3) is an indictment of the cold rigidity of law and church, the delays of the former and the smugness of the latter in the person of the self-righteous Reverend Chadband. Society, represented by Sir Leicester Dedlock – 'his family is as old as the hills and infinitely more respectable' – and his wife, is revealed as haughty and also as concealing a guilty secret. Such secrets are an aspect of the melodramatic character of much of Dickens' work. Such melodrama was very popular with the public, joining fiction and theatre, accentuated by the drama of public readings, such as those given with great success by Dickens. Modern television offers many instances of such melodrama. As with the orphan Smike in *Nicholas Nickleby*, society fails the poor in *Bleak House*, in this case Jo, a young crossing-sweeper, who also dies.

In *Hard Times* (1854), Dickens attacked utilitarianism in the person of the fact-obsessed, unloving hardware merchant Thomas Gradgrind. In *Little Dorrit* (1855-7), a satire that prefigures some today, society worships Merdle, a great but fraudulent financier, 'a new power in the country', while government, in the shape of the Circumlocution Office, is callously inefficient. 'Treasury hoped he might venture to congratulate one of England's world-famed capitalists and merchant-princes... To extend the triumphs of such men, was to extend the triumphs and resources of the nation'.

Not only a novelist, Dickens also launched the hugely successful weekly magazine *Household Words* in 1850. *The Old Curiosity Shop* (1840-1) sold 100,000 copies, and his weekly magazine begun in 1859, *All the Year Round*, as many as 300,000. A fine observer of people, Dickens was a recorder of a changing society, as in his short story 'Dullborough Town', published in *All the Year Round* on 30 June 1860:

Most of us come from Dullborough who come from a country town ... the Station had swallowed up the playing-field. It was

English Culture

gone. The two beautiful hawthorn-trees, the hedge, the turf, and all those buttercups and daisies had given place to the stoniest of jolting roads... The coach that had carried me away, was melodiously called Timpson's Blue-Eyed Maid, and belonged to Timpson, at the coach-office up-street; the locomotive engine that had brought me back, was called severely No. 97, and belonged to SER [South Eastern Railway], and was spitting ashes and hot-water over the blighted ground.

Dickens was not alone in such concerns. His one-time collaborator Wilkie Collins (1824-89) dealt with issues such as divorce, vivisection, and the impact of heredity and the changing environment. In *The Woman in White* (1859-60), Anne Catherick is incarcerated in an asylum in order to conceal a secret. Evangelical busybodies are attacked in the person of Miss Clack in *The Moonstone* (1868). *Man and Wife* (1870) castigates the cult of athleticism and criticises the marriage laws, while in *The New Magdalen* (1873) Collins condemns sexual hypocrisy. Wracked by gout, he took large quantities of laudanum and the drug had a major impact on his work.

Social issues attracted other successful and prominent writers. Elizabeth Gaskell (1810-65) tackled industrial strife, working-class living standards, and the role of entrepreneurs in *Mary Barton* (1848); she was more positive about entrepreneurs in *North and South* (1855). Her underlying theme was conciliation, rather than aggressive class conflict. George Eliot, the pseudonym of Mary Anne Evans (1819-80), depicted a seducing squire in *Adam Bede* (1859), social ostracism in *The Mill on the Floss* (1860), the cruel selfishness of two sons of the squire in *Silas Marner* (1861), corrupt electioneering in *Felix Holt* (1866), a hypocritical banker in *Middlemarch* (1871-2), and the decadent mores of society and antisemitism in *Daniel*

Deronda (1878). Her work also recorded the pressures of social organisation and mores. Social rank is seen as divisive in *Middlemarch*. These female authors were in the front rank of the nineteenth-century novelists, and they helped to boost female readership as female literacy rose. Influencing her realism, George Eliot was also the co-editor of the *Westminster Review* and an active reviewer.[1]

In novels such as *Far from the Madding Crowd* (1874) and *The Mayor of Casterbridge* (1886), and even more so in his poetry, Thomas Hardy (1840-1928) recorded the bleaker side of country life and the corrosive pressure of urban mores on rural ways. Rural society was presented as steeped in folk-lore and customs, and suspicious of new men of business. In *Tess of the d'Urbervilles* (1891), the machine operator spoke with a 'strange' (ie northern) accent. Hardy's *Jude the Obscure* (1895) dealt with exclusion from scholarship as a result of class. Earlier, the agricultural labourer John Clare had depicted the plight of the rural poor in *Poems Descriptive of Rural Life* (1820) and his long poem *The Village Minstrel* (1821).

George Gissing (1857-1903) presented urban poverty and the harsh binds of heredity in *Workers in the Dawn* (1880). In *Demos: A Story of English Socialism* (1886), however, he was biting about the motives and integrity of Socialist leaders. Other social comment novels included Andrew Mearns's *The Bitter Cry of Outcast London* (1883).

Many novelists were less noted for social criticism or handled society in a different way; *Vanity Fair* (1847-8), the panoramic masterpiece of William Makepeace Thackeray (1811-63), offered a realistic account of individual drives, rather than a prescription for social action. In *The Way We Live Now* (1874-5), Anthony Trollope (1815-82) condemned the corruption of what he saw as 'the commercial profligacy of the age', but much of his work was far less pointed. Trollope was particularly popular with contemporaries for his Barsetshire sequence (1855-67) which provided a realistic but essentially benign account of middle-class provincial, especially clerical, society. Trollope also wrote a successful series of political fictions, the six Palliser novels, which appeared in 1864-80. These and his other novels offered a fine and close account of character and an intimate understanding of human action, which provided the basis for his sympathetic yet ironic treatment of character. Trollope's productivity – 47 novels and much else including travel books and biography alongside an active career in the Post Office – surpassed that of his mother Frances Trollope (1780-1863) who had been driven by family debts to publish 41 books.

There was little social criticism in the works of Edward Bulwer Lytton (1803-73), now little known, but, in his prime, frequently seen as the country's foremost man of letters for works such as *The Last Days of Pompeii* (1834). A friend of Dickens who was an active MP before being raised to the peerage, Bulwer Lytton's career indicated the potential profit of authorship and the variety of styles and forms that gifted (and not so gifted) writers could employ. He wrote twenty-four novels, ten plays, eleven volumes of poetry, translations, essays, and historical and sociological studies, and was also a magazine editor. Among his genres was that of the 'silver-fork novel', the portrayal of drama or at least events in high society. Bulwer Lytton's *Pelham, or, The Adventures of a Gentleman* (1828) was a successful example, and the novels of Benjamin Disraeli, later Prime Minister, can also be located in this genre. In Lytton's *The Coming Race* (1871), a mining engineer encountered at the centre of the Earth a people who controlled 'Vril', a kinetic energy offering limitless powers; which has left us the legacy name Bo(vine)vril.

The writers of the age sought a mass readership, not only for personal profit but also because they thought it important to write accordingly. This was not seen as incompatible with literary excellence, and these attitudes reflected the distance between the literary world of the nineteenth century and that of two centuries earlier.

Poetry

In terms of what was conventionally seen as such culture, this was an age in which poetry made a major impact. In the early decades of the century this meant the Romantic poets, especially William Wordsworth (1770-1850), Samuel Taylor Coleridge (1772-1834), and Robert Southey (1774-1843), these poets a template for many others. The Cumbrian-born Wordsworth was a supporter of Revolutionary France in the 1790s who became the most celebrated of the English Romantics with works such as the *Lyrical Ballads* (1798, 2nd edn., 1800), *The Prelude* (1799; longer form 1805), and *The Excursion* (1814). Wordsworth was very much a poet of elemental forces with a fine eye for landscape. He lived most of his life in the Lake District, which he celebrated in poetry and prose. The poets attracted the attention of artists, Wordsworth deep in thought in Benjamin Haydon's portrait of 1842, pictured against rocks and clouds.

This matched the engagement seen in the preference for the picturesque style of landscaping, an abandonment of formalism. In *An Essay on the Picturesque* (1794), Uvedale Price argued in favour of a wilder, less regular and more natural, 'picturesque' beauty that would accord with 'all the principles of landscape painting'. Such arguments influenced Humphry Repton (1752-1818), author of *Observations on the Theory and Practice of Landscape Gardening* (1803), who transformed about 220 gardens. In contrast, the Brontë sisters were to idealise rugged Yorkshire moors.

The benign image of landed ease offered by stately homes and landscape gardening sits alongside a fierce agrarian control that extended to the sweeping away of villages. Based on his experience of Suffolk poverty, George Crabbe's poem *The Village* (1783) rejected the pastoral:

Fled are those times, when, in harmonious strains,
The rustic Poet prais'd his native Plains...
Theirs is your House that holds the Parish Poor,
Whose walls of mud scarce bear the broken door.

Like Wordsworth, Coleridge was another early radical who became reconciled to the Establishment. Famous works included *The Rime of the Ancient Mariner* (1798) and *Kubla Khan* (1797), while he was also an important critic. Southey was a less gifted writer, but, like Wordsworth, became both conservative in disposition and politics, and Poet Laureate. As a reminder of the transience of reputations, Southey for long attracted relatively little scholarly attention. A principled writer who supported the war against Napoleon but was more political reformer than reactionary, Southey was a social conservative who was a bitter critic of factories and supporter of the independent yeomanry against large landowners, who opposed atheism while relativising the Church of England.[2]

Underlining the individuality and variety that was Romanticism, several prominent poets of the period did not follow Southey's political journey. Percy Bysshe Shelley (1792-1822), the author of *Prometheus Unbound*, was a democrat who led what was, by the standards of the age, an irregular personal life, developing the radical potential of Romanticism in order to

Nineteenth Century: Sites and Styles

attack religion, law, the state and capitalism. For Shelley, politics and literature were not separable. The flavour of his critique can be gauged from some stanzas in his *The Masque of Anarchy* (1819):

As I lay asleep in Italy
There came a voice from over the Sea,
And with great force it forth led me
To walk in the visions of Poesy.
I met Murder on the way –
He had a mask like Castlereagh [Foreign Secretary] –
Very smooth he looked, yet grim;
Seven blood-hounds followed him;
All were fat; and well they might
Be in admirable plight,
For one by one, and two by two,
He tossed them human hearts to chew
Which from his wide cloak he drew.

Next came Fraud and he had on,
Like Eldon [Lord Chancellor], an ermined gown;
His big tears, for he wept well,
Turned to mill-stones as they fell,
And the little children, who
Round his feet played to and fro,
Thinking every tear a gem,
Had their brains knocked out by Them.

Clothed with the Bible, as with light,
And the shadows of the night,
Like Sidmouth [Home Secretary], next, Hypocrisy
On a crocodile went by.

English Culture

Shelley wrote it after hearing of the Peterloo Massacre in which the breaking up by the Yeomanry of a radical public meeting in Manchester had led to unnecessary fatalities.

The greatest 'betrayal' was by Wordsworth, at least in the eyes of Robert Browning in his poem 'The Lost Leader' (1845). The once radical 'semi-atheist' Wordsworth had accepted a pension from the government and in 1843 had become Poet Laureate on the death of Southey:

> Just for a handful of silver he left us,
> Just for a riband to stick in his coat...
> Shakespeare was of us, Milton was for us,
> Burns, Shelley, were with us,—they watch from their graves!
> He alone breaks from the van and the freemen,
> —He alone sinks to the rear and the slaves!

George, 6th Lord Byron (1788-1824) was another radical like Shelley with an irregular personal life, who went to live abroad and died there. Byron's satire was less comprehensive in its denunciation of society than Shelley's, but it could be barbed, as also his criticisms of writers, of Southey for example. Byron developed the image of the Byronic hero, a wandering outcast from an unjust society.

John Keats (1795-1821) was less melodramatic and political, and developed a more intimate style of Romantic imagination and expression, although he also captured drama as in *On First Looking into Chapman's Homer*:

> Or like stout Cortez when with eagle eyes
> He star'd at the Pacific – and all his men
> Look'd at each other with a wild surmise –
> Silent, upon a peak in Darien.

Nineteenth Century: Sites and Styles

His *Isabella, or, the Pot of Basil, Hyperion, The Eve of St. Agnes*, and *La Belle Dame Sans Merci* remained in the English Literature school curriculum into the late twentieth century.

Wordsworth's successor as Poet Laureate in 1850, Alfred Tennyson (1809-92), helped reconcile poetry and the Establishment. A favourite of Queen Victoria, Tennyson was raised to the peerage in 1883. Tennyson was no bluff rhymester, but a neurotic and withdrawn figure who grasped sadness. The self-sacrifice endorsed in poems such as *Enoch Arden* (1864) was very popular. As the protagonist of morality and Empire, who could pull out line stops for set-piece poems such as *The Charge of the Light Brigade*, Tennyson was also safe, and he was a master of poetry as understood in the period. It was self-sacrifice, not of the Byronic outcast, but of the servant of a social but not servile or excessively deferential morality.

Despite the importance of the prolific and talented Robert Browning (1812-89), Tennyson dominated the poetic world even more than Dickens did that of novels, but there were of course other poets. One of the most prominent was the multi-talented William Morris (1834-96), a member of the Pre-Raphaelite school. Yet none of the poets of the period approached the intensity and quality of the Romantics.

The expansion of publications provided opportunities for the arts, including comic publications, as with the 'Song of the Garotter' published in the comic London magazine *Punch* in 1862:

So meet me by moonlight alone,
Kind stranger, I beg and entreat,
And I'll make all your money my own,
And leave you half-dead in the street.

Drama

The nineteenth century is not generally seen as the zenith of the stage. English drama of the sixteenth, seventeenth and twentieth century enjoys a considerably higher reputation. Even the eighteenth century can boast playwrights of the quality of John Gay and Richard Brinsley Sheridan. The latter lived until 1816, but *The Critic* (1779) was his last first-rate play, and *Pizaro* (1799), his last really successful work.

The current theatrical repertoire includes very few nineteenth-century works, even with the fashion for the Gothic. Several of the Gothic novelists were also dramatists, notably Matthew Lewis, with *The Castle Spectre* (1797) and Charles Maturin's *Bertram, or The Castle of Aldobrand* (1816). Some of the Gothic stories were staged, notably Robert Jephson's adaptation of *The Castle of Otranto, The Count of Narbonne*, which appeared in November 1781. Its 21 nights at the Theatre Royal, Covent Garden in the 1781-2 season was a major triumph, and the play was repeatedly staged during the rest of the century. An edition of the text was printed five times in the 1780s. Other prominent Gothic plays included Francis North's *The Kentish Barons* (1791), J. C. Cross's *Julia of Louvain, or, Monkish Cruelty* (1797), Joanna Baillie's *De Montfort* (1798), and *Presumption; or, the Fate of Frankenstein* (1823), Richard Peake's adaptation of *Frankenstein*.[3] North was second son of the former Prime Minister and would become 4th Earl of Guilford.

The interplay between publication and theatre was shown with *The Black Castle* (1800), an inexpensive 48-page novel, which became *The Black Castle; or the Spectre of the Forest, an Historical Romance. By C. F. Barrett. Founded on the spectacle of that name, performed at the Amph-Theatre of Arts, with unbounded Applause, for Nearly One Hundred Nights*. The castle belongs to Alphar, a Moor who oppresses women, imprisoning,

Nineteenth Century: Sites and Styles

raping and killing Ravia, whose ghost helps Lamora escape her fate. A secret passage is part of the plot, as is a forest, a cave, storms, and the castle bell.

Maturin's *Bertram* begins with a terrifying storm over a monastery, the responses to which capture a major rift which novelists frequently deployed:

> 1st **Monk:** O, holy prior, this is no earthly storm.
> The strife of fiends is on the battling clouds,
> The glare of hell is in these sulphurous lightnings,
> This is no earthly storm.
> **Prior:** peace, peace – thou rash and unadvised man;
> Oh! and not to this night of nature's horrors
> The darker shadowing of thy wicked fears.
> The hand of Heaven, not man, is dealing with us,
> And thoughts like thine do make it deal thus sternly. (I, 1)

An actor-manager, J. C. Cross in his *Julia of Louvain* (1797) had a commonplace plot, with St Pierre, a cruel aristocrat, incarcerating a young woman in a convent because she will not marry him, setting up the need for a rescue. In the nunnery, presented with the choice of 'Death or St Pierre,' Julia is confined in a sepulchre, but an intervention by townspeople (a scene already seen in Lewis's novel *The Monk*, 1796) leads to the seizure of the nunnery and, near death, Julia is discovered and freed.

Joanna Baillie's *De Montfort* (1798 and staged at Drury Lane in 1800) was one of her 'Plays on the Passions', the hatred of the arrogant, doom-driven, Marquis De Montfort toward Rezenvelt leading him to breach restraints and to murder. There is a good woman (Montfort's sister, Jane) and a bad one (Countess Freberg), and a Shakespearean intensity to the characterization and action, with the Gothic settings of castle, forests and cathedral. In *Ethwald* (1802), Baillie (1762-1851), a Scot who moved to England in the mid-1780s, borrowed freely from *Macbeth*. Her other Gothic plays included *Orra* (1812). Set in the fourteenth century, Orra is exiled from Switzerland to a terrifying haunted castle in the Black Forest for turning down the son of her guardian, Count Hughobert. She wishes to retain control of her fortune. A sinister knight, Rudigere, also desires her. A subterranean passage and a ghost provide part of the action. Orra is driven by fear to madness. Again set in Switzerland, Baillie's *The Dream* (1812), in contrast, has a frightened male. Count Osterloo is guilty of murdering a rival in love, the brother of a prior whose monastery is haunted and from whose vaults a skeleton is exhumed. A secret passage again plays a role, again in an unsuccessful rescue attempt. Sentenced to death by the vengeful prior, Osterloo, instead, dies from fear of retribution in Hell.[4] Baillie as a religious moralist is to the fore.[5]

Far more lasting are the Gilbert and Sullivan operettas. The staple of the Regency and Victorian stage was not political commitment. In general, there was a preference for far less cerebral work. Leading actors, such as Edmund Kean and Charles Kean, offered Shakespeare or far less distinguished modern works. Melodrama, mocked in George Bernard Shaw's hilarious send-up *Poison, Passion and Petrification* (1905), was a regular, as was its sibling, a sickly romantic drama that centred on such plot devices as long-lost family members and mistaken identities. These devices were used and mocked in the Gilbert and Sullivan operettas.

For most of the century, the theatre was dominated, on the pattern of David Garrick the previous century, by actor managers such as Henry Irving (1838-1905), which helps explain its nature. A prominent actor, Irving in 1878 became lessee and manager of the Lyceum in London, where his emphasis was on the opulence

Nineteenth Century: Sites and Styles

and drama of the productions, not the novelty of the play. Thus, for example, Irving shunned the work of Shaw and of the realist Norwegian playwright Ibsen, preferring Shakespeare, or plays such as Tennyson's (now forgotten) *Becket* (1884), which he put on with great success in 1893. Other now-forgotten plays were also successes. For example, in the 1860s and 1870s Thomas Robertson's comedies such as *Society* (1865) and *Ours* (1866), *Caste* (1867), *Play* (1868), *School* (1869) and *M.P.* (1870) were produced with considerable success. Robertson (1829-71) has been seen as offering a detailed account of domestic life that laid the basis for the later revival of serious drama by Shaw. His plays were described as 'cup-and-saucer drama'. Has anyone heard of any of these?

Robertson was also seen as introducing a realistic note borrowed by Sir Arthur Wing Pinero (1855-1934), who wrote not only successful farces, such as *The Magistrate* (1885), but also social dramas that focused on the difficult position of women, for example *The Second Mrs Tanqueray* (1893), *The Notorious Mrs Ebbsmith* (1895), *The Benefit of the Doubt* (1895) and *Iris* (1901). In the first of these, Paula Tanqueray commits suicide because of the social stigma created by the engagement of her seducer to her step-daughter and her opposition to the match. Pinero also dealt with seduction in his controversial *The Profligate* (1889).

Irving, who was knighted in 1895, the first actor to be thus honoured, ran the most famous theatrical company of the period. It was also a touring company, something made possible by the railway, which led to a major change in the structure of the theatrical world. Earlier in the century, the London theatre had been complemented by 'stock' companies, which were located in one theatre or appeared in several that were joined in a circuit. This ensured a local theatrical life across urban Britain and also

English Culture

underlay the building of numerous theatres in the provinces. For example, the Duke of Grafton's Servants, based in the Theatre Royal in Norwich, and the Norfolk and Suffolk Company of Comedians toured East Anglia until 1852 and 1844 respectively. Such activity encouraged the construction of numerous theatres, such as at Ipswich (1803) and Bury St. Edmunds (1819).

The world of the stock company was swept aside by the development of the London-based 'long run' system. In place of the costly permanent companies, necessary for a repertory (range) of plays, managers preferred a long run of a single play, such as Brandon Thomas's upper-class comedy *Charley's Aunt* (1892) which took the record for longest run. Success could best be secured by undemanding plays with stars, such as Irving's leading lady Ellen Terry (1847-1928), spectacular productions with an emphasis on scenery and music, familiar plots, and uncontentious approaches. Augustus Harris, manager of the Theatre Royal at Drury Lane from 1879 until 1896, set the tone with spectaculars featuring avalanches, earthquakes, horse races and snowstorms. Furthermore, the success of the run could be increased either by sending the company on a rail-borne tour, or by using second and third companies at the same time as the main company, cornering the London market. This system scarcely encouraged adventurous drama.

Good runs financed new construction, such as Her Majesty's Theatre built in 1897. The Prince of Wales Theatre built in London in 1884 was financed by the profits of a forgotten work, *The Colonel*, the translation of a French farce, and then staged Charles Hawtrey's farce *The Private Secretary* (1883), disliked by the critics on opening but which ran in London for nearly 1,500 performances in its first run and succeeding revivals. The Lyric Theatre which opened in Shaftesbury Avenue in 1888 was the result of the entrepreneurial energy of Henry J. Leslie. He

Nineteenth Century: Sites and Styles

financed it with the profits he had already made with the now forgotten comic opera *Dorothy* (1886), which followed the well-trodden path of a rake falling in love with his disguised fiancée. It was transferred to the new theatre where it took what was then the record for the longest-running musical theatre production.

It is not until the 1890s with Oscar Wilde, an Irishman who preferred London, that one finds works still frequently acted today. *Lady Windermere's Fan* (1892), *A Woman of No Importance* (1893), *An Ideal Husband* (1895) and *The Importance of Being Earnest* (1895) were ironic and brilliant portrayals of high society. *Salomé*, which was refused a licence in 1892 and first performed in Paris in 1896, was a very different work – a highly charged account of the relationship between Salome and St John the Baptist. Musical comedy with a modern setting flourished with *The Gaiety Girl* (1893) by George Edwardes, and from 1894 at the Gaiety Theatre he put on a new version of this popular work each season. His 'Showgirls' were largely recruited from the middle-class suburbs.

The 1890s also saw the appearance of the first of the plays of George Bernard Shaw (1856-1950). Several – *Widowers' Houses* (1892), *Mrs Warren's Profession* (1893), and *The Philanderer* (1893) were only performed privately as they were thought unlikely to obtain a licence: the Lord Chamberlain, through the Examiner of Plays, had to give a licence before any public performances on the stage. This restricted new and different works.

Widowers' Houses (1892), Shaw's first play, which was produced for the Independent Theatre Club, was far more 'realistic' than those of Wilde, and Shaw emphasised its realism and didacticism. The play dealt openly with economic power and social relations in a way that was very different to the rest of nineteenth-century drama. It concerns the relationship between the aristocratic Henry Trench and Blanche Sartorius, whose father is wealthy through slum landlordism. Trench is appalled, only for Sartorius to point out that Trench's money has come from similar sources. A series of realistic works produced publicly began with Shaw's *Arms and the Man* in 1894. The politically committed Shaw pushed the notion of the dramatist as a public figure able to turn a searchlight on society.

Other works of the period, now all forgotten, included Alfred Celliser's play *Doris* (1889) and Edward Solomon's comedy opera *The Red Hussar* (1889). Ivan Caryll's and Gustave Kerker's burlesque opera *Little Christopher Columbus* (1893) ran for 421 performances. Wilson Barrett's historical-Christian drama *The Sign of the Cross* (1895) was highly successful. In 1932, Cecil B. DeMille's film adaptation was released, to the fury of Barrett's only daughter, Dorothea. Despite apparently holding 'the sole rights' to the play, she told *The Citizen* on 31 January 1933:

> It is not our intention to claim one single farthing from the makers of the film... I regard it as tainted money. I have the very strongest views on how it [the play] should be produced... As little money as possible should be spent on it... There should be no stars in the cast.

That's quite proscriptive for a story that includes Nero, his wife Poppea's unrequited lust for the Roman Patrician Marcus Superbus, and Christians being eaten by lions in the Colisseum.

There was investment in ever more spectacular productions. This theatrical world persisted until the 1910s and the cinema, although for the years prior to Shaw and Wilde it did not produce many plays that are still performed today.

Music-hall
Music-hall was variety – song, music, acrobatics, dance – and encouraged interaction between performers and audience.

Nineteenth Century: Sites and Styles

Music halls originally sold food and drink, although the latter was slowly abolished as they became more respectable. The Star at Bolton, founded in 1832, is considered the first music hall, although they were most successful in London. Charles Morton, who founded the Canterbury at Lambeth in 1851, is regarded as the 'father of the music hall'. The halls were born of the focus of Victorian culture on the expanding cities, but with a cockney input.[6]

Music-hall was performance art; although the songs were printed and sold in large numbers, the printed version paled in comparison with the impact of singers such as Dan Leno, Marie Lloyd, the Great MacDermott and Harry Lauder. They and other singers used songs such as 'Oh, Mister Porter, or 'The Galloping Major' (who gallops so much his new wife returns to her mother), to refer to a sexuality that was banished from public culture. Indeed, Marie Lloyd (1870-1922), though 'the Queen of the Halls', was not socially acceptable and was not invited to perform at the Royal Command Performance in 1912. She responded by adding to her posters, 'Every performance given by Marie Lloyd is a command performance by Order of the British Public.' This was big business, whereas the individual music of street entertainers was ended by the Vagrancy Act of 1824 and subsequent police action.

Architecture

Alongside new theatres and music halls, art galleries and museums proliferated in every major, and many minor, towns as they sought to proclaim their cultural status.

The civic building is a major part of the cultural heritage of the nineteenth century. In the twentieth century, especially during the post-1945 Modernist vogue, Victorian architecture was much castigated and many buildings were destroyed, famously most of

English Culture

Euston station, or left stranded amidst a new world of concrete and cars. Nevertheless, an enormous amount survives in city centres, and this remains an aspect of the culture that can be readily approached.

The early decades of the century witnessed a variety of styles, but neo-classicism played a major role in several of them. Greek Revival was particularly important. Classical porticoes decorated major buildings. Sir John Soane (1753-1837) was one of the most influential exponents of the new style. Having won a competition in 1788 to design a new building, he presided over work at one of the central institutions of national life, the Bank of England. Classical themes also played a role in the work of John Nash (1752-1825) who worked extensively in London for the Prince Regent, later George IV. Nash's style was more varied than that of Soane. He was responsible for the Pavilion at Brighton, built for the Prince in an ebullient Indo-Gothic style.

The neo-classicism of the late eighteenth century drew heavily on Roman models, but that of the early nineteenth was more influenced by that of ancient Greece, particularly the Doric and Ionic Orders. Architects such as William Wilkins (1778-1839), Sir Robert Smirke (1780-1867), C. R. Cockerell (1788-1863), and H. W. Inwood (1794-1843) all made lengthy trips to Greece. This inspiration was spread by training, as young architects served as apprentices in London. Greek Revival led to works such as Wilkins' Grecian-style buildings at Downing College, Cambridge (1807-20).

Greek Revival did not stand alone. Neo-Gothic was important, especially in ecclesiastical architecture and for country houses like James Wyatt's vast Fonthill Abbey for William Beckford and Sir Walter Scott's building of Abbotsford (1816-23). The case for Gothic Revival was pushed hard by Augustus Pugin (1812-52), an architect who felt that the Revival had a mission. Pugin

Nineteenth Century: Sites and Styles

saw Gothic as the quintessentially Christian style. Having made his case for the Gothic in *Contrasts* (1836), Pugin built a series of works including Alton Towers (1836), which since that date has experienced something of a rollercoaster ride. His arguments and designs hit home at the right moment as, after a long period in which *relatively* few new churches had been built, there was a period of massive church-building. This was largely due to the expansion of the cities, not least through immigration from the countryside. Furthermore, Catholic Emancipation was followed by the building of many Catholic churches. Gothic Revival was thus a counterpoint of religious activism (although far less so for Low Church congregations). It was favoured by the Oxford Movement and by the influential cultural commentator John Ruskin (1819-1900). Influential architects in the Gothic Revival style included Sir George Scott (1811-78), William Butterfield (1814-1900), G. E. Street (1824-81), Norman Shaw (1831-1912) and Alfred Waterhouse. They were active in building and 'restoring' churches. Butterfield's work includes All Saints, Margaret Street (1859) and Keble College, Oxford (1873-6).

There was also much secular building in the Gothic style, especially from the 1850s as this style replaced Greek Revival. Scott's work included the Midland Hotel at St Pancras Station (1865-71) and the Albert Memorial (1863), while other prominent buildings included Waterhouse's Manchester Town Hall (1869-77), and G. E. Street's Law Courts in London (1874-82).

Gothic Revival did not enjoy an unchallenged ascendancy. Sir Charles Barry (1795-1860) worked in both Gothic and Greek Revival styles, but also developed a neo-Renaissance style, using Italian *palazzi* as models. This neo-Renaissance style was also employed by other architects such as Gilbert Scott in his Foreign Office building. Barry's creations attest to the eclecticism that was, alongside stylistic disputes, a pronounced feature of the period. They ranged from the neo-Gothic Houses of Parliament and the Jacobethan Highclere Castle (the set for Downton Abbey) to the Greek Revival Manchester Athenaeum. As the century waned, the neo-Gothic became increasingly repetitive. The variety of the Arts and Crafts movement associated with William Morris (1834-96) helped, however, to lighten it. Morris popularised an interest in craftsmanship.

These names may seem of scant interest to some, but they created much of the iconic fabric of modern England. If they were all men, that reflected the socio-cultural context, including access to opportunities for artistic education and patronage. If they were all white, those factors were combined with the small numbers of non-white inhabitants until the late twentieth century.

At the close of the century, other architectural styles and themes included Art Nouveau, which drew on Continental developments. Functionalism had not of course been absent earlier in the century. Indeed, the railway and other examples of new industrial technology brought a requirement for new buildings and in new forms; while advances in construction techniques and in interior design requirements also encouraged a search for effective designs. The most famous individual work was Paxton's Crystal Palace, but railway stations, and, more generally, iron-fronted commercial and industrial premises helped popularise new designs.

Artistic styles do not exist and interact in an historical vacuum. Those of the nineteenth century are in fact largely comprehensible only in terms of the politics of a society experiencing rapid change. The functional works just referred to can be seen as engineered buildings, built without too much, or indeed any, theoretical reflection. However, there was also a cultural reaction to industrialisation. By the 1840s, the undeniable horrors of industrialisation encouraged a nostalgic return to medievalism

Nineteenth Century: Sites and Styles

in some quarters. Although there was no strict equivalence, this can be related to the High-Anglican Oxford Movement in the Church of England and also to the resurgence of English Catholicism. The most obvious manifestation of this cultural politics was architectural, notably the very historicist Gothic revival. Pugin was a Catholic stylistic polemicist, responsible for the Catholic cathedrals at Birmingham (1841) and Newcastle (1844), as well as for the rebuilding after a fire of the Palace of Westminster. Much, but by no means all, artistic patronage reflected institutional and personal commitments within these ecclesiastical contexts.

Painting

Modern popular interest in nineteenth-century painting generally focuses on J. M. W. Turner (1775-1851) and the Pre-Raphaelites. They were indeed important, and in some circles enjoyed considerable popularity. However, before discussing their work, it is worth noting that neither represented the mainstream. Instead, a far more established figure would be Queen Victoria's (and her subjects') favourite painter, Edwin Landseer (1802-73) who was knighted in 1850 and offered the Presidency of the Royal Academy in 1865. Although he died insane, Landseer was safe, in that he accommodated and expressed what was expected. Characteristic of his style was *Windsor Castle in Modern Times* (c.1842). This showed Victoria and Albert as an idealized family with the gardens of Windsor Castle visible through the open window. Albert has just been shooting, but the dead birds on the carpet do not bleed and have no visible signs of injury. Everyone is appropriate and devoted, including the dogs. Landseer was a specialist in animal paintings and noted for works such as *The Monarch of the Glen* (1851), the depiction of a stag. Engravings of these paintings were printed in large numbers. Landseer was

English Culture

not noted as an explorer of the urban scene, although he left his mark on London when he sculpted the lions at the foot of Nelson's Column.

Daniel Maclise (1806-70), Irish-born and London-settled, was a counterpart of Landseer, although today far less well known. Nevertheless, at the time he was much applauded as a great artist. A close friend of Dickens, and an accomplished draughtsman who painted statuesque forms, Maclise illustrated themes from Shakespeare, for example *Macbeth and the Weird Sisters* (1836), and from British history, such as *Alfred the Great in the Tent of Guthruyn* (1852). He painted *Wellington and Blücher at Waterloo* (1861), and *The Death of Nelson* (1864) for the Houses of Parliament. These paintings were regarded as a great triumph and Maclise received £7,000 for the two. Maclise was also a society portrait painter.

Another prominent figure of the period, now forgotten, was Sir Charles Eastlake (1793-1865), who became President of the Royal Academy in 1850. Eastlake was noted for portraits, historical scenes, and picturesque displays of Mediterranean scenes and people, for example his *Pilgrims Arriving in Sight of Rome* (1827), *Christ Blessing Little Children* (1839) and *Christ Weeping over Jerusalem* (1841). These were different to the pre-Raphaelites in tone and content, but similar in religious topic.

Animals, sporting pictures and exemplary historical, religious and military scenes were popular, for example the battle scenes of Elizabeth, Lady Butler (1846-1933), as were scenes of rural bliss. There were of course paintings reflecting the less benign aspects of life, but most of these were tempered in their realism. Thomas Kennington's *The Pinch of Poverty* (1889) did not provide a picture of smiling joy, but poverty was generally far harsher in its consequences than this genteel scene with its charming flower seller and romantically pale mother. The same was true of John

Nineteenth Century: Sites and Styles

Dollman's *The Immigrants' Ship* (1884). Despair and hardship were not generally emphasised, although George Frederick Watts' *Found Drowned* (1849-50) was a reference to the lists of women, mostly prostitutes, found dead in the Thames, while Luke Fildes' *Applicants for Admission to a Casual Ward* (1874) dealt with poverty.

Turner offered scenes of commercial life – for example his *Keelmen Heaving in Coals by Moonlight* (1835) – but was primarily, as in that painting, interested in light, or rather luminosity, colour and shape. His was Romanticism on canvas and was criticised for its lack of formalism by Sir George Beaumont (1753-1827), a major art patron and leading amateur painter who made the first major bequest to the National Gallery. Beaumont was an active defender of Reynolds and is a reminder of the inherently contentious nature of artistic debate. Turner himself moved from landscapes to more abstract works in the 1840s. Turner was to inspire the Impressionists and also to push the symbolisation of the elements further than hitherto. His was a different account of landscape from that of John Constable (1776-1837), although, like Turner, Constable departed from what they saw as the mannered interpretation of landscape in the eighteenth century and, instead, sought to present a total vision of nature. This, for example, involved blobs of pure colour to represent sunlight. Landscape painting became less original and more stereotypical in the hands of the successors of Constable and Turner.

After Constable and Turner, British painting in this century is mostly noted for the works of the Pre-Raphaelite Movement. This term was adopted in 1848, the 'year of revolutions', by a group, or, as they called themselves, Brotherhood, of young English painters, the most prominent of whom were John Everett Millais, William Holman Hunt and Dante Gabriel Rossetti. They sought

English Culture

to react against what they saw as the empty formalism of the then fashionable 'subject' painting, for example the Shakespearean and historical works of Maclise. The phrase Pre-Raphaelite was a reaction against current lodestars of artistic quality and the notion that beauty was essential to art, which was associated with Raphael. Instead, the Pre-Raphaelites stressed the moral purpose of art. In addition, they offered a primitivism that rested on the suggestion that the medieval period was purer and less artificial. There was thus a parallel to the Gothic Revival in architecture; and perhaps also an increasing sympathy with Catholicism, or, at least, hostility to Protestant criticisms of the medieval Church.

Purity was controversial, not least when focused on attempts to provide a realistic portrayal of the life of the Holy Family, as in Hunt's *Girlhood of Mary Virgin* (1849) and Millais' *Christ in the House of His Parents* (1850), the latter bitterly criticised, not least by Dickens. Such works exemplified the Pre-Raphaelite claim to focus on nature directly perceived and to show what life must have been like, rather than being guided by artistic classifications and rules. The Movement, which had been initially constituted as a secret Brotherhood, had dissolved by 1855, but its themes remained influential, including among many of those who were not members of the Brotherhood, or indeed of the second brotherhood founded by Rossetti, Edward Burne-Jones and William Morris. Thus, for example, Ford Madox Brown (1821-93), although never a member, was sufficiently impressed to depart from his earlier Romantic historical painting and paint in the Pre-Raphaelite manner, most famously *Chaucer at the Court of Edward III* (1851) and *Work* (1863). The latter dignified labour and was based on navvies whom Brown saw working in Hampstead. As a reminder of the frequent close interaction of art with the wider world, Brown depicted in the painting Thomas Carlyle, whose *Past and Present* (1843) had stressed the

Nineteenth Century: Sites and Styles

disadvantages of unemployment, and F. D. Maurice, the Christian Socialist principal of the Working Men's College where Brown had taught.

Among the Brotherhood, Hunt (1827-1910) remained faithful to its aims. He travelled on several occasions to Egypt and Palestine to ensure his paintings of biblical scenes were accurately grounded. The popularity of his paintings, such as *The Light of the World*, *The Scapegoat* and *The Hireling Shepherd*, is a reminder of the strong Christian commitment of Victorian society.

Millais (1829-96) followed a different course, becoming a fashionable painter and pillar of the artistic establishment. Created a baronet in 1885, Millais was elected President of the Royal Academy in 1896. He found favour with undemanding Shakespearean scenes and sentimental portraits, for example *Ophelia* (1852), *The Blind Girl* (1856), and *Bubbles* (1886). At the same time, there was a celebration of industrial enterprise and the new, as in William Parrott's *Building the Great Leviathan*, a dramatic celebration of scale and steam, executed shortly before the *Great Eastern* was launched on the Thames in 1858.

By Millais' death, the contours of the artistic world were very different to those the Brotherhood had reacted against. A sense of *fin de siècle* affected the mood of the 1890s. Paintings such as *Circe Invidiosa* (1892) by J. W. Waterhouse (1849-1917) exploited the appeal of the exotic. So did the artificial decorative patterns of Aubrey Beardsley (1872-98), the illustrator of the English version of Wilde's *Salome*, *The Yellow Book* (1894), and *The Savoy* (1896-8). Other Art Nouveau figures included the architect and designer Arthur Mackmurdo (1851-1942), a prominent figure in the Arts and Crafts Movement, Charles Ricketts (1866-1931), an artist, and theatre and book designer, and Walter Crane (1845-1915), an artist and book illustrator. They emphasised ornamentation in their reaction to academic 'historicism'. The aestheticism, self-absorption, and ostentatious of some Art Nouveau figures, especially Beardsley, was not akin to the moral purpose of the Pre-Raphaelites, although Crane can be seen as in the Pre-Raphaelite tradition.

Art Nouveau had less of an impact on British society than the Art and Crafts Movement of the second half of the century. This again can be seen as a reaction against industrialisation. The prime inspiration of the movement was William Morris, an advocate of personal production, not of mechanization and standardization. Morris influenced the leading craftsmen of the 1880s and 1890s, and the movement led to the foundation of the Guild and School of Arts and Crafts in 1888. The influence on public taste of such artistic movements should not be exaggerated. Landseer's *The Stag at Bay* (1846) was still very popular at the century's close.

Music

There were social distinctions in the response to music, in the willingness to engage with 'demanding' classical music,[7] but they were not absolute. There were types of music, such as church music, that were universally appreciated. The century was intensely musical, although it is today sometimes regarded as the dead period between Handel and the twentieth-century revival of Elgar and, even more importantly, Vaughan Williams and Britten. This is misleading. Musical life in Victorian England was active, very different to the situation today when people primarily *listen* to music. In the nineteenth century, people played and sang. The piano was the centre piece of the Victorian drawing room. The singing of songs and ballads was a family activity.

There was also much communal musical activity. Street ballads had been driven away as street entertainers were punished under vagrancy legislation, but brass bands became very popular in the

Nineteenth Century: Sites and Styles

1880s and 1890s. Amateur choral singing had developed in the eighteenth century and remained strong. Major choral societies were founded, such as that at Huddersfield in 1836. Concert halls provided forums for such societies.

London was more advanced as a centre of music than of drama, in part because it was more open to Continental influences. Much of the music performed was written by foreign composers, including Felix Mendelssohn. Possibly the most talented in the early decades was Dublin-born John Field (1782-1837), who spent most of his career in Russia. Later in the century, Sir Hubert Parry (1848-1918), Charles Villiers Stanford (1852-1924), Sir Edward Elgar (1857-1934), and Sir Arthur Sullivan (1842-1900) revived English music, Parry and Stanford playing a major role as professors at the Royal College of Music from its foundation in 1883, in training the next generation of composers. Elgar and Parry published early works under pseudonymous German names, while Henry Hugh Pierson (1815-73), a composer now totally forgotten but who taught Parry, lived in Germany from 1845 and worked under the name of Heinrich Hugo Pierson.

Victorian composers are generally known for their secular music, but they also composed religious works. Parry and Stanford both played a major role in the English choral tradition, and Sullivan's work included *Onward Christian Soldiers* (1871) and the oratorio *The Light of the World* (1873). These were popular works. So also were the fruits of Sullivan's collaboration with W. S. Gilbert, a series of comic operettas, famously *HMS Pinafore* (1878), *The Pirates of Penzance* (1879) and *The Mikado* (1885), that are far better known today. Gilbert's libretti held up a light-hearted and witty mirror to his audiences. It was what many of them wanted to see and the partnership was successful, sufficiently so for the entrepreneur D'Oyly Carte to build the

English Culture

Savoy Theatre (1881) for the operettas. The partnership dissolved after the relative failure of *The Grand Duke* in 1896. As more generally in an artistic world that largely existed without government subsidy, commercial motives were central.

Conclusions

As the nineteenth century closed, England cultural world was buoyant by Western standards. It rested on mass literacy, a highly urbanised society, and the wealth of one of the leading economies in the world. The metropolitan settings of culture were lavish and expanding in number. The London Coliseum, which opened in 1904, included tea rooms, a cigar bar, and an American bar. The London Palladium, which followed in 1910, included facilities for gentlemen to change into evening dress. The Bechstein Hall, now known as the Wigmore Hall, was built in 1901 at the cost of £100,000. From the 1890s, theatre syndicates from existing music hall managements built new venues such as the 'palaces' for more respectable customers.

Cultural inequality was class-based, but the working class (who had work) still had access to inexpensive forms of culture, such as newspapers and music halls. While not synonymous with mass entertainment, popular culture was well served by it. Furthermore, although the situation was very far from being one of equality, especially as far as the entrepreneurs were concerned, women were not denied the opportunity to be performers. Some of the leading music hall artistes were women, most famously Marie Lloyd, while women became stars in the more conventional theatre. Nevertheless, men enjoyed far more opportunities.

Mass culture was viewed with dismay by Socialists, who sought to transform the working class into a moral, united and educated force able to transform society. They hoped for self-improvement and 'rational recreation', not the rowdiness and vulgarity

Nineteenth Century: Sites and Styles

of football or music hall, and they founded bodies such as the Cooperative Holidays Association, the Clarion Vocal Unions and cycling clubs. These had scant impact on the bulk of the working class who were happy to make their own choices, which was part of the process, seen also with photography and book purchasing, in which individual participation and purchasing were to the fore. These choices, however, were and sometimes are sneered at by middle-class Socialists as 'false consciousness'.

Music-hall, meanwhile, lent itself to the new cinema. On 20 February 1896, the first films seen by a paying public in Britain were shown at the Regent Street Polytechnic, with 54 people paying a shilling each to see a sequence of short films by the Lumière brothers. This show was also seen in the Empire, Leicester Square, a fortnight later. Opened as a variety theatre in 1880 and reopened as a music hall in 1887, the Empire became a cinema in 1928.

Already by 1900, society had a strong sense of transformation. Later commentators have played down the significance of earlier changes, implying there was considerable continuity prior to the shock of world war and Modernism. That approach, however, underplayed the dynamic potential and reality of development within established forms and systems.

7

NINETEENTH CENTURY:
THE CULTURE OF EMPIRE?

The age of fiction is coming – the age when religious and social and political changes will all be effected by means of the novelist.
Arthur Conan Doyle, interview for *McClure's Magazine*, 1894

Empire as a greater Britain, and Britain as an overlap with England were both commonplace in the nineteenth century. The English tended not to differentiate themselves from Britishness in the nineteenth century, and there was a crucial multinational character to it, but though the English used the language of Britishness, they tended to focus on their own history and views. Guides to English counties and sites were frequently published, and the ability to travel by train, cycle and car brought the landscape nearer, an opportunity to link past and present in an exposition of English nationalism.[1]

Nineteenth Century: The Culture of Empire?

There was an English incorporation of ideas of Britain in the interest in British (though not Irish) landscapes. Romanticism focused strongly on identity with landscape and especially with mountains. The Lake and Peak Districts attracted attention, visitors and representation, as did the Scottish Highlands and Snowdonia. This was landscape somewhat denuded of people. The English read Scotland through Walter Scott, some of whose major novels were set in England. Scott did not tend to engage with the Scotland of the new. Instead, it was a 'Condition of England' movement which was linked to the cult of novels strong from the 1840s and had already been seen in William Cobbett's accounts. Sent from Derby in 1829 his thoughts on the diet of the poor ended with 'And this is ENGLAND!' Prefiguring J. B. Priestley, Cobbett was a very English writer, deeply committed to a geographical Englishness and steeped in English localities, and also a trenchant critic of the social and political situation. Free trade was seen as a way to ensure cheap food and thus restore a social contract, but also a means to reduce wages.[2] This Englishness could be very xenophobic. Thus, throughout the century, working-class Toryism included a robust anti-Catholicism,[3] and there was a broader hostility to the Irish, as well as an opposition to the utilitarianism of what Cobbett called 'Scotch Philosophy'.

And yet, there was also an Englishness, expressed as a Britishness, that was imperial in its ambition, scope and language, one expressed across the arts.[4] A sense of pride in imperial range, status, character and strength was very clear at the end of the nineteenth century. Consumer culture was important in this. Flags, images of Queen Victoria, and scenes of imperial activity were splashed across advertising and packaging, from tea and biscuits to new mechanical devices. Pride was expressed in

English Culture

London, the dominant city in England and the capital both of the United Kingdom and of the British Empire.

The confluence of themes was repeatedly captured across the arts. The English/British even walked in a different way to the foreigner, the idle boulevardier, Anna Jameson noting in *The Diary of an Ennuyée* (1826):

> The different appearance of the streets of London and Paris is the first thing to strike a stranger. In the gayest and most crowded streets of London the people move steadily and rapidly along, with a grave collected air, as if all had some business in view.

The stride, which became increasingly significant in England from the mid-1820s, was seen as more purposeful, healthy and safe than the then fashionable slouch, as well as making godly self-control possible. More accessibly, there was Gilbert and Sullivan's bombastic, though wry, 'He is an Englishman!' song from *HMS Pinafore* (1878), which ignored the fact that the Royal Navy was the British Navy. Navalism and the sea were significant. John Brett's very large painting *Britannia's Realm* (1880) was an almost empty seascape.[5]

This confluence of Britain and England was also seen in political speeches. In April 1904, Winston Churchill, breaking with the Conservatives, pressed the electors to 'proceed by well-tried English methods towards the ancient and lofty ideals of English citizenship', adding in April 1905 that the 'regular, settled lines of English democratic development' underpinned the 'free British Empire'. Popular stories for children included William Henry Kingston's set in the national drama, from *Peter the Whaler* (1851) to *Adventures in India* (1884),[6] and Charlotte Yonge's *Little Lucy's Wonderful Globe* (1871). G. A. Henty produced boys' adventure stories. There were also imperial styles in architecture, home décor and fashion. The early and mid-century vogue for

164

Nineteenth Century: The Culture of Empire?

Paisley shawls, Indian dress, Indian dress fabrics and architectural fancies such as the Royal Pavilion at Brighton reflected Britain's Indian empire. Imperial enthusiasm, nevertheless, varied by place, community and time.[7] Thus, the late century fashion for Oriental, especially Japanese, décor expressed an *avant garde* rejection of conventional, bourgeois culture.

There were frequent comparisons with America. Many commentators, notably Fanny Trollope and Dickens, saw America as the horrible outcome of a surfeit of democracy. American culture was presented as crude, backwoods and populist, a warning about potential developments in Britain.

At the same time as an awareness and expression of difference, there were multiple links with Continental culture. These were not only in the visual and literary arts, but also in theology, where English Biblical understanding drew heavily on German work. The Continent also provided many topics for English writers and artists,[8] more so than the empire.

Musical life was very cosmopolitan. Italian musicians were particularly important amongst the many foreign ones who suffused London's musical life.[9] Germans provided archetypical brass bands. And so also with fictional life. Sherlock Holmes is interested in learning about opera and music, as well as owning a Stradivarius violin which he delights in playing. In *The Hound of the Baskervilles* he goes to hear the two de Reszkes in Meyerbeer's *Les Huguenots*. Édouard and Jean de Reszke were notable Polish singers, appearing in *Les Huguenots* at Covent Garden every year 1880-1884, and in 1888-1893 and 1899; and Jean in the same in Covent Garden in 1888, 1889, 1891, and 1893. In 1869, the march from *Les Huguenots* was adopted as the slow march of the Grenadier Guards. In 'Black Peter' (1904), in an operatic joke, Holmes has just finished his 'famous investigation of the sudden death of Cardinal Tosca', a reference to the Puccini opera which had its British premiere in London on 23 July 1900. At the close of 'The Adventure of the Red Circle', Holmes exclaims to Watson: 'It is not eight o'clock, and a Wagner night at Covent Garden! If we hurry, we might be in time for the second act.' Holmes hears Pablo de Sarasate in concert in 'The Red Headed League', and in 'The Mazarin Stone' there is reference to Jacques Offenbach's opera *The Tales of Hoffmann* (1881). In 'The Retired Colourman' he wishes to hear Carina sing at the Albert Hall, which had been built in 1867-71. In *A Study in Scarlet*, Holmes wants to go 'to Hallé's concert to hear Norman Neruda this afternoon'.

English/British culture was nevertheless presented as morally superior to the decadence of French art and literature, while the British saw themselves, with reason, as having more freedom of expression than police states like Russia or in Catholic nations.

The closing years of Victoria's reign and the reign of Edward VII (r. 1901-10) saw empire at its height (as well as confronting difficulties, notably in the Boer War of 1899-1902) and Britain as a vibrant culture.[10] There was confidence in established cultural forms, as well as the development of new ones, notably cinema. Major novelists were in the shadow of Hall Caine (1853-1931), the most highly paid novelist of his day, whose *The Christian* (1897) was the first novel in Britain to sell over a million copies, although that claim is also made for his *The Eternal City* (1901).

Caine also wrote extensively on social matters, including those seen as women's questions, such as his attack on the divorce laws in *The Woman Thou Gavest Me* (1913). Other successful novelists of the period included Marie Corelli (1855-1924) who was fascinated by mysticism, notably in the Faustian *The Sorrows of Satan* (1895) and Charles Garvice (1850-1920), a successful writer of heart-tugging melodramas.

The irreligion of much urban life and culture troubled the clergy, and not only them. The left-wing journalist John Hobson

Nineteenth Century: The Culture of Empire?

claimed that 'the neurotic temperament generated by town life seeks natural relief in stormy sensational appeals, and the crowded life of the streets, or other public gatherings, gives the best medium for communicating them.'[11] In hot weather, the sweltering urban population was more volatile and strike-prone, as in 1911-12.

Poverty engaged attention in the 1890s to a degree not always so apparent a century earlier. Arthur Morrison's *A Child of the Jago* (1896) was a bestselling novel about children growing up in the Old Nichol slum in London's East End, depicting it as a dog-eat-dog world, full of parental neglect and police corruption, with crime, poverty, poor health and murders. Morrison was insistent that the book was entirely based on fact. The protagonist, Dicky Perrott, is corrupted by his upbringing and fatally injured during a gang brawl, as the real-life Charles Clayton, who inspired the incident, was, in 1892.

The end of the nineteenth century provided some cultural infrastructure that has lasted to the present. Thanks to the conductor Henry Wood and the impresario Robert Newman, the annual Proms series of classical music concerts began life at Queen's Hall in London in 1895. Another lasting legacy from the period is the Wimbledon Championship which began in 1877, a ladies singles competition being added in 1884, won by vicar's daughter Maud Watson, who beat her sister Lilian in the final.

Cultural icons could be reworked, a tribute to their strength but also to an independence of view. This was seen in 'The Battle of Edmonton,' published in the *Enfield Chronicle* of 17 February 1899. This riffed on Tennyson's 'Charge of the Light Brigade' in describing disturbances over the failure of the Great Eastern Railway to provide sufficient tickets for the last workmen's morning train.

English Culture

'Half a load, half a ham,
Sandwich-men onward!
Into the railway yard
Edmonton thundered;
Up by the workmen's train
More than six hundred!

As with other cases of *fin de siècle*, the emphasis can be placed very differently: 1890-1910 saw artistic decadence and socialism, imperial expansion and a sense of falling behind. It was and remains possible to offer differing emphases. Where the stress should be is a matter of debate not assertion, a situation more generally true of cultural assessment.

8

1900 TO THE PRESENT: SPHERES OF PATRONAGE

Sheffield Empire
Eve Kelland presents
'The Three Graces,'
A Musical Revusical [sic] Comedy, the actual production from the
Empire, London.
Music by Franz Lehar [sic] of 'Merry Widow' fame.
MUSIC, LAUGHTER, and SUPERB DANCING.
To drive dull care away
Latest important news will be shown on the screen at each
performance.
Advertisement in *Sheffield Daily Telegraph*, 7 May 1926.

There was growing artistic production: far more words, images and sounds claiming to be art appeared than in any previous age. A greater quantity was, and is, not the same as more diversity, true today. At the risk of considerable simplification, two broad categories are offered at the outset. First, works that engaged with human society at a large scale, and, secondly, those that focused on more intimate relations, especially issues of gender, family and self. These classifications can be contested, but they are a start and they provide an overarching structure for most sub-categories.

In 1938, on the road from London to Henley, one novelist observed: 'Even in what we now call built up areas, glimpses through gates and over fences revealed the blazing colours of massed flowers.'[1] As with environmental, economic, and social developments, cultural counterparts showed a mixture of international trends and of distinctive national ones, in this case gardening. There was a lessening of the national ones and a degree of homogenisation at the international level. Whether described as Americanisation or as globalisation, and both indeed were at play, the homogenisation was value-laden. It was an aspect of the consumerism that was central to both Americanisation and globalisation.

Advertising played a major role in this consumerism, but it was not the only element. There was also the more subliminal imagery of a desirable life presented by television programmes and with the lavish colour photography in Sunday colour newspaper supplements that began in 1962 with the first *Sunday Times* colour supplement, an issue entitled 'A Sharp Look at the Mood of Britain', that depicted a new sense of national purpose and classlessness. Such supplements provided a way for newspapers to raise revenue through advertising and to counter the competition of television. Beginning with the 'quality' press, supplements were subsequently introduced by lower-price popular newspapers, enhancing the magazine-type character of the press. This character affected other media, with varying social impacts and contexts. Élite very much became a pejorative term in cultural commentary, indeed a means to disparage activities, institutions and commentators. In part, there were political, social and generational divisions and angers at play, and the use of the term élite proved an easy 'dog-whistle' categorisation, although that term usefully saved élite critics of public opinion from the trouble of thinking.

The difficulties of categorising and analysing culture and the arts, meant it was felt necessary by some to use such terms in order to forward their views and interests. In part, there was also a question of 'false consciousnesses'. The charge of élitism was commonly directed against particular institutions and practices on behalf of a supposed democratic cultural impulse and world that was allegedly being deprived and thus left to an unwelcome demotic culture. In practice, this could be one group of the relatively privileged chiding another, while both condescended to the preferences of those with different interests and values. This was scarcely new. Indeed, the cultural politics of the country can be approached in these terms so long as it is appreciated that categories overlapped and were in large part matters of perception and rhetoric rather than clear objective measures. Thus, an emphasis in the coverage in 1997 of the funeral of Diana, Princess of Wales was very much on it being 'the people's funeral,' and notably so for ITV.[2] In practice, many were disengaged from a short-lived populist frenzy.

To use the terms Americanisation or globalisation was (and is) to make a choice about the source and direction of international influence. Americanisation was generally a pejorative term. It was an aspect of culture as politics in the broadest sense, which indeed was, and is, one way to approach culture, although not the sole one. The same is true of the word globalisation, which frequently and mistakenly serves as a description of international capitalism.

In Britain, the impact of international links and models, of contents and forms, interacted with transformations in identity and behaviour that contributed, in the broadest of forms, to the

English Culture

culture as well as politics of the period. Moreover, they were aspects of the incessant nature of change, and of unprecedented changes; the extent, rate and persistence of change leading, for many, to a strong sense of discontinuity and disruption, but for others, to a welcome excitement.

In addition more assertive gender and youth expectations, there were other broad currents that helped to give a character to the age. The decline of formality in all its respects was a major one. Informality in means of address and conversation became far more pronounced. Informality in dress, an expression of personality through spending on particular fashions, became commonplace. The visual identifiers of class, position and status were abandoned or became less common. Moreover, they were also mocked or caricatured, although the significance of this process for discarding the identifiers is unclear. Male hats were a classic instance: the bowler hat, let alone the top hat, of the upper class and the flat cap of the working class became very uncommon from the 1960s. In 1936, it was remarked that the new king, Edward VIII, arrived in London hatless, John Betjeman, in one of his poems writing 'a young man lands hatless from the air.'

So also with women wearing hats and gloves at social occasions, which had been the norm, with a major effort being put into having a matching outfit. Indeed, the covered-up nature of Muslim women took on greater significance as it was so much at variance with the far more uncovered nature of clothes for others.

The signifiers that were lost included those for unmarried and married women and for widows. Means of address, both verbally and in correspondence, changed with the decline of Miss (for an unmarried woman) and Sir (for an older man), and the rise of Ms, a form of address for women that removed attention from their married state. There was an increased use of first names, for example toward hospital patients. Writing conventions altered

1900 to the Present: Spheres of Patronage

greatly as letters were replaced by electronic communications: Facebook, Twitter and other formats were particularly significant.

In place of clothes and shoes that were altered, adapted, darned, mended, by mothers, by the owners, or by tailors and seamstresses, of shoes repaired by cobblers, and of coats reproofed against the weather, came 'disposable items'. Older women and men wore more casual clothes and shoes than in the past. Men ceased to wear ties. From the 1960s fashions changed greatly for the young with the mini-skirt and with brightly coloured flared trousers and shirts. The fashion among young women (and, less commonly, men) in the 2010s for trousers with holes, and increasingly large holes, in them was a clear example of a non-functional choice that appeared almost wilfully negligent, at the individual level, of considerations of staying warm and not wasting resources. Young men wore trainers, the old following.

Previous conventions in hairstyles and make-up were abandoned, as were restraints on tattoos, piercings and unusual jewellery in the shape of studs and chains. Noses, tongues, eyelids, tummy buttons, breasts, and genitals were among the parts of the body embellished with studs, rings and other objects. Men were part of the process, for example with their earlobes thus decorated. At the same time that fashion helped set the tone for appearance and behaviour, so both were deliberately unconventional in their content and presentation. In 2016, it was estimated that one in five people and one in three young adults had tattoos, and these percentages were higher by the mid-2020s.

Class and gender stereotypes were rapidly surmounted, notably so from the 2000s, but they had already changed greatly from the 1960s. Paradoxically, at the same time as these changes, there was a degree of continued and new division within national culture, not least in response to Britain becoming an increasingly multi-ethnic society. One description of this situation was multi-culturalism.

English Culture

There was a major breach in continuity, a breach of the 1960s, although prefigured in the 1950s. The earlier situation was outlined in *Death at the President's Lodging*, a detective novel by J. I. M. Stewart published in 1936. Of one character, he wrote that he reflected an epoch 'of English life. Dodd, heavy, slow, simply bred, and speaking with such a dialectical purity that a philologist might have named the parish in which he was born, suggested an England fundamentally rural still.'[3] To Stewart, this situation was already changing in the 1930s, as indeed was the case, due to the major impact of internal migration, the motorcar, and mass education. So also with the role of the landed orders, hit hard by agricultural depression, the First World War, and taxation. Stately homes were abandoned and some major ones that had stood for centuries, such as Beaudesert, the Staffordshire home of the Pagets, pulled down.

In the 1960s, a set of values and practices that had provided cohesion and continuity, at least since the mid-nineteenth century, and often for far longer, was greatly challenged or, in part, collapsed. Respect for the monarchy, the Church of England, Parliament, the legal system, the military, the nation's past, unwavering support for the Union in Scotland, for the landed Protestant ascendancy in Northern Ireland, and for much else, were all eroded. This erosion occurred in response to shifts in the understanding of gender, youth, class, place, nation and race. This challenge greatly affected the content and reception of culture, both new culture and the cultural past that was presented, revived (or not), and reviewed (or not).

It would be possible in a chapter on culture, after an initial introduction, to move to a discussion of particular cultural forms, with so many words on theatre or on poetry. However, to do so would be to underplay common themes and also to over-emphasise the autonomy of these individual forms. In practice, the trends that were most apparent across the world of culture were the rise of television and the complex interaction of government, the market and consumers. That world does not make the discussion of individual forms and specific arts less consequential, but a focus on trends puts this discussion and these forms in context.

In practice, contexts are the correct term, not context, because there are many that affected and reflected cultural life. Particularly important ones related to the means of transmission and reception of cultural forms and opinion. This was even more the case if sport and other leisure activities are also understood as forms of culture, rather than being separated from it. This very classification is a matter of controversy, but rests on a rejection of élite definitions of culture, a rejection that became increasingly important in this period and, indeed, was an aspect of its cultural history. A sign of the flexibility of these divisions is the way in which professional sport, especially football, moved from a predominantly working-class concern to the centre of élite politics and society, although the social background of professional players has hardly changed. There is also, and repeatedly so, the question of the very meanings of words, one captured in her first Prime Minister's Questions on 20 July 2016 when Theresa May responded to the Labour leader Jeremy Corbyn: 'He uses the language of austerity – I call it living within our means.' Culture was similarly a matter of linguistic debate, or, rather, disagreement.

State Intervention

Devastation is one of the bluntest forms of political activism. There was relatively little in England after the wartime devastation by German air and (from 1944) rocket attack from 1940 to 1945 during World War Two, bar the IRA terrorist bombings, for example that in 1993 in London that devastated St Ethelburga's in Bishopsgate. The cultural devastation seen with urban

English Culture

transformation, such as the destruction of the old Euston Station, was legal. The situation changed with the illegal throwing of a statue into Bristol harbour in 2019 which kicked off a would-be iconoclasm of racist and imperialist symbols. Such destruction was not new. In 1914, Mary Richardson, a suffragette attacked with a meat cleaver Velasquez's *Rokeby Venus* in the National Gallery, inflicting at least five slashes. This was very much commentary on culture.

In a much more frequent and destructive form, but, as noted, a legal one, so was the large-scale demolition of buildings (and their fittings) that was part of new construction projects. There was also the neglect or destruction of buildings no longer considered viable, from churches to stately homes.

In organisational terms, in contrast, the principal tension in the culture industries (to think of the situation from one particular angle) in the twentieth century arose from state intervention. It would have been surprising in a century in which government increasingly intervened in large areas of society, and taxation played a much greater redistributive role than earlier, for the world of culture and leisure to have escaped such intervention.

There were also particular reasons for intervention in this sphere. An inherited concern with morality, or at least propriety, had left the government with powers of censorship and a widespread expectation that censorship would be exercised in order to `protect society'. Established cultural forms, such as books and theatre, were subject to censorship. It focused on morality and language, but the culture of the age also had powerful political cross-currents.

The Lord Chamberlain, through the Examiner of Plays, had to give a licence before any public performances on stage. This restricted new and different works. D. H. Lawrence's novel *The Rainbow* (1915) was banned on grounds of obscenity, and when his novel *Women in Love* was published in 1921, it had been altered to avoid a similar ban and a threatened libel action. Lawrence's novel *Lady Chatterley's Lover*, written and privately printed in Florence in 1928, was published in England in an expurgated version in 1932, and in a complete version only in 1960. The publishers were prosecuted, unsuccessfully, for obscenity in 1962. In 1929, thirteen of Lawrence's paintings were seized in a London exhibition. James Joyce's novel *Ulysses* (1922) was banned until 1936 and copies were seized by the Customs. In addition, censorship was extended to new media: film, radio, television and videotapes. Cinema censorship began in 1912.

Censorship was exercised in a number of ways. The most obvious was the suppression of works. The three editors of the satirical magazine OZ were imprisoned in 1971 for publishing obscene literature. Aside from government action, there was also self-censorship by authors or publishers in order to avoid the prospect of action. Lawrence was initially unable to find a publisher for *Women in Love*. The British Board of Film Classification was established in 1912, and films were designed to avoid certificates by the censor that would limit viewing: in the late 1950s, the Rank Organisation refused to show any X-rated films in its cinemas. Yet, more significant, was the censorship created by the institutional structure of particular industries, as well as expectations about their goals and roles.

The two combined with the state control of radio and television for much of the twentieth century. Although not a government body, the BBC was a public one and it enjoyed a monopoly on television transmissions until 1955 and on radio broadcasts until 1973, which it tried desperately to preserve in each case, and it has succeeded in perpetuating a licence fee. Even when permission was granted for an independent television channel, ITV, the times within which television could be broadcast were still set by the government.

There was a political direction to the dominant social ethos, with Stanley Baldwin, the Conservative leader from 1923 to 1937 and Prime Minister in 1923-4, 1924-9 and 1935-7, keen to advance a culture that provided a vision of England in which there were Christian and ethical values and an emphasis on continuity, paternalism and pastoralism. In what was both an extension of pre-1914 pastoralism and a reaction against subsequent turmoil, Baldwin presented the countryside as representing eternal values and tradition. Anti-Communist thrillers, such as Dennis Wheatley's *Black August* (1934), that ends up in a (temporarily) Communist-controlled Ipswich, and Geoffrey Household's *A Time to Kill* (1951), with Bournemouth as a backdrop, presented an existential political threat across southern England.[4] *Black August* was published in 1934 but was set at some time in the future, when there was

> ... starvation rampant in every city in Europe... Balkan and Central European frontiers disintegrating from month to month, while scattered, ill-equipped armies fought on broken fronts, for whom, or for what cause, they now scarcely knew. (Chapter 1)

However, Labour's electoral victory in 1945 encouraged an emphasis on urban and industrial settings and topics.

Television

Both the BBC and ITV were expected to conform to an agenda that reflected the culture of society. Thus, they were expected not to broadcast material that was deemed obscene, cruel or blasphemous, or to encourage people to break the law. In the widest sense, the prime agency for cultural transmission became an adjunct of society. This was a matter not only of proscriptive (what could not be broadcast), but also of prescriptive (what

1900 to the Present: Spheres of Patronage

was encouraged) content. For much of the century, radio and television encouraged a sense that 'family values', as traditionally understood, were normal. These were very much the values that predominated until the 1960s. The BBC had a specific sense of mission, that of promoting serious culture and excluding vulgar elements of popular culture or too much American culture. BBC Radio, which was far more comprehensive in its social following than the television, created a 'popular' culture as well as a 'highbrow' one with programmes such as the 'Brains Trust'.

The rise of television culture was dramatic: increased television ownership, longer broadcasting hours, more channels, and rising viewer numbers, each of which altered greatly over the period from 1945 to the present. These trends were interlinked and interdependent. As a result, individual television programmes, as well as the very process of watching the television, could acquire an iconic force within society, expressing values and encouraging a sharing of experience. The sharing was particularly pronounced when there were relatively few channels. For both families and individuals, mealtimes were organised round the television.

Initially, television was very much a state concern. Established in 1926, the BBC was a public monopoly acting in the 'national interest', supported by a licence fee charged on every household with a television. It had an exalted, self-referential, and self-congratulatory sense of its mission for public enlightenment. There were no advertisements and scant regionalism. A culture already developed by the BBC for radio was applied from 1936 to television, which was a more challenging and expensive medium. However, at that stage, there was only one channel, only limited transmission hours, including no daytime or late broadcasts, and only black and white images. For much of the day, only the unchanging 'test card' was shown on the television, proving that it worked.

English Culture

Only 20,000 households had television sets at the beginning of the Second World War, and it was decided that the resources it took up could be better used elsewhere during wartime. TV shut down for the duration. Television returned to the air in 1946 but did not expand greatly until the coronation of Elizabeth II in 1953. The regulatory situation did not alter until 1955 when the BBC monopoly was deliberately breached as the Conservative government allowed the foundation of ITV (Independent Television) which first broadcast on September 22, 1955. This was a national channel based on a federation of new independent regional companies, which both produced and transmitted material, while the central organisation provided the ITN news. ITV, which received none of the licence fee, was funded by advertisements and provided a more consumerist account of life, and one that was focused on viewer interests. The companies, which had potentially highly profitable franchises, sought to make money, and advertisers favoured and pushed for programmes with high viewing figures. The terms on which the franchises were awarded (and later renewed) aroused controversy, appearing to some as aspects of a 'crony capitalism', a term that might possibly be widened to include the license fee. Had more been known about the process, then this perception would have been stronger, but there was little public clarification. Also in 1955, an increase in television running time from 41 to 50 hours weekly was authorised.

Reflecting a reaction against the state-planning and control of the late 1940s, ITV helped usher in a profound change in the national psyche, one of mass consumerism, although, looked at differently, a desire for the latter was the basis for the success of ITV. I once heard the veteran far Left-wing politician Tony Benn claim that ITV had made true Socialism impossible in Britain. The obvious parallel is between the iconic role of the BBC and that

1900 to the Present: Spheres of Patronage

of the NHS which, in a very different context, did not have to accept any equivalent to ITV: private health provision remained the choice of a minority, less than ten per cent of the population.

Ownership of goods, as pushed by advertising, was represented in the 'soap operas' that ITV carried, with actors depicted surrounded by material goods and, in part, defined by them. Such goods became a major topic of conversation, with gender norms coming into play. Men were expected to talk about cars, women about shopping and washing machines. Television ownership was linked to the acquisition of novelty and to one-upmanship among neighbours. It granted status, as when neighbours and relatives who lacked televisions were invited over for 'television suppers'. In time, video/DVD players became the status symbol.

Like the liberalization of borrowing by means of 'Hire Purchase,' ITV was important to the spread of car-culture in the 1950s, and also to the increased vogue for 'white goods' such as washing machines and, later, dishwashers. American soaps, such as 'I Love Lucy,' were prominent in ITV's schedules, as were American-style advertisements. The soaps and the schedules helped make particular aspects of British life appear anachronistic and unattractive. This was the case, for example, with coal fires, with living in terraces ('row housing'), and with internal twilight due to poor lighting. Beards and moustaches seemed out of place in the 1950s given the clean-shaven men on American programmes. Instead, ITV's 'soaps' encouraged the preference for electricity, and for living on modern estates of detached or semi-detached houses with a car parked on the drive. The emphasis was very much on nuclear families.

ITV was therefore part of the enormous American contribution to English life and culture, as were films, music, fashions, consumer goods, and the idea of the teenager. Without American influence and participation, life in England, at least up to 1960,

English Culture

might have appeared boring for some, and was subsequently to be presented in this light. However, the 1950s provided high levels of employment, more television, unprecedented access to holidays, including inexpensive travel to Europe, the expansion of paperback publications, participation in European football, and a still vital sense of patriotism; there was still national service.

By August 1959, 80 per cent of the population could receive ITV and its network was completed in 1962. However, partly in response to the Pilkington Committee on Broadcasting, which in 1962 condemned the 'trivial' nature of many television programmes, particularly on ITV, only the BBC was allowed a second television channel, BBC2, in 1964. Independent television had to wait until 1982 for a second channel.

To respond to ITV, BBC had to adapt, and in a chase for ratings it increasingly adopted a populist approach, both on television and on radio, one that did not reflect its founding principles and long-held precepts, and that some commentators decried. The BBC produced its own soaps, some of which were indistinguishable from their ITV counterparts, and this was more generally true of much of the production of the two rival systems.

Television decimated cinema audiences in the late 1950s. They fell from over 900 million in 1954 to 450 million in 1959. which ensured that financing was a problem, fewer films were made, and most were on safe topics such as *The Colditz Story* (1955) and *The Battle of the River Plate* (1956), both war epics. Many cinemas were eventually to close.

The tension between BBC and ITV was an aspect of a more general tension between state provision of culture and popular interests. It was seen, for example, in the contrast between patronage by the Arts Council, a government body, and the activities it subsidised, and the desires of much of the public for a more populist tone and content to culture. This tension increased

1900 to the Present: Spheres of Patronage

over time, and it remains significant at present. Arts programming and commentary on the BBC, both television and radio, provides a particular instance. There is a marked tendency to focus on the *avant-garde* or critically fashionable, and not on the popular, still less the populist. The popular press takes a very different approach.

Alongside print, television was the predominant cultural technology from the 1960s. There was a period when challenging television drama did have a popular audience, for example the television plays of Dennis Potter (1933-95), such as *Pennies from Heaven* (1978). Nevertheless, on the whole, television contributed to a situation in which popular culture was the dominant culture, but set out to offer few challenges. 'Difficult' work was marginalised. Potter's *Brimstone and Treacle* (1977) was banned by the BBC.

Television created a shared context in which common memories developed. Families were encouraged to sit down together to watch '*the* television,' for at this stage it was very rare to have more than one per household. Popular programmes became common experiences as they were watched by more than 50% of television viewers. Phrases or jokes from such shows as the *Morecambe and Wise Show* entered the national vocabulary of the period. This process was accentuated because Britain is only on one time-zone. The impact was varied. ITV took to broadcasting the first television showing of James Bond films on Christmas Day at 3.05 pm and the pressure on the National Grid as people switched on their electric kettles during the intermissions was such that a large stand-by capacity had to be made available. Colour television, introduced from 1967, and fully operational across all three channels in 1969, dramatized a sense of change: everything before then appeared grey, unattractive, dull and redundant.[5] Colour made television far more attractive. Living in North-West London, the fictional Chen household in Timothy Mo's novel *Sour Sweet* (1983) had

English Culture

added no furniture to that purchased from a previous tenant, 'bar a gigantic television'.[6]

Television viewing (like reading in the eighteenth century) was to move from an intensive experience to an extensive one. Television provided a 'TV culture,' with common points of reference. In contrast, in the channel boom and format proliferation that gathered pace from the 1980s, that shared culture was lost and was replaced by a fragmented, extensive media culture. The same has happened since with social media. Under the Broadcasting Act of 1980, Channel 4 was launched in 1982, followed by TV-AM in 1983: a second independent (non-BBC) channel had been anticipated by the Conservative government in 1963, but Labour had not been supportive.[7] Although largely commercially self-funded, Channel 4 is ultimately publicly owned. Originally a subsidiary of the Independent Broadcasting Authority, the station is now owned and operated by Channel Four Television Corporation, a public corporation of the Department for Culture, Media and Sport, and attempts in the early 2020s to privatise it were abandoned.

By 2015, the average commercial channel viewing on a TV set had increased to 2 hours 24 minutes daily. Attempts to recreate common memories by revivals, for example in 2016 of *Are You Being Served?*, *Porridge* and *Cold Feet*, suggested a lack of confidence in the ability to create convincing new inclusive programmes. Lazy stereotypes of class differences continued to be produced, as in the BBC sitcom *Home From Home* (2016).

Television is changing fast. Terrestrial television has already been diminished in importance by satellite and cable services. These are all now being diminished by streaming services such as Netflix, and by YouTube and social media. The rapid rise of the latter is of importance in its influence on culture, and not just in the changes that it has made in the social interactions of the young.

1900 to the Present: Spheres of Patronage

Which Culture?

State intervention was fairly apparent as an issue in radio and television. Elsewhere, it was frequently important, but not always so apparent. Moreover, there were significant changes, for example in the extent and nature of censorship. The word 'fuck' was first allowed in films in 1970. Attempts to introduce press censorship were kept at bay in the 2010s and 2020s.

Yet, one obvious sphere in which the role of the state was important was patronage. In the twentieth century, the state was the single most important patron of the arts, far more active than any other body. This reflected, in part, the extension of the state's role in the economy with nationalizations, notably in the late 1940s and 1970s, but also more generally in the growth of government. As a consequence of the formation of the NHS in 1948, the major roles of the churches in charitable functions and the provision of social welfare were largely replaced by the state.

Patronage was most apparent in architecture. Public bodies were the biggest commissioners of buildings. This was true both of large individual works, such as universities and hospitals, and of multiple units, especially council houses. Once constructed, buildings also had to be decorated. The *avant-garde* sculptors Jacob Epstein and Eric Gill produced important work for the London Transport headquarters (then the London Electric Railway Company) including 'Day' and 'Night' by Epstein. The importance of public commissions encouraged the production of designs that were believed likely to appeal, and this moulded the profession more widely than the actual commissioning process itself. Approved techniques and styles were reinforced through the planning process. Buildings required planning permission, and this provided many and insistent opportunities for the propagation and enforcement of specific agendas.

In architecture, proscriptive and prescriptive public pressures were (and are) readily apparent. They were (and are) less so in

English Culture

other fields where state patronage has been less important and where planning permission was not required. Nevertheless, the state still played a role in these fields, and increasingly so during the century. This owed much to the institutionalisation of state patronage. Such patronage was not new. In the 1910s, Joyce received grants from the Royal Literary Fund and the Civil List while working on *Ulysses*. Nevertheless, as with much else, total war set the cultural agenda, with both world wars, notably the second, seeing massive government intervention.

The wartime situation was sustained with the formation by the postwar Labour government of the Arts Council in 1946 (the economist John Maynard Keynes was the first chairman), and the beginning of a programme of continual public subsidy of the arts. This explicitly statist, leftwing policy was both an opportunity and a problem. It was an opportunity because it freed the arts from dependence on the marketplace, making possible the Modernist idea of the planned environment. State sponsorship, subsidy and control was a problem, however, because it created another marketplace. This was politicised, not so much in terms of public politics, but, rather, less public, but still bitter, artistic politics.

The two could overlap in the debate over 'the Two Cultures', the title of a 1959 lecture by the scientist and realist novelist C. (Charles) P. Snow, in which he argued that science offered the answers which the unscientific and literary 'traditional culture' could not provide. In turn, in 1962, F. R. Leavis, a Cambridge academic, focused on the 'Great Tradition' in English literature, attacked Snow and a stress on material objects and emphasised instead the role of ideas and language. This launched a major debate about the nature of progress and the character of merit, one that continues to the present, not least over the content and funding of education.[8]

1900 to the Present: Spheres of Patronage

Stylistic fashions and notions of relevance played a major role in this marketplace, but so also did pressure on behalf of particular cultural institutions, for example the establishment-backed Royal Opera House at Covent Garden in the 1990s. The National Lottery grant in 1997 of £78.5 million to update the building was very controversial.

Public patronage attracted much attention and considerable controversy. Each year, grants led to debate, especially with particularly difficult works of art, such as those of Damian Hirst in the 1990s. Whatever the views on their individual merits, the common note in these controversies was whether public funds should be used for such ends at all. In one sense, this was an aspect of a culture war between the criteria and ranking set by the artistic establishment that influenced and directed government funding, and those that made sense in the vernacular culture of popular taste. This led, and leads, to issues of taste and influence that divided commentators. Were, for example, the most influential and `best' novels of the 1950s, the James Bond novels of Ian Fleming (1908-64) or the early novels of Iris Murdoch (1919-99), *Under the Net* (1954) and *The Bell* (1958)? Whatever judgments are made, it is the case that the latter type of work tended, and tends, to attract far more critical attention. That was central to the cultural politics of the twentieth century. Critics such as Q. D. Leavis, in *Fiction and the Reading Public* (1932), were sceptical of, if not hostile to, bestsellers.

The most commercially successful British films of 1959, 1962, and 1974 respectively – the smutty comedy *Carry on Nurse*, part of a long-running series, the Cliff Richard musical *The Young Ones*, a vehicle for a very conventional English type of popular singer, and the soft-porn *Confessions of a Window Cleaner* – have not attracted much critical or scholarly attention. In 1963, however, Sir John Davis, Managing Director of the

Rank Organisation, the owner of the important Odeon cinema chain, commented on the critically acclaimed realist films of the period: 'I do feel that independent producers should take note of public demand and make films of entertainment value. The public has clearly shown that it does not want the dreary kitchen sink dramas.' This was made clear to Rank by the commercial failure of Lindsay Anderson's film *This Sporting Life* (1963). In the play *Comedians* (1975), by the left-wing playwright Trevor Griffiths, those comedians who remain true to their trainer's ideals and believe that jokes should not exploit prejudices and sustain stereotypes are rejected by the agent, who is 'not looking for philosophers but for someone who sees what the people want and gives it to them'. There was, more generally, a profound ambivalence on the Left about consumerism.[9]

From the 1990s, there was repeated criticism of the 'dumbing down' of culture, and critics such as William Best, in his *The Strange Rise of Semi-Literate England* (1991), blamed institutions such as public libraries and the BBC for failing to maintain cultural standards. This was hardly a new charge. In July 1969, the Arts Council working party recommendation of the repeal of regulations against obscene publications provoked a critical parliamentary motion by Sir Gerald Nabarro who appealed to the silent majority: 'I shall campaign vigorously throughout to obtain the support of 90 per cent or more of intelligent, law-abiding and decent British people,' as opposed to 'the lunatic fringe, believing in unbridled licence and sex'.

The Establishment emphasis in cultural politics was challenged not only by the marketplace, but also by increasing critical interest in popular culture, especially from the 1960s on; although much of that attention was from a self-consciously intellectual position. This was the case, with the treatment of the two most successful categories of novel produced in the century: the adventure novels,

1900 to the Present: Spheres of Patronage

which reached their height in the works of John Buchan and Fleming, and the detective novel, most famously the works of Agatha Christie (1890-1976), the best-selling novelist of all time.

Both the categories indicated that popular art tended to be realist in style, rather than Modernist. To use the term 'realist' to describe the generally improbable plots and limited characterisation of Fleming and Christie may appear confusing, but they were realist in that they purported to represent the world as it is, using traditional means to do so.

Modernism

Modernism, in contrast, was a characteristic of a range of international artistic movements that challenged traditional forms and assumptions and, instead, preferred an experimental moulding of form in order to shake the reader and viewer from established patterns of response. Modernism was a reaction against the positivism and representational culture that had dominated the Victorian period. In part, Modernism drew for inspiration on the new social sciences and their challenge to established assumptions, for example on works such as Sigmund Freud's *The Interpretation of Dreams* (1900) and Sir James Frazer's classic of anthropology, *The Golden Bough* (1890-1915).

On canvas, the first chance for many to see the works of Manet, Cézanne, Gauguin and Van Gogh was offered by Roger Fry, when, in 1910, he organised the Manet and Post-Impressionists exhibition. The impact this had on British artists was indicated two years later with the contents of Fry's 'Second Post-Impressionist Exhibition'. Modernism had an effect on a number of artistic movements, including Vorticism, Expressionism and Surrealism. The very terms used by the Vorticists indicated their determination to shock. In 1914, the Vorticists led by Wyndham Lewis (1882-1957) founded the Rebel Art Centre, and

English Culture

Lewis adopted the term Vorticism to describe the transforming energy of Modernism. The Vorticist magazine was called *Blast: The Review of the Great English Vortex* (1914-5). Its first issue, in June 1914, stated: 'We only want the world to live, and to feel its crude energy flowing through us.' Vorticism helped open English art to Modernism. Such activity centred on London, but there were also important provincial centres. In 1903, Alfred Orage and Holbrook Jackson founded the Leeds Arts Club to propagate the most recent departures in the cultural world. Orage lectured on Nietzsche, while the club sponsored exhibitions of *avant-garde* paintings. Although Orage left for London in 1906, the club continued until 1923.

Modernism's impact in literature was multifaceted, although more in poetry and the novel than drama. Its distinctive characteristics included the use of stream of consciousness and a fascination with myth. Free verse was used to bring together very different voices and fractured ideas in the influential poem *The Waste Land* (1922) by T. S. Eliot (1888-1965). Major Modernist works are held to include the novels of Dorothy Richardson (1873-1957) and Virginia Woolf (1882-1941), as well as the novel *Nostromo* (1904) by Joseph Conrad (1857-1924). Richardson's fictional sequence *Pilgrimage* (1915-67) created an impact with its early use of stream of consciousness writing. Conrad had been born in Poland, Eliot in America, but both settled in England. Their careers are a reminder of the difficulties of placing national categories on writers. They also underline one of the central features of British culture, its use of the most influential language in the world. English benefited from the spread of British empire and trade, but, increasingly, from the impact of American power and culture. At the same time, Modernism reflected the role of Continental émigrés settling in Britain, notably Lucian Freud in painting, Ernö Goldfinger and Erich Mendelssohn in architecture,

1900 to the Present: Spheres of Patronage

Eugen Wellesz and Berthold Goldschmidt in music, and Gerard Hoffnung in both art and music.

Cultural Divisions?

If film remained dominated by Hollywood values, this was part of a general shift in which America became more influential among both the cultural élite and mass culture, certainly more so than the earlier influence of European models for part of the élite. However, cultural forms other than film were less influenced, still more set, abroad. English architecture enjoyed a rise in its international reputation with architects such as James Stirling producing major works at home and abroad. Nevertheless, Modernism in architecture, notably the work of Denys Lasdun, was increasingly criticised by conservation movements and on aesthetic grounds. It was attacked as the 'New Brutalism', lacking a human scale and feel, and this attack was popularised by Prince Charles in the 1980s and 1990s, not least with his description of the initial plans for the extension to the National Gallery as a 'monstrous carbuncle'. He also condemned the plans for the new British Library as 'a dim collection of brick sheds and worse'. By the 1980s, Modernism was being challenged by a neoclassical revival pioneered by Quinlan Terry.

The prestige of English painting and sculpture was also high. It was recognised and celebrated with prominent exhibitions, such as the Hayward Gallery's account of British conceptual art, 'The New Art', in 1972. Established figures, such as Francis Bacon, Barbara Hepworth and Henry Moore, were joined by younger figures like Peter Howson. With increased interest in performance art, there was a growing determination to bridge the gap between performer and audience. This was especially true of sculpture and culminated in 1998 with Antony Gormley's *Angel of the North*. Situated on a hill south of Gateshead, overlooking both the A1(M) and the East Coast railway line, this work was seen by over 90,000 people daily, making it the most viewed piece of sculpture in England.

The *Angel of the North* was a product of public patronage. Gateshead Urban District Council was keen on sculpture as a way to raise artistic consciousness and somehow improve the quality of life. There was also money available in the 1990s from the National Lottery. The Arts Council of England Lottery Fund provided £791,000 for the *Angel*. This was a very different cultural context to working men's clubs, which were especially prominent in Northern England, and in the 1990s still numbered more than 3,000, with a total membership of three million. Entertainers there had to be immediately responsive to their audiences, and they tended to focus on traditional themes. It was too easy to overlook such institutions but it was harder to ignore the fact that Sheffield's Crucible Theatre was best known from 1977 as the venue for the world snooker championships, and not for plays.

The use of public money ensured that in the 1990s culture became increasingly a political issue, although it had scarcely been free from controversy in the 1970s and 1980s. In that period, although there was no consistent widespread popular interest in the place of the arts in society, individual artists had taken political positions. For example, influenced by Brecht, Howard Brenton probed the nature of power in plays such as *Magnificence* (1973), *The Churchill Play* (1974), and *The Weapons of Happiness* (1976), and caused controversy with his criticism of government policy in Northern Ireland in *The Romans in Britain* (1980). Edward Bond attacked capitalism and the Establishment from a revolutionary Socialist perspective in plays such as *Saved* (1966), and *The Worlds* (1979). David Hare's powerful play *Plenty* (1978), which was subsequently made into a film, was a striking account of post-war disillusionment.

English Baroque. Portrait of John, Duke of Marlborough by Sir Geoffrey Kneller. Soon after Marlborough's total victory over the French at Ramillies in 1706.

The Match between Aaron and Driver at Maidenhead, 1754, *Aaron Wins the Second Heat* by Richard Roper (1730-75), who exhibited extensively in London in the early 1760s.

The Neo-Gothic as Art: Henry Fuseli's *The Nightmare*, 1781, first exhibited at the Royal Academy in 1782 sold for 20 guineas. The work became better known in a best-selling engraving of 1783 by Thomas Burke.

Charlotte Raikes by George Romney, 1787. Charlotte Finch, granddaughter of Daniel, 2nd Earl of Nottingham, wife of the merchant and banker Thomas Raikes. Son of a provincial cabinet maker, Romney (1734-1802) became a fashionable London painter noted for portraits, but, disliked by Sir Joshua Reynolds, Romney was never invited to join the Royal Academy.

Utilitarian Art. *A Delineation of the Strata of England and Wales, with part of Scotland* (1815), the first detailed geological map of the country, was produced by William Smith (1769-1839), the self-educated son of a blacksmith. Alongside his map, with its colour-coded key, Smith produced a stratigraphic table, geological section and county geological maps, collectively intended to form a geological atlas.

Sarah Siddons as the Tragic Muse by Sir Joshua Reynolds, 1783-4. Siddons (1755-1831) was particularly famed, from 1785, for her depiction of Lady Macbeth. Having failed initially at Drury Lane, she made her name in provincial companies in Birmingham, Bath, Bristol and York, and returned to Drury Lane in triumph in 1782.

Captain Samuel Sharpe Pocklington with his wife Pleasance and possibly his sister Frances, by George Stubbs (1724-1806), 1769. Stubbs was noted for his depiction of horses. Pocklington was an army officer.

Granville Leveson Gower's children, by Thomas Phillips (1770-1845). Born in Dudley, he was initially a glass painter but became a major portraitist, painting over 700 portraits and becoming Professor of Painting at the Royal Academy from 1825 to 1832.

The Clarendon Building, Oxford, 1711-15. Built to a design by Nicholas Hawksmoor, a leader of the English Baroque who had worked with Christopher Wren.

Windsor Castle in Modern Times by Edwin Landseer, 1841-5. Landseer presents Queen Victoria and her husband, Prince Albert, Ranger of Windsor Park, in a domestic scene that was a contrast to the medievalism of the Neo-Gothic that celebrated the origins of the castle.

Above left: Circe Invidiosa (1892) by John William Waterhouse (1849-1917) captured a fascination with mythology also seen in his three versions of *The Lady of Shalott*.

Above right: Salome (1893) by Aubrey Beardsley (1872-98), a key figure in the Decadent movement and the development of *Art Nouveau*, who sought to push the boundaries of the acceptable in the pursuit of a new aesthetic. An illustration for Oscar Wilde's play *Salome*. Beardsley's use of the monochrome and of strong lines corresponded to the content in rejecting Victorian values.

Wilton's Music Hall (here set up for a wedding). Originally a pub in part of the London East End, it became a 'Magnificent New Music Hall' in 1859, able to take an audience of 1,500. Destroyed by fire in 1877, the building became a Methodist Mission.

An early cinema. Alongside purpose-built cinemas, and initially more important, came the conversion of existing leisure facilities, notably music halls, as well as the showing of films as part of a broader leisure programme.

Above left: Virginia Woolf (1902), studio photograph by George Charles Beresford (1864-1938). Woolf (1882-1941) used stream of consciousness as an arresting narrative method, her major novels including *To the Lighthouse* (1927) and *The Waves* (1931).

Above right: Skylon, Festival of Britain, 1951. A futuristic steel structure, illuminated at night, that became the symbol of the Festival. Dismantled in 1952.

MI6 Building, Vauxhall Cross. Designed by Terry Farrell with an eclectic industrial Modernism looking to 1930s power stations, but also Central American temples. Much of the building is below street level. The style is assertive rather than accommodating. Frequently depicted in James Bond films. (Geograph.org.uk, 4541871)

Cross-section of a Mini, on display at the Science Building, London. A two-door, four-seater car produced from 1959 that became a British icon. Designed for the British Motor Corporation by Alec Issigonis (1906-88) in response to the demand for small cars due to the fuel shortage arising from the 1956 Suez Crisis. (By permission of cc-BY-SA GFDL)

2012 London Olympic Games Opening Ceremony. London's third Olympic Games were opened on 27 July 2012 with 'Isles of Wonder', a problematic account of national culture and history, with music to the fore and a measure of humour. (Korea.net / Korean Culture and Information Service under cc-BY-SA)

George Orwell identified 'gloomy Sundays, smoking towns … green fields and red pillar-boxes' as continuous, distinctive aspects of English civilization (see page 267). He was wrong on most counts, except in terms of nostalgia. The red pillar-box survives of course, like this one at Tower Bridge. It looks old but it was only installed in 1989, a replica of a 'Penfold' design (1866-89). It's a 'gentique'. Perhaps in this sense the pillar-box really has 'entered into the English soul' as he claimed, nostalgia being 'the English disease'.

1900 to the Present: Spheres of Patronage

Culture was a highly political matter for some Thatcherites and they publicly criticised subsidised 'left-wing' theatre. Community theatre, which had flourished in the 1970s, was hit as subsidies were withdrawn, on essentially political grounds, from companies like 7:84, Joint Stock, and Belt and Braces. Many arts figures, such as the playwright Harold Pinter, attacked the Thatcher government. Its appointment of businessmen as trustees to national museums and galleries led to controversy, although there was no issue comparable to that of the use of Lottery funds in the 1990s. Meanwhile, once-banned works became lauded classics. Whole areas of experience that had been expressed covertly, such as homosexuality, were given prominence. E. M. Forster's novel about homosexuality, *Maurice*, written in 1913-14, was not published until 1971, a year after Forster's death (it was filmed in 1987).

The 1990s also brought the Department for Culture in 1997, and a fierce controversy over whether it was appropriate to charge for entry to museums. The Labour government elected in 1997 attacked what it termed cultural elitism, and sought to redirect public patronage in line with its 'Cool Britannia' image. It quickly found itself embroiled in controversy, not least because it was unable to free itself from major commitments of public funds to the Royal Opera House.

The geographical location of culture was also an issue. There was strong criticism of London's dominant position, not least over the decision to locate the Millennium Dome at Greenwich. Nevertheless, a part of the Tate Gallery opened in Liverpool in the 1980s, and there were major developments in Birmingham and Glasgow.

A different aspect of culture was offered by the popular 'heritage' films of the 1980s and early 1990s, for example *Heat and Dust* (1983), *A Room with a View* (1986), *Maurice* (1987), *Howard's End* (1992) and *The Remains of the Day* (1993). They were undemanding literary adaptations that provided attractive

English Culture

period costume accounts of upper-class life. The same was true for several successful television series.

Technology

The spin of technology was a major factor in a changing cultural context that entailed consequences for content. The overlapping categories and contents of culture, entertainment, news and personal relations were readily presented and catered for by the Internet. Whereas, in the late 1970s, 60 per cent of 17- and 18-year-olds said they read a book or magazine almost every day, by 2016 only 16 per cent did. Electronic forms did not inherently mean differing content, as the reading of books indicated. Yet, there was a more bitty response by many readers. In addition, the financing of culture changed as free provision became more significant, notably for music and news. Electronic purchasing helped ensure that the factors that influenced purchasing and consumption online, for example algorithms, were of great significance. There was certainly an alteration in the nature of artistic criticism, in that 'influencers' could be far more varied in their formats, methods, and experience. Comparisons were also easier. Thus, on 6 May 2001, 'Culture Vulture' in the *Sunday Telegraph* produced a chart of the reviews of new films and new productions of plays, operas and ballets, carried in the *Daily Telegraph, Times, Guardian, Independent, Financial Times, Daily Mail, Daily Express* and *Evening Standard*, the chart using a pictorial key of 'Great Carrion!', 'On the Turn' and 'Rotten'.

Television was in effect advertised by the press and by social media, both with reviews and schedules and with discussion of prominent programmes such as *The Great British Bake Off, Strictly Come Dancing* and *Love Island* as news. Newspapers covered contestants and controversies. Magazine-type articles became more prevalent, as did celebrity news values. On

1900 to the Present: Spheres of Patronage

4 March 2011, Richard Peppiatt published in the *Guardian* his resignation letter from the *Daily Star*: 'On the awe-inspiring day millions took to the streets of Egypt to demand freedom, your paper splashed on "Jordan ... the movie."'[10] Somewhat differently, Mike Bartlett, the writer of the BBC 1 series *Press*, noted of a research visit to the *Sun*: 'These people are not brash or stupid. They know exactly what they're aiming at, what their audiences want, and they're just striking a different balance between entertainment and content. And they're very proud of that.'[11]

The audience selective nature of cultural activity was shown by the differences between platforms, whether television channels, theatres, publication series, or even the online and print editions of individual newspapers. On 1 September 2018, the *Daily Mail* led on 'Schools turn down children who live one minute away' and the *Mail Online* with 'Roxanne Pallett Walks out of the Celebrity Big Brother house amid backlash over the ex-Emmerdale star's false claim that former Coronation Street actor Ryan Thomas punched her.' There was scant difference between the tone of such online issues and social media items; but the relevant journalism rested in providing a mass of material of this kind. Rob Rinder, a columnist in the *Evening Standard*, began an article on 31 August 2018 with:

> I was flicking through the paper, shaking my head at another week of showbiz stories about spoilt pop stars making unreasonable demands, spending small fortunes on bling, holidays and cars, and demanding "Don't You Know Who I Am!"

Technology was not only a matter of social media, its impact and context. It was also seen across the arts and throughout culture, providing opportunities for artistic and entrepreneurial innovation. Thus, in the 2020s, whereas in popular music, legacy

English Culture

acts continued to dominate (although guitar bands continued to have a role in local scenes), the trends for recorded music were for shorter songs, faster beats per minute, speeded up vocals and digitally enhanced hyperpop. Digital enhancement was also very important to cinema, while architecture and design saw experimentation with new materials.

Conclusions

Alongside the rhythm of cultural change, continuing fissures between élite and popular cultural forms can be traced, a wide disjuncture between 'highbrow' and 'lowbrow' works. There were of course also parallels. For example, both detective fiction and children's literature from the 1960s tackled issues that would have been generally regarded as inappropriate prior to that decade. By doing so, they lessened the gap in content with more 'highbrow' works. For example, Roald Dahl produced surrealistic children's stories, such as *James and the Giant Peach* (1961) and *Charlie and the Chocolate Factory* (1964), as well as verses, such as *Revolting Rhymes* (1982). By the 1990s, Dahl's books were the most popular children's works, but in 2023 a focus on his anti-Semitism made him highly contentious. Ironically, the same submerging of reputation, but with far less cause, happened to his successor, J. K. Rowling, the author of the Harry Potter stories, who became contentious because of her views on gender identity.

Dahl was an experimenter, but the overwhelming characteristic of popular 'lowbrow' works was a reluctance to experiment with form and style. This division in approach was more widespread, and also affected other arts, such as architecture, music, painting, and sculpture. As a consequence, a pattern of contrast that was essentially set earlier in the twentieth century with the impact of Modernism remained important to the cultural life of the country. It ensured that there were very differing understandings and

1900 to the Present: Spheres of Patronage

experiences of culture and the arts. This difference was more than a matter of stylistic pluralism. It also reflected the wider cultural politics of a society containing very different levels of income, education and expectation. There was no automatic link between these differences and the contents of cultural 'consumption' and 'production', or artistic awareness, but they were very important to the configuration of the cultural life of the people.

So also was the role of intermediaries, both public and private, from the BBC to publishing, the latter a field in which public patronage was limited. Thus, 'Bookworm' in *Private Eye* on 30 April 2015, reviewing forthcoming novels, noted:

> The only other literary novels the Penguin General group is publishing next season – there will be plenty of crime and chick lit novels from other divisions of course – are [3 named ones] ... it seems that only books by the publisher's established and usually senior literary authors are still safe: young first-timers now stand little chance of being picked up by Penguin.

The *Critic* produced similar pieces about publishing in the early 2020s. These sources are unlikely to receive sufficient attention in the future.

Also affecting artistic intermediaries such as publishers was legislation and government intervention. Some was very indirect. Thus, the Holidays with Pay Act of 1938 helped lead to the development and flourishing of holiday camps which, in turn, became an important aspect of the entertainment industry. Far from this being an aspect of cultural manipulation of the workers, the camps succeeded by providing what was wanted, not least by women.[12] What such contexts and developments indicate is the need to understand culture in a broad fashion, and particularly so if the 'response' to the arts is assessed, for 'response' was and is far from a passive process.

9

1900 TO THE PRESENT: SITES AND STYLES

1900-39

Continuity was most clearly the case in the continued prominence of printed works, both in the wider culture, and particularly in artistic terms. Although poetry remained significant, it was less prominent than in the nineteenth century. Instead, novels dominated literary culture, as they continue to do.

Human society is central to the works of two of the most influential writers at the start of the century, the playwright George Bernard Shaw (1856-1950) and the novelist H. G. Wells (1866-1946). Science fiction played a major role in Wells' work. It was not simply a matter of scientific futurism. Instead, he used fantasy to discuss what he saw as social realities in *A Modern Utopia* (1905) and offered portraits of the travails of those born without silver spoons in their mouths in *Love and Mr Lewisham* (1900), *Kipps: The Story of a Simple Soul* (1905), and *Tono-Bungay* (1909). In the last, landed wealth, religion and commerce

1900 to the Present: Sites and Styles

all appear as weak panaceas, and scientific experimentation, instead, is revealed as fulfilling, although not always profitable. Education as a means for personal development and social advancement was also an important theme in Wells' work, as it was to be in many novels of the century, such as those of C. P. Snow (1905-80).

In *The New Machiavelli* (1911), Wells attacked the obsession over bureaucratic reform, and this links his work to the far more sombre vision of Aldous Huxley (1894-1963), in his *Brave New World* (1932). Set in the 26th century, this used a vision of the future to criticise powerful intellectual trends in the present. People in *Brave New World* are engineered biologically to make them fit for their tasks, and drugs are used to keep them happy. Technology offers not heaven but a bureaucratic hell of ordered control.

If the future could be a discussion of the implications of the present, there was also much social comment that was more direct. Shaw was a determined opponent of social hypocrisies, which he saw as morally destructive and poisonous for society. He directed his vigour against both bourgeois greed and do-gooding liberalism, the latter satirised in his play *Major Barbara* (1905). In the preface to the play, published the following year, Shaw claimed that by giving the workers a sense of the immorality of the system, 'We produce violent and sanguinary revolutions, such as ... the one which capitalism in England and America is daily and diligently provoking.' This was a world away from the playful probing of hypocrisies in the works of Oscar Wilde, who had died in exile in 1900.

A less cerebral account of social problems was offered by the highly successful novelist Arnold Bennett (1867-1931). In *Anna of the Five Towns* (1902), there was not only paternal pressure and the harshness of religious conviction, but also the divisiveness

English Culture

of wealth and poverty in the Potteries. The debtor Prices both commit suicide. *The Old Wives' Tale* (1908) was about the travails of two sisters. The difficulty of escaping one's background was also a theme of Bennett's novel *Clayhanger* (1910).

John Galsworthy (1867-1933) was another popular writer of the period, although his role as a dramatist tends to be forgotten. His plays frequently commented on social problems: *Strife* (1909) on the impact of a strike, *Justice* (1910) on solitary confinement in prison, and *The Skin Game* (1920) on social inequality. Galsworthy's plays frequently contrasted wealthy and poor families. His sequence of novels *The Forsyth Saga* (1906-21) focused on social mores and matrimonial break-up, not political or social issues. Galsworthy was rewarded with honours, the Order of Merit in 1929 and the Nobel Prize for literature in 1932, but was criticised in fashionable circles.

Those circles had little time for popular writers of the period, such as Bennett, Galsworthy, Rudyard Kipling (1865-1936), who received the Nobel Prize for literature in 1907, G. K. Chesterton (1874-1936), and Hillaire Belloc (1870-1953), let alone for adventure writers such as John Buchan. Chesterton and Belloc offered a Catholic critique of modern society, as well as detective fiction and literary biography (Chesterton), and travelogue and poetry for children (Belloc). J. M. Barrie (1860-1937), the author of many successful plays, most famously *Peter Pan* (1904), received the Order of Merit in 1922, as well as a baronetcy and honours from the Universities of Cambridge, Edinburgh, Oxford and St Andrews.

Instead, the Bloomsbury Group sought to further the *avant-garde* in a deliberate reaction against Victorian styles and assumptions. Bloomsbury was essentially a group of friends with similar views who saw themselves as playing a crucial role in reviving a stale literary tradition. The best-known novelist in the

1900 to the Present: Sites and Styles

group was Virginia Woolf. She had no time for what she saw as the 'materialist' writing of Bennett and Galsworthy and instead sought a Modernist focus on aesthetic sensibility. In 'Mr Bennett and Mrs Brown', an essay of 1924, Woolf distinguished between what she considered Bennett's false 'realism' of surface description and a 'modernism' that searched for true realism. In place of narrative, Woolf advocated a view of life as a 'luminous halo'.

Her novels explored such ideas. In *Mrs Dalloway* (1925), she employed interior monologue and stream of consciousness to reveal character; in *To The Lighthouse* (1927), Woolf offered a pointillistic meditation on time and fulfilment; and in *The Waves* (1931) provided another experimental form, including a series of interior monologues, to reveal personality and consider the role of memory. Another such form was offered in 1923 when *Facade*, an innovative set of poems by Edith Sitwell was performed with music composed by William Walton.

Woolf was not alone among inter-war writers in focusing on people as individuals, building up or frustrating the personalities of others (and themselves), rather than as vehicles for narrative and/or commentary on social issues. An emphasis on imagination and the emotional focus was clear in D. H. Lawrence's *Women in Love* (1920). These subjects were not incompatible with comments on wider issues, however, as E. M. Forster (1879-1970) showed in *A Passage to India* (1924), at once a novel about sensibility and a searching investigation of the psychological tensions of empire. In contrast, Aldous Huxley's *Antic Hay* (1923) depicted, in the aftermath of the wartime challenge to social values, a new London society of jazz clubs, drug-taking, and birth control.

Modernism had only a limited appeal and unsurprisingly had little airing on the radio. In Christie's radio play 'Miss Marple Tells a Story' (1934), she remarks that her novelist nephew,

English Culture

Raymond West, 'writes those very modern books and about rather unpleasant young men and women'. In *Death on the Nile* (1937), Salome Otterbourne, a very different fictional novelist, offers 'strong meat' about sex in her outspoken, unconventional *Under the Fig Tree* before pressing on with the absurd *Snow on the Desert's Face.*

Although 'middle-' and 'lowbrow' writers might not find favour with Bloomsbury and the reviewers of the *Times Literary Supplement*, such writers tended to dominate sales. They benefited from the rising disposable income of the inter-war period, especially in the 1920s, from the ready availability of inexpensive books, the spread and popularity of cheap lending libraries, notably those run by Boots and Smiths, and from increased leisure. Women readers were of growing importance, as indeed were children. There are suggestions that society was more literate in the 1920s than it was to be in the 1990s. By the 1920s, as a result of free education, literacy was in theory universal, and consumerism had resumed after the war. Reading thrived.

These markets did not necessarily see themselves as 'middle' brow. Their favoured authors were not necessarily too different in style to Kipling or Galsworthy. In *The Herries Chronicle*, a family saga set in Cumberland, Hugh Walpole (1884-1941) produced a work that was closer to *The Forsyth Saga* than to *The Waves*. Popular works in this saga included *Rogue Herries* (1930). Walpole also wrote popular school stories.

Walpole's one-time collaborator, J. B. Priestley (1894-1984), also won popularity with an accessible novel, *The Good Companions* (1929), an engaging account of a touring theatrical company. A Yorkshireman whose World War Two radio broadcasts brought a north country accent to the popular ear, Priestley had an interest in English character, but his distance from cosmopolitanism did not make him a provincial drudge.

1900 to the Present: Sites and Styles

In his plays of the 1930s, such as *Dangerous Corner* (1932), he used time cleverly for intellectual as well as dramatic effect, a theme to which he was to return in *An Inspector Calls* (1945). Another Yorkshire writer, the feminist Winifred Holtby (1898-1935), also offered a strong sense of place in *South Riding* (1936). This tradition continued in much of the popular novel writing of the later twentieth century, for example the works of Catherine Cookson (1906-99), which were mostly set in her native Tyneside.

'Lowbrow' works of the interwar period included popular romantic stories, for example those published by Mills and Boon, as well as adventure stories and detective novels. In Freeman Wills Crofts' *Sudden Death* (1932), Rose, a young servant, 'made herself comfortable before the kitchen fire and buried herself in a shocker which she had got for a few pence at a second-hand shop in Ashbridge, and with which she was deeply enthralled'.[1] Such works were not especially profound but they were important, and are valuable today as accounts of the mores of the period. Thus, for example, to take particularly well-written cases, many of Dorothy L. Sayers' detective novels, including *Whose Body?* (1923), *Clouds of Witness* (1926), *Unnatural Death* (1927), *Strong Poison* (1930), *The Five Red Herrings* (1931), *Murder Must Advertise* (1932), *The Nine Tailors* (1934), and *Busman's Honeymoon* (1937) are still in print. They are fantasies, in that Lord Peter Wimsey, the detective, although shell-shocked at the outset, is wealthy and improbably perfect. In *The Saturday Review* of 7 January 1939, the Communist journalist John Strachey dismissed detective novels as escapism:

The detective story is the opium of the contemporary British reading public ... the terrors of the detective story world are strictly controlled; they are small, manageable events, such as the murder of an individual; and, above all, they are invariably overcome.

English Culture

In practice, Sayers' novels also offered guidance on contemporary attitudes to women, in the person, in particular, of the independent-minded Harriet Vane. Furthermore, they showed such milieux as the new world of advertising.

At the same time, the weight of the literary past was still there in libraries and and reprints, although new works, some foreign ones, were not excluded. In Christie's novel *Evil Under the Sun* (1941), a hotel room includes:

A Bible, a battered copy of Shakespeare's plays, *The Marriage of William Ashe* by Mrs Humphry Ward, *The Young Stepmother* by Charlotte Yonge, *The Shropshire Lad*, Eliot's *Murder in the Cathedral*, Bernard Shaw's *St Joan*, *Gone with the Wind* by Margaret Mitchell, and *The Burning Court* by Dickson Carr.

In Christie's *Three Act Tragedy* (1934), the elderly Satterthwaite can cite Tennyson but notes that he 'was very little thought of nowadays' and that he dislikes the current openness about sex.

On the stage, the equivalent were readily accessible domestic comedies, such as the plays of Noel Coward, for example *Hay Fever* (1925), or Priestley's *When We Are Married* (1938). P. G. Wodehouse's comic novels about Bertie Wooster and Jeeves, characters first introduced in 1917, were adapted for the stage by Ian Hay.

A musical equivalent to the sense of place can be sought in the pastoral work of Ralph Vaughan Williams, for example his *Pastoral Symphony* (1921). This was criticized by the composer and critic Constant Lambert as the 'cow pat school' of English music, but it was very popular. Elgar emphasized an elegiac tone, and remained conspicuous in concert programmes, gramophone record sales and BBC broadcasts. The cult of the countryside was also seen in A. A. Milne's popular dramatisation in 1929 of

The Wind in the Willows by Kenneth Grahame (1859-1932), as well as in Milne's books *Winnie-the-Pooh* (1926) and *The House at Pooh Corner* (1928). The popular *Shell Guides* of the English counties began in 1934 with John Betjeman's of Cornwall.

Similarly, many of the painters of the period produced portraits or landscapes that paid scant tribute to fashionable themes. In the inter-war years, the Royal Academy Schools were characterised by a conservatism greatly at odds with Modernism. Works by painters such as Picasso could be bought in the galleries in Cork Street, London, but their impact on the wider world was limited.

It was only in 1945 that the Trustees of the Tate Gallery in London agreed to the opening of a small room devoted to abstract art. The Gallery, founded in 1897, was way behind the Museum of Modern Art in New York, not least because it lacked funds. In the inter-war period, the Treasury was loath to increase support for the arts, and this contributed to a weak, in many respects absent, cultural policy. Taste was also an issue. James Bolivar Manson, the Tate's Director in the 1930s, was a painter of flowers opposed to Post-Impressionism, Cubism, Expressionism, Surrealism and to living British artists such as Sickert and Moore. This rather predictably affected the Tate's acquisition policies.

Modernist ideas were spread in the Architectural Association and the *Architectural Review* in the 1920s and 1930s, notably by Howard Robertson.[2] However, despite works by architects such as the Georgian-born Berthold Lubetkin, who emigrated to Britain in 1931, as well as Giles Gilbert Scott's Battersea Power Station and Charles Holden's Senate House of the University of London (1932-7), Modernism also had little impact in architecture. Liberty's in Regent Street, built in 1924, using Elizabethan timber, better expressed the widespread desire for a style suggesting continuity, not the new. It was matched on the screen by the success of Alexander Korda's *The Private*

Life of Henry VIII (1933). In her novel *Murder Is Easy* (1939), Christie depicts in idyllic and fictional Wychwood-under-Ashe 'an anachronism, a large white modern building, austere and irrelevant to the cheerful haphazardness of the rest of the place'. It was built and endowed as an Institute and Boy's Club by Lord Whitfield, who remarks: 'Employed the best architect in the country! I must say he's made a bare plain job of it – looks like a workhouse or a prison to me – but they say it's all right, so I suppose it must be.'

Yet in a longstanding fashion continuing that of adaptability and transition, there were also combinations: suburbia offered Tudorbethan fronts, mock-Jacobean panelling, Modernistic Art Deco features, geometric lino and labour-saving devices.[3] There was also a continuation of traditional patterns in church architecture, as in Guildford Cathedral or the many memorial chapels erected in the aftermath of the First World War, such as that at St Barnabas, Ranmore, to the three sons of Lord Anscombe.

Modern art was mocked. In Christie's 'Miss Marple Tells a Story' (1934), the protagonist has scant time for the remarkable pictures of square people with curious bulges, preferring instead the Victorian works of Frederic Leighton and Lawrence Alma-Tadema, while Christie's 'Swan Song' (1934) mocks the ambitious artistic Lady Rustonburg, who has a private theatre where there has been 'a play of the ultra new school, all divorce and drugs, also a poetical fantasy with Cubist scenery'. In her novel *Murder Is Easy* (1939), considering disguise as an artist, Luke reflects 'I can't draw, let alone paint,' earning the rejoinder 'You could be a modern artist... Then that wouldn't matter.' Christie continued her themes after the Second World War. In *Third Girl* (1966), Christie has Poirot visit a London gallery where he sees

1900 to the Present: Sites and Styles

... a picture which depicted three aggressive looking cows with vastly elongated bodies overshadowed by a colossal and complicated design of windmills. The two seemed to have nothing to do with each other or the very curious purple colouring.

Much of the culture of the period was not designed to challenge established practices and the social order. Sayers' Harriet Vane, introduced in *Strong Poison* (1930), had a lover before she married another man, and was more independent than the women in Christie's detective novels. But other female novelists, for example Ivy Compton-Burnett (1892-1969) and Daphne Du Maurier, presented stable sexual and class identities. This was part of a conservative disposition that was very pronounced in the 1930s. Du Maurier's novels, such as *Jamaica Inn* (1936) and *Rebecca* (1938), had a particularly strong sense of place, in her case Cornwall.

Women won equal suffrage with men in 1928, when they reached the age of 21. As a result of wartime casualties and differing long-term death rates, they were a clear majority of the electorate. There were no uniform gender cultural preferences, however. Aside from the customary differences that also affected men, on social, ethnic, religious and ideological lines, there were also specific divisions between, for example, housewives and employed women, married and unmarried, older and younger, feminists and non-feminists; and these categories clashed. In 'Street Haunting: A London Adventure' (1927), Woolf suggested that London threatened the established order by offering liberation to women who had formerly been marginalised. In the event, many of the new female voters supported the Conservatives and were closer to Christie than Woolf.

Alongside works that were about and/or for the affluent, there was also much that might be termed 'Condition of Britain' culture, attempts to present the life of the less fortunate. These included George Orwell's social criticism in his *Down and Out in Paris and London* (1933) and his bleak and bitter description of working-class life in northern mining communities in *The Road to Wigan Pier* (1937), as well as Walter Greenwood's depiction of the harshness of unemployment in *Love on the Dole* (1933) and Walter Brierley's *Means Test Man* (1935) on a similar theme. A sense of the nobility of ordinary people was presented in *The Dustman* (1934), a painting by Stanley Spencer (1891-1959), that showed a dustman and other labourers being reunited with their wives after the Last Judgment.

A more accurate portrayal of working-class life was offered by *10am* (1937) by Harry Wilson (1899-1972). This view of coalmining in North Seaton depicted daily routines, such as cleaning boots, and the scene included the ubiquitous coal heap. Writing as Josephine Bell, Doris Bell Collier, a doctor who practised for a while on the Thames, presented the extent and nature of misery in *The Port of London Murder* (1938), 'the grime and squalor and ugliness', with grinding poverty and terrible housing. In this world of expedients, sickness is to the fore, as is humanity and individuality, and the characters interact with scant sentiment.

The Road to Wigan Pier was published by Victor Gollancz for The Left Book Club, a scheme to encourage the reading of committed works launched in 1936, that had over 56,000 subscribers by 1939. There were also radical publications for children.[4]

Meanwhile, the cinema boomed. In 1934, out of a population of 46 million, 18.5 million went to the cinema on a weekly basis. Birmingham alone had 110 cinemas and Britain close to 5,000. Cinemas such as the Ilford Hippodrome and the Rex at Stratford were converted theatres, part of the assault by film on music-hall. Nevertheless, music-halls remained part of the equation, now largely dominated by musicals, but the offerings were still 'variety'. In her novel *Murder on the Links* (1923), the performance at the Palace in Coventry is described by Christie:

> Japanese families balanced themselves precariously, would-be fashionable men, in greenish evening dress and exquisitely slicked hair, reeled off society patter and danced marvellously. Stout prima donnas sang at the top of the human register, a comic comedian endeavoured to be Mr George Robey and failed signally ... the Dulcibella Kids ... danced neatly, and did some clever little acrobatic feats. The words of their songs were crisp and catchy.

Dance halls were also important, their music and style part of the Americanisation of English leisure.

One tradition that has survived began in 1924, the sound of Big Ben and the Greenwich electronically produced 'pips' on BBC radio.

The Second World War

Total war led to government support for measures to raise morale and to help energise the activity of artists. There was less demand for landscapes and portraits, but under the War Artists' Scheme established by the Ministry of Information several thousand paintings and drawings were commissioned, some showing bomb damage, such as Graham Sutherland's *Devastation in the City* (1941). Modernist artists benefited greatly. Henry Moore and Feliks Topolski depicted people sheltering from German air raids in tube stations. Stanley Spencer glorified shipyard work. Evelyn Dunbar was the only salaried woman war artist. She recorded the home front and in particular the contribution of the Land Girls.

English Culture

The popularisation of painting exhibitions was a deliberate attempt to propagate a common culture, but it was not value-free. The WAAC kept abstract and non-objective art largely at bay.[5] The Ministry gained the services of the GPO Film Unit, renamed the Crown Film Unit, and they produced propagandist documentaries. Graham Greene (1904-95), author of *Ministry of Fear* (1943), was employed in the Ministry of Information.

Dorothy Sayers abandoned detective stories in the 1940s. As for many authors, the war provided the occasion, if not the cause, for a shift to a new seriousness, in Sayers' case a series of radio plays about the life of Christ, *The Man Born To Be King* (1941-2).

This seriousness did not drown out other themes or styles, and the war years saw, for example, the introduction of vigorous jive and jitterbug dances by American soldiers (GIs). Such exuberance was rarer in the world of high culture, but Michael Tippett's oratorio *A Child of our Time* (1944) incorporated Negro spirituals.

The war had a major impact on the audience. Aside from loss, suffering and fear, there were wartime restrictions. Although far less prosperous and with other claims on their time, including Home Guard duties and vegetable growing, the reading audience had little else on which to focus their leisure, although paper rationing hit the publishing world hard. Printing and distribution were affected by bomb damage and by the staff shortages arising from conscription. Theatrical audiences were reduced by wartime restrictions. Collections were removed for safety, the National Gallery to a Welsh quarry, although, to maintain morale, public musical recitals were held in the Gallery in London and a major painting exhibited each month.

The war of course presented writers with new topics and contexts, such as the blackout, with food shortages, gloom, official regulations, and officious bureaucrats, as in E. C. Lorac's wartime stories such as *Checkmate to Murder* (1944) and *The Fell Murder* (1944). Yet, at the same time, as with the previous conflict, a refusal by artists and writers to focus on the war could be a phlegmatic response, a stoical emphasis on keeping going.

'There'll always be an England' was a widespread message of the war, as in Churchill's speeches. Humphrey Jennings' documentary-style film *Fires Were Started* about the work of firemen during the Blitz used real firemen, not actors. The same message was to be found in J. B. Priestley's broadcast 'postscripts,' the upper-class whimsy of Noel Coward, T. S. Eliot's poems 'East Coker' and 'Little Gidding', and G. M. Trevelyan's *English Social History* (1942).[6]

1945-62

The late 1940s and 1950s saw a revival of pre-war patterns in a society that very much sought such continuity after the trauma of war. The ruralism of much 1930s culture was revived, as in continued interest in landscapes,[7] and the appearance in 1950 of Vaughan Williams's *Folk Songs for the Four Seasons*. The classics were celebrated, notably on film, as in David Lean's 1946 version of Dickens' novel *Great Expectations*. In the visual arts, *avant garde* ideas competed with a more conventional mainstream. The latter prevailed at the 1951 Festival of Britain. Its dominant artistic mood was neo-Romantic. Only one abstract work was selected for display in connection with the Festival, and that work caused a public controversy. The Director of the Tate in the 1950s, John Rothenstein, was criticised for his lack of enthusiasm about Cubism.

But there were wide-ranging works engaging with the modern, with George Orwell's bleak political satires, *Animal Farm* (1945) and *Nineteen Eighty-Four* (1949), making a considerable impact. The theme of authority and its dangers was at the forefront.

English Culture

Winston Smith is punished for thought crimes in a Britain that is dominated by a Party under Big Brother that rewrites history and manipulates the language in order to control thought.

Carol Reed's film *The Third Man* (1949) was set not in the future but in a corrupt and devastated present. Occupied Vienna could echo the situation in austerity England. The screenplay was by Greene, who in *The Heart of the Matter* (1948) had tackled the failure to maintain moral standards in the face of a pitiless world. *Brideshead Revisited* (1945), by another Catholic convert, Evelyn Waugh (1902-66), also dealt with faith assailed and the search for some sign of divine purpose.

The legacy of the war was a touchstone of value and values that produced a potent set of assumptions. The war provided plots, a guide to character and a framework for characters. Casualties, figures and episodes from the war were memorialised across the arts.[8] It is very difficult for modern readers, none of whom in England have had that experience of a struggle for national survival, to appreciate its weight, resonance and implications, not least the sense of war as a moral struggle. The imaginative strength of that experience can be dissipated by the attempt to 'update' plots in order to make them 'relevant'.

The music of Vaughan Williams and Edward Elgar was rejected by young composers, especially Benjamin Britten and Tippett. Britten's operas, the most important English ones of the century, notably *Peter Grimes* (1945), *Billy Budd* (1951) and *The Turn of the Screw* (1954), were disturbing works. The Ealing film comedies of the late 1940s and early 1950s, such as *Passport to Pimlico* (1949), *Kind Hearts and Coronets* (1949) and *The Lavender Hill Mob* (1951), were far less bleak, but their satire could not conceal a sense that the world was rarely benign. On radio, Britain was challenged by sinister schemes that had to be thwarted in the 711 episodes of *Dick Barton, Special Agent*

1900 to the Present: Sites and Styles

(1946-51), who also starred in three British films (1948-50). Barton, an ex-commando with a VC, had a peak audience of 15 million. The Boulting Brothers made *High Treason* (1951), the nearest British equivalent of the Hollywood 'red scare' films, about Communists trying to sabotage power stations.

Change became more apparent from the late 1950s. Artists such as the sculptor Barbara Hepworth (1903-75) were experimenting with abstract forms. *New American Painting*, a big exhibition of large abstract works held in 1958, had a major impact. Looking at art and design from a different perspective, there was a shift in fine and decorative arts, graphics and industrial design from the austerity and functionalism that had characterised the late 1940s to a more affluent tone, as shown, for example, in the Coventry Cathedral exhibition of 1962. Architecture was now dominated by Modernism.

There was more of an engagement with the urban experience under the 1945-51 Labour governments, and notably with the welcome to modernity seen in the 1951 Festival of Britain, centred on buildings constructed on a site on the bombed South Bank of the Thames in London. The architect Basil Spence made his name with the Sea and Ships Pavilion there, as well as with his prize-winning design for Coventry Cathedral. Offering a Labour vision of progress, the Festival, which was visited by close to 8½ million people, and that included exhibitions outside London, reflected confidence, or at least interest, in new solutions.[9] The rocket-like, cable-tensioned Skylon hovered over the site. Boldness was intended to replace the drab dullness of the 1940s. Nevertheless, most people were less confident than at the time of the Great Exhibition in London in 1851. Modernism was seen in projects that were aspects of a planned environment, a key theme in the politics and public culture of the period.[10]

English Culture

The progressive style of the 1930s became an orthodoxy that was used for the widespread post-war rebuilding, for urban development, and for the new construction made possible by the investment in hospitals, schools and New Towns. W. H. Auden began his poem 'The Chimeras' with the line 'Absence of heart – as in public buildings'. A centrepiece was the first major post-war public building, the Royal Festival Hall (1951), designed for the Festival of Britain's South Bank Exhibition by Robert Matthew, the Chief Architect to the London County Council. The Modern movement in public architecture transformed British cities from the 1960s, although less so in domestic architecture.

The novelists of the 1940s were concerned, at times despairing, but not angry. In the late 1950s, in contrast, there were the 'Angry Young Men', a group of writers who felt very much at odds with their country. Their problems were not those of faith in a hostile world (Greene, Waugh) or the pressure of totalitarianism (Orwell), but, rather, a sense that the post-war reforms of the Labour governments and 1950s' Conservative affluence had produced a vulgar materialist society that was disagreeable in itself and frustrating to them as individuals. They were impatient alike with the values of ITV and with traditionalism. In contrast to the liberal worthiness of C. P. Snow's Lewis Eliot, the protagonist of his sequence *Strangers and Brothers* (1940-70), came Charles Lumley in John Wain's novel *Hurry on Down* (1953), a graduate who flees self-advancement and becomes a window-cleaner, and Jim Dixon, the hapless protagonist in Kingsley Amis' *Lucky Jim* (1954). The latter novel also struck at the 'phoniness' of social mores in the period. Social values were lacerated in John Osborne's bitter play *Look Back in Anger* (1956), a classic 'kitchen-sink drama', John Braine's novel *Room at the Top* (1957), Alan Sillitoe's novel *Saturday Night and Sunday Morning* (1958), and David Storey's novel

This Sporting Life (1960). Sillitoe's account of working-class life in his native Nottingham was an example of the 'grim up north' school that became fashionable in the 1950s. More generally, this extended to a stronger interest in 'the North'. This had a number of manifestations. Northern accents became fashionable; northerners, such as the dramatist Alan Bennett, 'made it' on the national stage; and northern males were said to benefit from the alleged southern preference for a bit of 'rough'.

The works of the 'Angry Young Men', however, were a long way from the successful staples of the West End stage, the lending libraries, and W. H. Smith. In the West End, audiences flocked to see plays by Noel Coward, both old, such as *Private Lives* (1930, there was a London revival in 2023), and new, for example *Look After Lulu* (1959), as well as plays by Terence Rattigan (*The Winslow Boy*, 1946) and William Douglas-Home (*The Chiltern Hundreds*, 1947, *The Manor of Northstead*, 1954). The audiences were also very large for the short stories Christie adapted for the stage: *The Mousetrap* (1952) and *Witness for the Prosecution* (1953). Christie's *Mousetrap*, a play very much located in a world of conventional social distinctions, unexpectedly, became the world's longest-running play and is still running. In contrast, the works of *avant-garde* playwrights, such as Samuel Beckett, scarcely appeared. Nicholas Blake, the pseudonym of the Poet Laureate Cecil Day-Lewis, in the novel *The Worm of Death* (1961), satirised such West End conventions, A young man sets out to supplant an elderly husband in his wife's affections:

A hand comes out from a secret panel while the husband's back is turned, shakes a powder into the young man's glass. He dies… The husband is suspected. But the poisoner turns out to be their faithful old housekeeper, whose daughter has been seduced by the young man.

English Culture

The 'Angry Young Men' were not the only voices in print, and this yet again underlines the difficulty of defining a cultural period. Studies of middle age by Angus Wilson (1913-91) – *Hemlock and After* (1952), *Anglo-Saxon Attitudes* (1956), and *The Middle Age of Mrs Eliot* (1958) – enjoyed solid sales. The lending libraries continued to buy and lend large quantities of Christie and other secure genre writers. There was much continuity with inter-war authorship, notably with Christie in detective fiction and P. G. Wodehouse in light satire continuing to publish as if there had been no change in society. In Christie's 'Greenshaw's Folly' (1960), Raymond West, who deals bleakly with the sordid side of life, is described as having a name in literature, but not being a best-seller. In Patricia Wentworth's detective novel *The Listening Eye* (1957), Ethel Burkett writes critically about her sister: 'who had taken the unjustifiable step of leaving an excellent husband whom she complained of finding dull'.

Popular genres did not necessarily alter, although the detective novel was to change with more troubled detectives coming to the fore. *Casino Royale*, the first of Ian Fleming's James Bond novels, was published in 1953 and depicted a hero who was a comfortably off gentleman, at home in Continental casinos and eating *pâté de foie gras*. Like most heroes in fiction and films of the period, he had had a 'good war,' as indeed had Fleming. The war helped define that generation of British males, as the First World War had defined their predecessors.

At the cinema, Hammer's *The Curse of Frankenstein* (1957) began a series of successful horror films that made the reputation of their leading actors, Peter Cushing and Christopher Lee. Modern themes were attempted for example in the film *Seven Days to Noon* (1951) which deals with a scientist threatening to set off an atomic bomb in London as a warning about the dangers of nuclear destruction. In the 1989 edition of his *Film Guide*,

1900 to the Present: Sites and Styles

Leslie Halliwell described the film as a 'persuasively understated suspense piece which was subsequently much copied,' so that it now seems rather obvious.' In 1952, Churchill, a critic of the Festival of Britain as Socialist, had the Skylon taken down.

In the real world, clothes in the early 1950s were more similar to those of the 1930s than the 1970s, and reflected hierarchies of class, gender and age. They could do so as clothes rationing had ended. In addition, this was very much the 'New Elizabethan Age,' forecast at the time of the accession of Elizabeth II in 1952 and her coronation in 1953. The latter was a highly traditional occasion, albeit with the addition of deferential television coverage, broadcast live and watched by over twenty million people, 56% of the population. The coronation encouraged many to get televisions. Christianity and the class system defined the ceremony. Moreover, the Christianity of the period was mostly Establishment in tone, very much a matter of old white men telling others what to do. A standard subheading in the popular press, notably in the *News of the World*, a Sunday shocker, was 'Bishop speaks out', usually in response to reported moral outrages that challenged the established moral code.

Due to the focus on the 1960s as the period of transformation, a focus that directs attention on the young of that period, it is easy to forget that the 1950s was also a decade of change. The popularity of American 'Rock and Roll' music represented a rejection of established English popular entertainment. Women in Bond novels did not seek matrimony or motherhood. Bob Dylan first performed in London in 1962, but the Musicians Union opposed the entry of American pop stars.[11]

'Kitchen-sink drama' was had a clear social and, often, regional setting. These were not plays depicting the lives and mores of the social élite, as with the plays of Coward and Rattigan. Instead, they portrayed people in difficulties, and in commonplace milieux, as with

English Culture

Arnold Wesker's *The Kitchen* (1957). They focussed on the North of England, which was understood as a tough environment, or on the world of London bedsits. The net effect was a new 'Condition of England' literature, one that looked back to the interwar writing of Orwell. In fiction, Colin MacInnes wrote of the West Indian community in London and on race relations in his novel *City of Spades* (1957), going on, in *Absolute Beginners* (1959), to address youth culture and the anti-black Notting Hill race riot of 1958 in London. The content, tone and language were scarcely conventional: 'his chief exploit ... had been to wreck the Classic cinema in the Ladbroke basin, and, with some of his four hundred, drop the law's coach-and-four into a bomb site, while others engaged the cowboys [police] in pitched battle with milk bottles and dustbin lids.'[12]

'Kitchen-sink drama' and its novel equivalent spanned the late 1950s and early 1960s. It was often iconoclastic in tone and it sought to question, even subvert, existing genres. For example, in spy fiction, Fleming's Bond was joined from *The Ipcress File* (1962) by Len Deighton's Harry Palmer, a working-class spy who had to cope with betrayal from within the Secret Service by a social and professional 'superior'. This was certainly not a Bond theme, but it was an aspect of the real history of the post-war Secret Service, notably with the spy Kim Philby, an Establishment figure who was revealed in 1963 as a Soviet spy. In a less iconoclastic fashion, Alan Hunter, in his 1957 novel *Landed Gently*, referred to 'jingoism' as doomed alongside other aspects of the Old World, especially the 'satanic mills' and social injustice.

Change in a distinctive form came with the Mini, designed in 1959 for the British Motor Corporation by Alec Issigonis. This was a car very different in design to those earlier in the decade, and it reflected an inventive engagement with the possibilities of the new. Indeed, design was to become a major cultural theme, one that concentrated on new products.

1900 to the Present: Sites and Styles

Focusing on traditional assumptions of social structure, Marxist New Left thinkers largely failed to engage with youth or the variety of working class culture.[13] Nevertheless, there was a relationship between cultural changes and the rise of Labour to power in 1964. This relationship was indirect, but significant. A sense that a distinct and anachronistic 'old order' existed and needed replacing by a new meritocracy, one able to use planning,[14] provided a way to stir up opposition to the Conservatives, as well as to encourage the Tories, especially from the early 1960s, to show more interest in reform policies. These themes were very much part of the public culture of these years, and they helped fuel the 'satire boom' that became significant in the early 1960s, with clubs, such as The Establishment Club in London, live shows, and radio and television programmes.

Programmes such as 'That Was the Week that Was' on television, and the new satirical periodical *Private Eye*, made existing class distinctions and social conventions appear ridiculous as well as dated. Failure in government, economy and society could thus be traced to the alleged incompetence of national arrangements. The satirists were largely well-educated young men, and were scarcely representative of society as a whole, but that did not lessen the force of the charge. There were particularly strong attacks on the last years of the Macmillan government and on its aristocratic character.

At the same time as all this witty sniping, on 13 August 1961, a Sunday, 900 played bingo at the Trocadero, Elephant and Castle, London, the biggest cinema to have started bingo sessions.

1962-70

The 1960s were already offering less Establishment and more radical models in novels and on the stage before what is generally understood as 'the sixties' began, a process variously dated to

English Culture

1963-6, with Philip Larkin claiming in his poem *Annus Mirabilis* (1967):

Sexual intercourse began
In nineteen sixty three...
Between the end of the 'Chatterley' ban
And the Beatles' first LP.

The sense of 'the sixties' owed much to popular music. It emanated from every transistor radio, linking culture, technological provision, and entrepreneurial ability. Initially, the key change was the response to the Beatles, a northern group who, with their debut single 'Love Me Do,' released in October 1962, set the 'Mersey beat' and gave working-class experiences prominence.[15]

Youth culture was not an invention of the 1960s, but it became much stronger then and greatly influenced the overall cultural life of the country. Furthermore, the Beatles were home-grown. In the late 1950s, singers had essentially imitated American models, Cliff Richard initially looking towards Elvis. One newspaper posed the question in a banner headline: 'Tommy Steele – the new Elvis Presley?', which cannot fail to bring a smile to the face of anyone who has seen both *Jailhouse Rock* and *Half a Sixpence*. In the winter of 1960-1, however, the Beatles established themselves as the band for Liverpool teenagers and developed the distinctive Mersey sound. To become national, the Beatles had to be repackaged. In 1961, the band abandoned their leather jackets for smart suits, and their manager, Brian Epstein, got them a recording contract with the music giant EMI. The company was newly responsive to the commercial possibilities of pop and understood that it was no longer appropriate to expect performers to behave as they had been told to do in the 1950s.

1900 to the Present: Sites and Styles

Pop music challenged the 'received pronunciation' of the English language, regional differences were accepted by the BBC where the importance of conformity in diction, style and tone declined from the 1960s. The film director Guy Hamilton later noted:

> The combination of angry young men, Michael Caine and the Beatles killed the leading men who all spoke with Oxford accents... Unless you had a Brummy accent, forget it. I think the Beatles and the pop scene in general had a major influence on the cinema at this time.[16]

Other groups and performers also came from Liverpool, including Cilla Black, Gerry and the Pacemakers, and the Swinging Blue Jeans. Popular music lent itself to female as well as male performers. If the bands, with their emphasis on electric guitars, were male preserves, many singers were women. This was not the case with the the alternative Liverpool cult, football. Interest in Liverpool was also shown by the popularity of *The Liver Birds*, a television sit-com set there that began in 1969. Working-class voices and themes were increasingly present, not only in popular music, but also in fiction and theatre. The growing willingness of television to focus on working-class life was crucial. 'Situation comedies' ceased to be preponderantly middle-class: both *Steptoe and Son* (1962-5) and the *Likely Lads* (1964-6) made a lasting impression.

In practice, in the context of 'Beatlemania' in 1963-4, the Beatles went south, to London. Working class plays and films set in the North of England, like *Room at the Top* (1959), *Saturday Night and Sunday Morning* (1960), *The Loneliness of the Long Distance Runner* (1962), *Billy Liar* (1963), *This Sporting Life* (1963) and *Get Carter* (1971), had a vogue, but were absorbed

English Culture

by a more metropolitan focus, and the same was true of popular music. British youth culture was reconfigured towards fashionable middle-class interests. Thus, the hippies and drugs of the 1960s reflected the affluence, ethos and Americanism of middle-class south-east youth, rather than the experience of the northern working class. The Beatles came from the latter, but unlike the later exponents of 'Northern Soul' they took to this new culture, especially to drugs and Asian mysticism, providing it with a 'sound'. The role of students in the 'pop culture' of the 1960s was particularly important, and the majority of them came from a middle-class background. Many of these students had the money to spend on drugs and attending pop concerts because of the affluence of their parents. The social impact of 'pop', however, was far broader.

Pop art was an aspect of a determined assault on conventional apprehension of artistic content, meaning, and production. 'Just what makes today's homes so different, so appealing?', a satirical collage by the influential pop art exponent Richard Hamilton, appeared in 1959. Pop art of the 1960s included Peter Blake's collage for the album cover of the Beatles' *Sgt. Pepper's Lonely Hearts Club Band* (1967), and the Beatles' animated film *Yellow Submarine* (1968). Pop art, deliberately unconventional and irreverent, was followed by op art, the iconic, pulsating black-and-white spirals painted by Bridget Riley. 'Different' art had entered the mainstream and public consciousness. This was not only a case with the visual arts. In 1966, Tom Stoppard's play *Rosencrantz and Guildenstern are Dead* wittily and successfully reinterpreted *Hamlet*. Stoppard followed up with *The Real Inspector Hound* (1968), a play that subverted theatrical conventions, not least by playing on the audience's sense of certainty. Like many other innovative and influential figures of the period, Stoppard, born in 1937, was young.

One feature of the literature of the period that should be noted is the major role of women novelists, which, while scarcely new, was more pronounced than in the 1950s. Aside from the already well-established Iris Murdoch (1919-99) and Doris Lessing (1919-2013), women writers who made an impact included Margaret Drabble (1939-) and Angela Carter (1940-92). Lessing's *The Golden Notebook* (1962), a key text of the decade, engaged with feminism and psychoanalysis. Like many earlier novelists, Drabble took the familiar theme of a sensitive individual's attempt to break free from the limitations of a conventional background, and her novels, such as *A Summer Birdcage* (1963), *The Garrick Year* (1964), and, in particular, *Jerusalem the Golden* (1967), permit us to see the working out of that theme for 1960s women.

At the same time, attitudes towards shape and colour that owed much to cultural currents rather than functionalism affected the context of everyday life, from the lines of motorcars to kitchen design. Experimentation with new forms that were still functional became widespread and affected manufactures. For example, the potter Walter Keeler made pots with practical uses, taking particular interest in attractive domestic tableware. To that end, he, like other potters, sought inspiration from foreign forms, in his case raku, the moulded earthenware used in Japanese tea ceremonies, and probed the possibilities of the medium. Keeler developed salt glazing, using changes in texture to highlight design.

Aspects of 'high' culture, especially architecture, were influenced by new design values and a striving for relevance in a 'post-industrial society'. This was clearly seen in museums and art galleries. New attitudes to building design and layout and to the presentation of exhibits rapidly took hold. For example, in the Tate Gallery muslin ceilings and plywood walls brought an airiness to where there had earlier been heavier surfaces.

English Culture

This was a national shift, as were most of the cultural developments in the period. The role of radio, television and the record industry helped ensure the national, indeed international, character of popular music. Yet, alongside commercially induced homogeneity, there was also a diversity of cultural roots. There was an interest in ethnic music, for example, in the 1990s, Bangra and the revival of Irish traditional music via Riverdance. Furthermore, those roots could influence the mainstream. This was true of Afro-Caribbean influence: Bob Marley had a major influence on popular music from the 1970s.

The Beatles contributed powerfully to the idea of a 'New Britain,' an idea that was very powerful in the mid-1960s. This idea was linked to the policies advocated by the Labour Party, which governed the country from 1964 to 1970 and which titled its 1964 general election manifesto 'The New Britain'. Labour introduced a range of social legislation. This idea of a new beginning was related to a variety of cultural and product developments, including the clothes fashions pioneered in Carnaby Street in London and modern technology, symbolised by the supersonic Concorde aircraft and the Post Office Tower in London (1964). Harold Wilson, a northerner who cultivated his image as a northerner, ensured that the Beatles were given honours, although this proved controversial.

In the mid- to late 1960s, male hair became longer and the dress code changed from shirt, tie and sports jacket to jeans and sweaters. Women wore miniskirts, showing an expanse of flesh that would have amazed their predecessors, corsets were out, tights replaced stockings, suspenders and garter belts, and birth control was transformed with the contraceptive pill, giving women control over their fertility. Working-class talent provided a powerful infusion of energy in a world in which pop stars, hairdressers and photographers were celebrities. In a different

1900 to the Present: Sites and Styles

fashion to kitchen-sink drama, the working class emerged into the light of day. At the end of his poem 'The Clothes Pit,' published in his *Terry Street* (1969), Douglas Dunn captured the centrality of music:

> Three girls go down the street with the summer wind,
> The litter of pop rhetoric blows down Terry Street,
> Bounces past their feet, into their lives.

Beat-music drove the rhythm. The mid-1960s saw a cycle of 'Swinging London' films, including *Darling* (1965) and *Blow-Up* (1965), both of which examined the morals and mores of a permissive society in which family and church values were largely redundant. For Alfie in the 1966 film of that name set in London, women, clothes and cars were commodities that proved one could get on in the world without the privileges of birth and education. Supermarkets provided new, anonymous, shopping experiences and spaces.

Change accelerated. By 1967, the Beatles had become hippies and drugs were in the air. The Beatles changed music in a number of respects. With *Sgt. Pepper's Lonely Heart Club Band*, the lyrics were printed on the back of the album for the first time, and the meaning was a long way from their earlier 'She Loves You, Yeah, Yeah, Yeah.' Half a million people attended an open-air pop festival on the Isle of Wight.

The young were not the only ones to the fore. A focus on change also affected the built environment, with much torn down in the 1960s by well-meaning but often misguided, or sometimes corrupt, developers, planners and city councils. They embarked on a rebuilding that was very different in style and tone. As a result, cities such as Newcastle saw major, indeed fundamental, damage to their centres. The needs of road transport played a central

English Culture

role, with major roads driven through the cityscape, in London (with the Westway), Birmingham, Exeter, Glasgow, Newcastle, and Wolverhampton.

Modernist functionalism drove the pace of architectural development, as with Richard Seifert's uncompromising slab-sided Centre Point (1967) skyscraper in central London. This Modernism was seen in hospitals, schools and other buildings, as well as housing. Considerable confidence in the new style was expressed, as in the *Daily Telegraph* of 23 November 1943 when discussing the appointment as architect for the South Bank building of Denys Lasdun, a choice made by the National Theatre Board without going to competitive tender:

> If he succeeds with it, as he has already done with his public and commercial work we should get one of the finest theatres of the age. If it stands up to its neighbour the Shell skyscraper, he will have achieved the impossible.

Completed in 1963, the Engineering Building at Leicester University, which was designed by the Scottish architects James Gowan and James Stirling, was deliberately Futurist, and was proclaimed as Britain's first postmodernist piece of architecture. The Engineering Building was actually rather a bolder Modernism than that of Le Corbusier, and was influential in using industrially produced materials. The auditoria in the Engineering Building were topped by protruding cuboid skylights.

Bold architectural schemes responded to the cult of the new, leading to much 'New Brutalism' in architecture. Seven greenfield, plate-glass universities were opened, beginning with Sussex in 1961 (for which Basil Spence did much of the architectural work), and ending with Kent and Warwick in 1965. The new universities offered new initiatives in teaching and organisation, notably with interdisciplinary curricula. Meeting in 1961-3, the Committee on Higher Education chaired by Lord Robbins recommended a marked increase in the number of students. The thesis of the committee report, which was presented to Parliament by Prime Minister Harold Macmillan in October 1963, was that every child with the potential to enter higher education should receive it and, if not at state expense, then with a significant state subsidy.

Ironically, Modernism was often far from functional, not least due to a misguided preference for flat roofs, a mistaken design in a rainy climate. Concrete cladding also frequently proved a problem. Erno Goldfinger, after whom Fleming named a villain, was responsible for Modernist horrors including Trellick Tower in West London.

There was resistance to, or, at least, criticism of, many of the cultural changes of the period. For example, alongside novels pressing for new experiences and for the experience of the new came the anti-sixties novel, such as A. S. Byatt's *The Game* (1967) and Kingsley Amis's *I Want it Now* (1968).[17] The *Carry On* films continued with classics such as *Carry On Screaming* (1966), a spoof on horror films.

1970-9

The 1970s opened with a cultural world of bewildering complexity. *The Mousetrap* was still running on the London stage (as indeed it still is in 2024), and James Bond was saving the world on screen: *Diamonds Are Forever* appeared in 1971. Yet, alongside this apparent, but somewhat misleading, continuity in 'lowbrow' interests, it was harder to see the main configurations of *avant garde* culture. Although `arty' films and television programmes were produced, both those media were essentially populist in content. *Avant garde* film did not attract a major following.

English Culture

Youth and novelty, key elements in the 1960s changes, continued to be significant in the 1970s. However, optimism was shadowed by the economic recession and political tension that gathered pace from 1973, and this shadowing affected the arts. A darker tone was evident in some spheres. The television police drama *The Sweeney* (1975-8) brought to an abrupt end the cosy image of the kind-hearted London policeman which had been built up in *Dixon of Dock Green* (1955-76), a comforting popular television series that was much at variance with the world of London crime and policing in the 1960s, a world that had included police corruption. Similarly, *Taggart* (1983-2010) provided a bleak view of Glasgow crime and policing.

Novels repeatedly registered problems. The 'social revolution' became for some novelists self-deception, adultery, and confusion, as in Iris Murdoch's *The Sacred and Profane Love Machine* (1974).[18] Complaining about a decline in radicalism, Melissa Todoroff, a self-obsessed character in Malcolm Bradbury's mordant satirical novel *The History Man* (1975), says, 'There was action. People really felt something... They just don't feel any more... Who's authentic any more?'[19]

A darker tone was more generally apparent with the fracturing of 'the sixties', which, in practice, had always been a diverse experience, a movement lacking unity and coherence. In 1971, the English rock band The Who declared 'We don't get fooled again,' and in 1978 they asked 'Who Are You?' A denial of the first and an answer to the second had already been supplied by the savant John Lennon on his first album after the Beatles breakup, released in 1970:

A working class hero is something to be...
Keep you doped with religion and sex and TV
And you think you're so clever and classless and free
But you're still fucking peasants as far as I can see.

1900 to the Present: Sites and Styles

The 'look' of the age was highly diverse. David Bowie relished the role-playing of his androgynous persona.[20] His albums, such as *Ziggy Stardust* (1972), tested established boundaries. So also with enthusiasm for the reggae of Bob Marley.

Some themes continued, not least the role of popular music in introducing working-class language and values into mainstream culture. This, however, proved to be a trickier process than in the 1960s. Then, massive open-air concerts focused the potent combination of youth culture and pop music, but this music, and its commercialism, was, in turn, to be challenged by punk, a style that set out to shock and to transform popular culture. To reach a wider audience, punk, in turn, had to be taken up by record companies and television. It also entered the cultural mainstream, affecting style in fashion and design. The role of punk in style and design was part of a more general bridging between popular culture and design themes, a bridging that was driven by the pressures of commercialism in a society that affected novelty. Design values came to be seen as more important in manufacturing and retail, and they changed more rapidly. The violence of the rebellious 'punk' aesthetic, as in the Sex Pistols' debut single *Anarchy in the UK*, released on 26 November 1976 and their album *Never Mind the Bollocks, Here's the Sex Pistols* (1977), was mirrored by 'Oi!' music, that of skinheads, mostly working-class youth, which was often racist and misogynist. Regional social differences were exposed. In 1976, Johnny Rotten and the Sex Pistols made their first appearance outside London, playing in a nightclub in Northallerton, a small Yorkshire town. The noise and lyrics did not go down well, and much of the audience promptly left. The Sex Pistols became a sensation, and there was criticism in the popular press, not least for their song *God Save The Queen*, which attacked Elizabeth II as head of a 'Fascist regime' and claimed 'There is no future in

English Culture

England's dreaming.' This and *Anarchy in the UK* were banned by the BBC.

Such differences were more generally present. If, for example, the 1960s was a period of pop concerts and drugs, it also saw a burst of Christian evangelism, embodied by the American Billy Graham and his revivalist missions to Britain, while trainspotting and making jam remained popular hobbies, and the 1970s began with the election of Edward Heath, a Conservative Prime Minister, just as America had elected Richard Nixon in 1968 and France Georges Pompidou in 1969. In 1974, the London stage provided *Two and Two Make Sex*, *The Danny La Rue Show*, *No Sex, Please – We're British* and *Oh! Calcutta*, as well as *Heidi*, *Why Not Stay for Breakfast?*, *Sherlock Holmes*, *Pygmalion*, *Billy*, *Birds of Paradise*, *Jesus Christ Superstar*, *The Debbie Reynolds Show*, *The Ken Dodd Laughter Show*, *The Mousetrap*, *Hair*, *Carry on London*, the *Max Bygraves Show* and *Pyjama Tops*.

For an older generation than the punks, dyspeptic novels, such as Kingsley Amis' *Jake's Thing* (1978), included much criticism of the new cityscape and of fashionable social mores. Drugs and self-indulgence were not acceptable behaviour for most commentators. The destruction of the grand theatre is symbolic of urban decay in the spoof horror film *Theatre of Blood* (1973).

1979-90

The arts were far more of a political battleground during the Thatcher years. These saw a degree of counter-cultural reaction. Margaret Thatcher, Prime Minister from 1979 to 1990, openly attacked what she termed 'the progressive consensus' and called for a return to older norms, telling *The Times* on 10 October 1987 that children 'needed to be taught to respect traditional moral values'. The radical world of universities, once

1900 to the Present: Sites and Styles

potent models for an apparently improvable future, was criticised in a series of television series.[21]

More specific policy failures contributed to the counter-cultural reaction, notably those of the high-rise public housing projects that had represented a civic culture focused on planning and technocratic solutions, rather than on the views of individual consumers.[22] This housing all too often became denigrated as 'slums in the sky'. Lifts that did not work, the use of stairways as urinals, issues with noise and criminal activity, especially drug-dealing, all helped make many high-rises undesirable and dangerous, and they tended to be admired by those who did not live in them. Similarly, public transport was often advocated by those who found a reason why they still needed cars. This was significant because of the major role of car-culture in popular experience.

There was a determined effort by many artists to use their work as part of an assault on Thatcherism. This was particularly apparent on the stage, as with the plays of David Hare, for example *Plenty*. An attack on Thatcherism was seen in art, popular music, poetry and cultural commentary. Films of the period, such as *Mona Lisa* (1986), showed England, or, at least, London, as permeated with crime. Class, sex and race were suffused by themes of individualism that some critics linked to Thatcherism. *Bread*, a television series that ran for more than 70 episodes from 1986, and whose audience grew to over 20 million, sympathetically depicted a Liverpool family whose younger members were mostly unemployed and ready to cheat the Social Security system. It was followed by *The Royle Family* (1998-2000), a sitcom about a television-fixated family living in a Manchester council house, which ran for three series.

There was criticism by the government of the automatic assumptions of public financial support made by the Arts Council.

English Culture

This criticism was justified, but that did not make it popular. The BBC came under government attack, not least over the reporting of security matters and the IRA. To counter IRA propaganda, their statements when reported on the BBC had to be read by actors.

Differences between the Thatcher government and the Arts (as well as the Church) were not driven to the point of breakdown (whatever that would mean), not least because the government continued to provide much patronage for culture, while there was no united artistic bloc. However, there was a degree of tension not seen in the 1970s, and one, moreover, that prefigured much of the self-conscious politicking over art seen in the 1990s.

Thatcher herself had been happy to win the support of Rupert Murdoch's tabloid newspaper the *Sun*. It put the pop into populism, and also provided page three nudes. In 2018, as an instance of the cultural misunderstanding of the very young, Charlotte Riley, an actress, recalled that when she was little, she wanted to be a Page Three Girl:

> I was always sent round to the corner shop to get my grandparents the *Mirror* and the *Sun* ... sightly weird, delivering my grandad boobs ... my granny said 'What d'you want to be when you're older?' and I said, 'I want to be a Page Three girl' ... I'd heard the term pageboy and thought a page girl was a professional bridesmaid.[23]

The *Sun*'s most arresting headline was carried on 13 March 1986: 'FREDDIE STARR ATE MY HAMSTER.' Starr, a comic, claimed the story came about because of an offhand remark he made, and that the incident was a total fabrication invented by Max Clifford, a prominent publicist, in order to focus interest on the star.

1900 to the Present: Sites and Styles

1990-

In the 1990s, politicisation in culture continued to be a theme, but despite this, the impact of consumerism and internationalism on the arts were more significant. Elected in 1997, 'New Labour' under Tony Blair sought to leave a cultural footprint comparable to that of Labour in the 1960s, but did not do so. Nevertheless, there were developments, including the foundation of museums, notably outside London, and the attempt, with the 2000 Millennium Dome, to stage a revival of the spirit of the 1951 Festival of Britain. The theme was one of taking culture to the people. Ultimately, however, 'New Labour' and its language of 'core values' et al proved superficial as a cultural movement – and was increasingly seen in that light.

Continuity was provided by a financial model in which public provision, while significant, notably with the central taxation that paid for BBC and museums, providing free entry to all permanent collections in national museums, was also limited, obliging many institutions to seek commercial sponsorship. This situation was an aspect of Britain as a hybrid society, one that can be compared with another hybrid in the shape of the relationship between cosmopolitan tendencies and national perspectives.

There was a general grounding of culture across England with a range of regional initiatives and experiences, most notably the greater cultural consequence of Manchester and Birmingham, as well as similar, but less prominent, developments in a number of smaller provincial cities, especially Bristol and Newcastle/Gateshead. Thus, the cultural dimension replicated the developments, tensions and alignments seen in other aspects of British life.

This process is likely to gather pace as the regional devolution of government functions within England becomes of greater import. The tendency to search for identity for new governmental entities will encourage the funding of regional arts, and the emphasis will probably be on distinctiveness, rather than on regional voices of British or English nationalism.

Cultural variations between social groups remained, although they were frequently underplayed. A YouGov poll in 2014 revealed that on television, Labour voters preferred urban and unexalted settings, especially *Phoenix Nights*, *Coronation Street*, *The Office* and *The Royle Family*, while Conservative voters preferred costume dramas and rural settings, as with *Downton Abbey*, *Foyle's War* and *To The Manor Born*. Labour voters particularly favoured accounts of working-class life. This group had been largely ignored by television up to the 1960s, until such creations as the memorable character of the bigoted working-class Conservative Alf Garnett in *Till Death Us Do Part* (1965-75) and, also, the gritty and highly popular soap opera *Eastenders* (1985-), another series set in East London, and one that has depicted topics such as rape, homosexuality, child abuse, violence and murder.

There was a more general change in plots. In 2016, the leading BBC radio soap, *The Archers*, for long regarded by those who did not listen to it as somewhat conventional in its subject matter, covered a controlling husband driving his distraught wife to stab him, and outlined the legal and psychological issues involved, including advising women being controlled in this fashion as how best to seek help. This BBC soap, which produces a new mini episode on six days of the week, had earlier moved a long way from its conventional origins. From the late 1970s, it portrayed social division more frequently and it subsequently engaged with a range of challenging topics, or ones that would have surprised its early listeners, including divorce, homelessness, homosexual marriage, and dementia. There was certainly continuity in the attraction of the sensational and the lurid. On 30 August 1901, the *Western Times* reported on a current moral panic: 'There is no holding back with the London *Express*, and its efforts to save innocent girls from the vile clutches of a few dramatic and music-hall agents and managers.'

Concern about the content and morality of modern culture was a recurrent theme among some commentators, but this concern had very different manifestations. From the late 1980s, much of the criticism focused on the conceptual 'Britart' that became increasingly influential, passing rapidly from its anti-establishment origins in 1998 to become an affluent new enclave. The presentation of parts of animals fixed in formaldehyde by Damien Hirst, including *The Physical Impossibility of Death in the Mind of Someone Living* (a dead tiger shark), *Away from the Flock* (a dead sheep), and *A Thousand Years* (the head of a slaughtered cow being assailed by flies), and *House of Ghostly Memory*, the concrete cast of a house by Rachel Whiteread, did not strike everyone as art. Striving for immediacy, these artists drew on punk and pop culture, and deliberately set out to shock with their works and provocative lifestyle, presenting this shock as enhancing their relevance. In response, some commentators, who were willing to accept these works as art, did not see them as *good* art, and were unimpressed by the glamorous freakiness that was apparent in Hirst's work.

Criticism of artistic fashionability reached a height with the 'Sensation' show at the Royal Academy in London in 1997, which led to unprecedented media attention being devoted to British art. Hirst's animals were on display, but much of the controversy related to Marcus Harvey's large portrait of murderer Myra Hindley. Painted in 1995 with the template of a child's hand, this painting led to controversy, with ink and eggs thrown at the painting and the resignation of some Academicians. The range of printed opinion on the exhibition indicated the ability of the arts

English Culture

to provoke debate, including about social developments. There was the clash between individualism and social convention, and also the sense of a continuous rhythm of cultural change. One critic, Julie Burchill, felt herself in an age of

> ... the politics of Why Not ... perfect for the ageing dirty-minded children ... at the Nursery for Wayward Youth. These are the days in which the most obscenely oppressive images are not challenged but actually celebrated as some sort of liberation.

Other critics saw the show as part of the rhythm of cultural change. Richard Cork of *The Times* claimed 'The rebels have stormed the bastions of conservatism.' Value and values appeared to be in conflict. For some, 'BritArt' was a critical comment on Blairism, for others a condemnation of capitalism, or of the cult of celebrity and its questionable value. Subsequently, the graffiti art of 'Banksy' also led to controversy.

The debate over fashionable art was given an annual outing in the popular media with the award of prizes to faddish works that did not strike most of the population as art. This was especially so with the Turner Prize, which was won in 1993 by Rachel Whiteread's *House of Ghostly Memory* and in 2001 by a light installation. Each year, the judges threw the modern to the fore and tested popular assumptions about what was art. In 2016, the Charles Wollaston award for the work judged the most significant of the Royal Academy's Summer Exhibition went to David Nash for 'Big Black,' a large standing section of redwood, charred by Nash in a fire pit and then painted black. In 2002, Ivan Massow was forced to resign as Chairman of the Institute of Contemporary Art, after he described most conceptual art as 'pretentious, self-indulgent, craftless tat'. He was particularly unimpressed by the work of Tracey Emin, a leading figure in

1900 to the Present: Sites and Styles

BritArt, which notoriously included displaying her unmade bed in an exhibition.

The 1990s were also the decade of 'Britpop' in which the band Blur played the leading role. Pursuing the idea of 'Cool Britannia', Blair sought to associate himself with this music and to appeal to the young through his links with musicians, whom he invited to No 10. His success in doing so was limited and ephemeral. The modish arts overlapped. For example, Hirst's works and those of Emin were among the modern British art collected by David Bowie. Such patronage drove prices up.

Plays that attracted controversy also increasingly attracted picketing or complaints. *Behtzi Behtzi*, a play by Gurpeet Kaur Bhatti which featured rape, abuse and murder among Sikhs, was greeted by a riot when it opened at the Birmingham Rep in 2004. The police were unable to maintain order, and the play was rapidly cancelled. In 2009, there were demonstrations when the National Theatre staged Richard Bean's play *England People Very Nice*, claiming that its account of immigration in London was critical of Bangladeshis.

Most art, however, was far less controversial, by intent or response, than the 'Sensation' show. Harvey's painting of Hindley said less about the 1990s than Howard Hodgkin's explorations of colour and its use to depict emotion. Winner of the Turner Prize in 1984 and knighted in 1992, Hodgkin was a member of a group of painters who began exhibiting in the 1960s, including Patrick Caulfield and David Hockney, who were of international significance.

Hockney's luminous depiction of British landscape had a great impact in the 2010s, as did his successful exploration of the possibilities of producing art on screen, notably on iPhones, which he described as 'a luminous medium and very good for luminous subjects. I began to draw the sunrise seen from my bed on the

English Culture

east coast of England... It was the luminosity of the screen that connected me to it.'[24] In the biggest exhibition of 2012 in Britain, 600,989 people visited the Royal Academy to see *A Bigger Picture* with Hockney's paintings of the Yorkshire Wolds where he lives, providing, as was accurately noted, 'an extraordinarily moving and cheering homecoming', one in which 'he paints the passing moment, but does not mourn its passing.'[25] Trees in different seasons were the subject matter. In 2016, at the Royal Academy, Hockney followed up with portraiture in the Royal Academy exhibition, *82 Portraits and 1 Still Life*.

Popular art classes, and lectures on art, concerned themselves with traditional means and themes. Watercolour painting was most popular for art classes, and the standard subjects were landscapes and flowers. For lectures, it was the grand tradition of famous painters that engaged most attention. The choice of lectures at NADFAS (the National Association of Decorative and Fine Art Societies) branches was instructive, as were the attendance figures for particular lectures. Far more people went to lectures on Dutch Masters or the Impressionists than to those on BritArt.

A less optimistic note can be struck. Alongside cultural change and continuity was the fissure between élite and popular cultural forms, the 'high'- and 'lowbrow' works. This breach in cultural politics frequently mapped social assumptions. There were overlaps, and some were very striking, as in the popularity of J. R. R. Tolkien's somewhat arcane *Lord of the Rings* trilogy, or the ability of Harrison Birtwistle, a producer of characteristic modern music, also to write *Grimethorpe Aria* (1973), a first-rate piece of brass-band music. Many cultural figures, however, failed to show, or even to seek to show, this range, a situation that readily paralleled the political landscape. A lack of engagement with the experiences of the bulk of the population was frequently

1900 to the Present: Sites and Styles

exposed. An example of cultural discontinuity was provided by the decision of English Heritage in 1998 to list five housing blocks on the Alton Estate in Roehampton as an architectural masterpiece, which made their replacement or alteration less likely, a decision widely deplored by the tenants.

In new architecture, a continued determination to embrace modern shapes and materials, and to focus on functionalism, was seen in important works of the 1990s, 2000s and 2010s, such as Nicholas Grimshaw's Eurostar rail terminal at Waterloo and the Serpentine Gallery extension designed in 2000 by Zaha Hadid. Moreover, far from being seen as a redundant form, skyscrapers were planned and built, notably in London where successive mayors encouraged them. Work that was far removed from Neo-Classicism included Norman Foster's Swiss Reinsurance Tower (2002), and his egg-shaped Greater London Authority building (2002), and Richard Rogers' Tate Modern (1999) and Millennium Dome (2000). Such buildings, followed by the rebuilt Charing Cross station, the MI6 building, and the Shard, provided the background for tourist perceptions of Britain, for, as in previous centuries, London was the most visited site and for many tourists the only destination. In 2015, around nineteen million foreign tourists visited London. This made it the most visited city in Europe, and the second most visited in the world, after Hong Kong. London surpassed Britain, which, in 2014, was the sixth most visited country by foreign tourists, after France, the US, Spain, Turkey and Germany, with 32.6 million, and its average annual growth rate in this category in 2010-14 was 3.6 per cent, lower than all these bar France.

Rogers' unimaginative 2008 plans for the redevelopment of the Chelsea Barracks site to produce a new, crowded barracks of high buildings providing expensive residential property indicated that, at least in this major case, little appeared to some critics to have been learned about reconciling the profit motive with the needs of the lived-in environment, let alone about aesthetic considerations. Architecture was certainly not the most popular expression of culture. It greatly affected the built environment in which people lived and worked, and many doubted the aesthetic or utilitarian contribution of new buildings. Such themes resonated strongly in fiction. In *The Body on the Beach* (2000), Simon Brett, who lived in the South Coast region he depicted, wrote:

> The architect who'd designed the new supermarket (assuming such a person existed and the plans hadn't been scribbled on the back of an envelope by a builder who'd once seen a shoebox) had placed two wide roof-supporting pillars just in front of the main tills. Whether he'd done this out of vindictiveness or ... incompetence was unknowable.[26]

The forms change, the issues remain.

Sport

Sport was and is a major public activity and preoccupation of the people, one that benefited greatly from television. Football profited from the finance available from television rights, from major global interest in English football, and from the increase in the average real earnings of the working population and the reduction in their working hours. In 2016, Football League clubs spent over £1 billion in the transfer season, something made possible by the £5 billion-plus made from the latest television rights.

Some narratives, such as the underdog team Leicester City winning the Premiership in 2016, engaged much of the nation. So did international results, both triumphs, the victory for England in the 1966 World Cup, which was held in England,

and humiliations, such as the Euro 2016 defeat of England at the hands of Iceland.

Football is practically a model for the process of globalisation. In place of the 1950s teams of local players, managers, owners and sponsorship, came international players, managers, owners and sponsorship for leading teams. There was sometimes opposition on the part of the supporters' clubs to the policies of foreign owners, for example in Liverpool in the 2010s to American owners, but, in general, this opposition was speedily overcome. The prices charged to see football matches rose speedily, not least because stadiums became all-seater. As a result, what had originally been a working-class sport very much became a middle-class one, with others having to watch on television.

Other sports also had major public followings and showed the impact of globalisation and money, notably cricket, rugby and tennis. These sports could attract the attention of the arts, as with L. S. Lowry's football painting *Going to the Match* (1953) and his *Lancashire League Cricket Match* (1964-9). They certainly received large-scale television coverage. So also with the Olympics where, in 2016, Britain had the second highest number of medals after America and in 2020 the fourth highest, a result that owed a lot to support organised by UK Sport and financed by the National Lottery in a policy introduced by John Major when he was Prime Minister.

The 2012 Olympic Games held in the UK displayed a remarkable level of social cohesion. London 2012 went over budget by 76% in real terms, measured from bid to completion. The cost per athlete was £800,000. Yet, more than two-thirds of the UK public believed the £8.77bn cost of the Games was worth the money, according to a ComRes poll for the BBC. International Olympic Committee President Jacques Rogge declared the London 2012 Olympic Games 'happy and glorious' and thanked

English Culture

London. The security operation was staggering: 10,000 police officers were supported by 13,500 Armed Forces personnel. The 2012 Cultural Olympiad ran alongside the Games, involving over 500 events nationwide such as the World Shakespeare Festival and the Bandstand Marathon. Artists David Hockney, Lucian Freud, Rachel Whiteread, Budget Riley, Tracey Emin and Howard Hodgkin were all involved.

Conclusions

Aside from sport, other aspects of public life and experience also engaged much of the nation. The doings of television stars, such as Jeremy Clarkson on *Top Gear* or Simon Cowell on *The X Factor*, of the judges and contestants on *Strictly Come Dancing*, the objects in *Antiques Roadshow*, the plots in *Call the Midwife* or the accuracy of *Downton Abbey*, were all subjects for public discussion, as measured by entries on social media in the 2010s. Allowing viewers at home to vote, as in *Strictly Come Dancing*, enhanced public interest.

The media very much supported the personality-driven account of sport. Television programmes such as 'Sports Personality of the Year' attracted large viewing figures. 'Celebrity' was very much a function of the media, which defined a national hierarchy of attention. Alongside the success of new programmes, there was much continuity. *Midsomer Murders*, which began in 1997, is still running, with many echoes of the novels of Agatha Christie, including no shoot-outs or sex scenes.

10

1900 TO THE PRESENT: 'NATIONAL, AMERICAN, EUROPE, OR WHAT?'[1]

Despite elements of popular xenophobia, the intellectual and cultural world of the eighteenth and early nineteenth centuries had not been closed to Continental influences. In the second half of the nineteenth century, Continental influences increased, in philosophy, theology, political and economic theory, and science. For example, the work of the German philosopher Hegel had an impact on Oxford. In the 1880s, Karl Marx's views were disseminated. In 1883, H. M. Hyndman's *The Historical Basis of Socialism in England* appeared, offering a view of class development that drew heavily on Marx. In 1885, the group variously termed the 'Hampstead Marx Circle' or 'Hampstead Historic Society', which included George Bernard Shaw and Sidney Webb, began meeting to discuss Marx's work, which they approached through the French translation. Two years later, an English translation of *Das Kapital* appeared in London.

English Culture

Writers such as Oscar Wilde played a role in the cosmopolitan *fin de siècle* movement. At a distance from the *avant garde*, other arts also were influenced by Continental developments and practitioners. In the fashionable field of portraiture, Franz Winterhalter and Jacques Tissot were key figures, although the painter John Everett Millais was also celebrated.

Continental developments continued to have an impact in the early decades of the twentieth century. The stress on the subconscious and, in particular, on repressed sexuality, in the psychoanalytical methods developed by the Austrian Sigmund Freud and the psychological theories of the Swiss psychiatrist Carl Jung, challenged conventional ideas of human behaviour, and affected both literature and drama as many writers sought to explore psychological states. Continental composers were influential after the Great War: Rimsky-Korsakov, Schönberg, Hindemith and Prokofiev. Ballet was greatly affected by the *Ballets Russe*, a company created by the Russian impresario Sergei Diaghilev.

Yet, there was also much resistance (and even more indifference) to Continental trends. Literary modernism, for example, had a smaller impact than on the Continent. There were important English modernists, including D. H. Lawrence, who left England in 1919, and Virginia Woolf, both outsiders in an English cultural world largely focused on more conventional styles and authorities. Realism in literature and art remained more influential, as did empiricism in philosophy. In music, Vaughan Williams was more popular than Hindemith, and not all critics or audiences enjoyed Schönberg's atonal and serial music.

This response was cultural in the widest sense, part of a suspicion of the foreign that was strongly marked in the period. The sense of challenge to the economic and political position, combined with widespread immigration and an awareness of

1900 to the Present: 'National, American, Europe, or What?'

cultural shifts, led to a fear of alien forces and an overt racism, as in the forcible repatriation of gypsies in the 1900s. Attitudes towards refugees in the mid-nineteenth century had been open, although, in part, this was due to a chauvinistic sense of national superiority. Attitudes hardened, however, in the late nineteenth century, in reaction to Jewish immigration, fears about anarchists, and anxieties about the national 'stock'.

One aspect was concern from the 1890s about sinister Chinese using opium dens to corrupt men and, in particular, women. Limehouse in East London, with its Chinese population, became synonymous with the seductions of opium. Thomas Burke's *Limehouse Nights* (1917) and the *Fu Manchu* stories of Sax Rohmer (the pseudonym of Arthur Sarsfield), the first of which, *The Mystery of Dr Fu-Manchu*, appeared in 1913, sustained this concern into the 1920s, and Brilliant Chang, a real Chinese drug-dealer, became the most notorious criminal of the period. Sarsfield had been a crime reporter in Limehouse. Imaginative fiction more generally registered a theme of foreign threats to Englishness operating in England, as in the popular *Bulldog Drummond: The Adventures of a Demobilized Officer Who Found Peace Dull* (1920) by Sapper (Lieutenant-Colonel H. C. McNeile), a novel that spawned a number of sequels. Detective novels often contrasted rugged English heroes who relied on their fists with foreign residents of London, who were generally presented in terms of supposedly undesirable characteristics, such as shifty looks and yellowish skins, and as using knives. Alexander Waugh, a London-based novelist, described Soho in 1926 as having 'a swarthy duskiness, and oriental flavour; a cringing savagery that waits its hour'.

The same threat was represented in drama, as in Arnold Ridley's highly successful *The Ghost Train* (1923) in which a spectral passenger train turns out to be a real one used by

English Culture

revolutionaries to smuggle Soviet arms, an English agent eventually defeating them. As an instance of the continuities that so often defy periodisation, Ridley had been seriously wounded on the Somme in 1916 and was to become a familiar figure in his comic role as Private Godfrey in the popular 1968-77 television series *Dad's Army*.

Communism could be grafted onto the sense of alien threat. It was generally presented as foreign, and the prominent role of Jews in the movement was emphasised. Jingoistic tendencies had been encouraged during the First World War, leading to propaganda such as Horatio Bottomley's newspaper *John Bull*. After the war, a sense of threat to what was seen as traditional patriotism led in 1923 to the foundation of the British Fascists.

The First World War, Britain's problems, and the threat of Communism combined to challenge cosmopolitanism in national life, and to encourage a search for national character. This had a number of cultural manifestations, not least the cultural style termed realism and also a stress on supposedly rural values. The development of a new suburbia demanded gardens for display, with flats in contrast seen as un-English. Speaking on the West of England radio programme on 2 January 1939, the poet John Betjeman attacked the slum-clearance schemes of the London County Council: 'Londoners, like all English people, prefer to live in a house.' Others had a bleaker perspective. *Jipping Street* (1928) by Kathleen Woodward (1896-1961) covers her early years in South London. Born into a very poor family, the story is of a child obliged to begin factory work at twelve and then to leave home at thirteen for another factory job north of the river.

Gardening became increasingly significant as an expression of Englishness, although it was not to receive proportionate attention in the arts after the 1940s. Earlier, the cult of the landscape that was especially strong in the 1920s and 1930s

246

1900 to the Present: 'National, American, Europe, or What?'

was focused on such southern features as downland. Henry Williamson in *The Linhay on the Downs* (1929) referred to 'the harmony of nature'.

One of the most successful disseminators of the ruralist image of England was H. V. (Henry Canova Vollam) Morton (1892-1979). Born in Birmingham and a journalist, he was one of the most popular writers of his day and was close to many leading figures accompanying Churchill to the Atlantic Charter negotiations with President Roosevelt in 1941. Morton's *In Search of England*, published on 2 June 1927, went through two more editions in 1927, three each in 1928, 1929 and 1930, four in 1931, and its twenty-fourth in 1937. It was the most influential of a whole genre of tour guides to England that were very popular in the inter-war period. There were about two million cars on the road by 1939. This was linked to the spread of suburbia, but not simply the result of it. England was being 'discovered', as cars and rural bus services reached many areas not readily accessible by train, while posters encouraged rail travel for tourism. To Morton, the countryside was integral to national life:

The squares of London, those sacred little patches of the countryside preserved, perhaps by the Anglo-Saxon instinct for grass and trees, hold in their restricted glades some part of the magic of spring. I suppose many a man has stood at his window above a London square in April hearing a message from the lanes of England... the village that symbolizes England sleeps in the subconsciousness of many a townsman. A little factory hand whom I met during the war confessed to me, when pressed ... that he visualised the England he was fighting for – the England of the "England wants You" poster as not London, not his own streets, but as Epping Forest, the green place where he had spent Bank Holidays. And I think most of us did. The village and the English countryside are the germs of all we

English Culture

are and all we have become: our manufacturing cities belong to the last century and a half; our villages stand with their roots in the Heptarchy [Anglo-Saxon period].

At the close of the book, the reader, having been taken by car to Land's End, then to the Scottish border and back to Kenilworth 'in the heart of England,' is offered at the last a rural idyll where Morton meets a vicar who provides an attractive account of timelessness:

> We are, in this little hamlet, untouched by ideas, in spite of the wireless and the charabanc. We use words long since abandoned. My parishioners believe firmly in a physical resurrection... We are far from the pain of cities, the complexities. Life is reduced here to a single common denominator... We are rooted in something firmer than fashion ... the newspapers are only another kind of fairy story about the world outside.

Morton's book closes with an assertion of faith and a powerful account of an identity of people and place:

> I went out into the churchyard where the green stones nodded together, and I took up a handful of earth and felt it crumble and run through my fingers, thinking that as long as one English field lies against another there is something left in the world for a man to love.

Morton saw the peasantry as 'the salt of the earth' and a kind of well of virtue and character from which the nation received constant refreshment, and called for 'a happy countryside ... guarding the traditions of the race'. This view might now seem conservative, but Morton was a Labour supporter, a populist, and moderately collectivist. The last was a position seen with

1900 to the Present: 'National, American, Europe, or What?'

both rural and urban commentators. Similarly, Ernest Barker, who sought national identity in his *The Character of England* (1947) in the 'cults' of the amateur and the gentleman, eccentricity, social harmony, the volunteering habit, and an ability to recreate Englishness, was from a Northern working-class background.

In some quarters, there was also a sense of the occult power of the landscape. This was the case with interest in ley lines, as in novels such as Sylvia Townsend Warner's *Lolly Willowes* (1926), with its satirical account of Chilterns' society including a Witches' Sabbath. Similar ruralist themes echoed in the second half of the century, although not continually: in the 1950s, rather than in the 1960s, for example.

Although such themes helped maintain an idea of the idyll of rurality, they could not preserve the countryside. Morton's vicar is pensive about the lord of the manor: 'Poor now as a church mouse but rooted to the land... When he dies ... I suppose they will sell to pay the death duties and then...' Nancy Mitford's 'Uncle Matthew,' a traditional landed aristocrat, in her semi-autobiographical novel *Love in a Cold Climate* (1949), embodied the same values, as well as being anti-Catholic and xenophobic. Many landowners did indeed sell up, as parts of the countryside were built over. The organic account of identity is fundamentally ruralist and conservative, although not in the sense of conservatism as the creed of capitalism, far from it.

Some sought to look abroad, within the Empire, to new Britains. The Society for the Overseas Settlement of British Women (1919-62) hoped that these latter-day pioneers would 'marry and produce the children essential to the preservation of a white Australia or a British Canada', that they would instil in the young a love of Britain, and ensure the purchase of British goods.

National culture was celebrated in a number of works. One of the most weighty was completed in 1928. The first edition of the

Oxford English Dictionary contained 240,165 main words and 400,000 entries. Started in 1859, it was a triumphant statement of the importance, longevity and character of the language, and a presentation of English as just that, not American.

America did not offer the security of the Empire. It was a source of competition, commercially, and of values challenging national social, cultural and political norms, although political and economic tensions between the two powers were handled peaceably. Disagreements in the New World in the 1900s – over South America and the Canadian frontier – were settled. America supported Britain in the First World War, coming into the conflict in 1917. The rise of one great power as the other faded was managed without conflict between the two.

America had a strong appeal to many British commentators, and this was part of its competitive threat. Those who looked to America for new developments in jazz or the cinema were looking in some respects to a very different America from that seen by those attracted by a notion of Anglo-Saxon cultural or racial affinity, but their common element was a potentially challenging frame of reference. Any stress on America represented a very different cultural emphasis from that of Europe, with its much stronger sense of the living past and its greater hesitation about novelty. Jazz, for example, was very much a novelty. American soldiers introduced it during the First World War. In 1919, the Original Dixieland Jazz Band visited London, and in the 1920s English emulators took to dances such as the Charleston and the Black Bottom. Part of the appeal of jazz was that it *was* American. Piano sellers added gramophones and records to their stock. In the 1930s, jazz was increasingly successful as dance music. English bandleaders such as Ted Heath and Ray Noble trumpeted their big brass sound on the radio.

1900 to the Present: 'National, American, Europe, or What?'

In the cinema, English culture, history, and society were interpreted and presented for American, and, thus, also English, audiences by American actors, directors and writers, or by their British counterparts responding to the American market. Thus, Lord Peter Wimsey, a fictional epitome of the best of the British aristocracy, was played by an American, Robert Montgomery, in *Busman's Honeymoon* (1940) and Walter Pigeon appeared as Clem Miniver in *Mrs Miniver* (1942). English audiences were encouraged to 'buy British', but generally preferred American films, a pattern also seen in the empire.[2] Cinema represented wholesale Americanisation. The only British films seen as competitive were films of literary classics or historical dramas.

American links, a positive image of America, and a habit of looking at Britain through the American prism, were all greatly accentuated by the Second World War.[3] Britain's eventual role was as a junior ally, more obviously saved and supported by the Americans than in the First World War. This co-operation was sustained after the war. The Anglo-American geopolitical and strategic alignment in the early stages of the Cold War was supported by a stress on common Anglo-American values. Truman's Democratic administration (1945-53) was far from identical with the Attlee Labour governments (1945-51), with their nationalizations and creation of a welfare state, but it was possible to stress common language and values, easy to do so in comparison with the Communist Soviet Union. This co-operation was supported by the memory of wartime co-operation and fraternisation. The large number of British women who went to America as GI brides was an obvious indicator of the latter: the length of the American forces' stay in wartime Britain ensured that it was far greater than comparable figures from elsewhere in Europe.

Co-operation with America did not separate England from the Continent. Other European states were also founder-members

English Culture

of NATO, American economic assistance under the Marshall Plan was important in the recovery of western Europe, and the Americans played a role in thwarting Communist activity in France and Italy. Cultural Anglo-Americanism was matched by closer links between America and western Europe as a whole: France, Italy, and, in particular, Germany were exposed to strong American cultural forces. The sway of Hollywood reached to the Elbe which, marked the frontier between what was to become West and East Germany. In 1947, G. M. Trevelyan, a leading historian, spoke of living in 'an age that has no culture except American films and football pools'. Its cultures weakened or discredited by defeat, collaboration or exhaustion, much of western European society was reshaped in response to American influences and consumerism, which were associated with prosperity, fashion and glamour. Changes in consumer taste were to have important economic consequences. Britain's economy, and society were wide open, like others in western Europe, to the stimuli coming from the most developed and powerful global economy.

Britain's cultural, social and political influence in former imperial possessions ebbed rapidly, the engagement of national image and a Greater Britain fading in both Britain and the former empire.[4] The percentage of the Australian and Canadian populations that could claim British descent fell appreciably from 1945, as they accepted immigration from other countries. Constitutional links with Britain, for example the right of appeal to the Privy Council in Great Britain from the superior courts of Commonwealth countries, were severed or diminished in importance. Republican sentiment grew markedly in Australia from the 1980s. America came to play a more important cultural role in both Australia and Canada, with, for example, American soap operas being shown frequently on television. In 1951,

1900 to the Present: 'National, American, Europe, or What?'

Australia and New Zealand independently entered into a defence pact with the United States (ANZUS). Britain was irrelevant as the Pacific became an American lake. In 2008, when Liverpool was European Capital of Culture, the role of empire in its history was largely ignored.[5]

In some respects, America served as a surrogate for Britain in the Dominions, providing crucial military, political, economic and cultural links and offering an important model, as well as supporting the 'Mother Country'. The strength of these links compromised Britain's European identity, but from the 1970s, they slackened. Anglophilia became less pronounced in America, and Britain had less to offer in the special relationship.

On the other hand, through the role of American TV programmes and American-derived products in British consumer society, the American presence in the economy, and the more diffuse but still very important mystique of America as a land of wealth and excitement, grew. The US became an essential part of culture in the widest sense of the term. The suburban culture and society that was prominent in the 1950s was particularly accessible to American influences. This was seen in popular music, the cult of the car, the allure of 'white goods', especially washing machines, and electricity rather than coal, the rise of television, and well-kept lawns.

Although there are obvious problems with 'measurement', it is apparent, not least for linguistic and commercial reasons, that post-war American cultural 'hegemony' was stronger in Britain than in the other western European countries. American influence in the 1950s became the currency of the affluence that replaced the austerity of the 1940s. American soap operas set standards for consumer society. America also became a topic for study. The Atlanticism of the 1960s led to the creation of Schools of English and American Studies in new universities, such as East Anglia

English Culture

and Sussex. At the same time, the engagement with the culture of national history declined; civic historical pageants died out.[6]

There were also important Continental influences, although far less so at the level of popular culture and most strongly in cosmopolitan milieux, such as Soho.[7] These influences, in part, came through personal links. Many artists trained or travelled abroad, and they were affected by what they found there. In the two decades after the Second World War, culture was greatly influenced by existentialism, a nihilistic Continental philosophical movement closely associated with Heidegger, Kierkegaard and Sartre, that stressed the vulnerability of the individual in a hostile world, and the emptiness of choice. Novels affected by these notions, such as those of Camus, had an impact, as did plays, most obviously the work of Sartre. From the war until the mid-1950s, French plays, especially the works of Sartre and Anouilh, were frequently performed in translation, in London and elsewhere. Sartre's work, for example, greatly affected the novelist Iris Murdoch.

The popularity of French plays was eventually challenged by the indigenous kitchen sink drama of, in particular, John Osborne. This was not, however, a simple case of 'British' versus foreign; for other Continental playwrights became influential from the mid-1950s, moulding authors, directors and audiences. Bertolt Brecht died in 1956, but it was only from the mid-1950s that his works had a major impact: productions were staged by leading national companies, such as the National Theatre and the Royal Shakespeare Company, especially in the 1960s. Brecht's works also became very popular as school plays.

Another powerful Continental influence on drama was the 'theatre of the absurd'. This term was applied in 1961 to a type of non-realistic modern drama that was centred in Paris, but followed in London. The works of Samuel Beckett, an Irishman

1900 to the Present: 'National, American, Europe, or What?'

resident in Paris, and the Romanian Eugene Ionesco were produced frequently. The author of *Waiting for Godot*, Beckett influenced Harold Pinter, one of the leading English playwrights from the 1960s.

Alongside the theatrical influence came that of French cinema, the French New Wave films. From the 1970s, there was also a significant influx of German films.[8]

Classical music was influenced by Continental composers. The works of the Russian Dmitri Shostakovitch were frequently performed in the 1950s and 1960s, the genius whose works were banned under Stalin, and who, according to the Russian actor Uri Lyubimov, 'waited for his arrest at night out on the landing by the lift, so that at least his family wouldn't be disturbed'. In Christie's *They Do It with Mirrors* (1952), Inspector Curry has never heard of Hindemith and Shostakovich, but finds, inside the music stand, the 'old-fashioned stuff', Handel's *Cargo*, Czerny's *Exercises*, Chopin's preludes, and the 1930 song 'I know a lovely Garden,' which the vicar's wife used to sing when Curry was young. In the 1970s and 1980s, living Continental composers whose works were often heard included the Italian Luciano Berio, Pierre Boulez, the French conductor of the BBC Symphony Orchestra (1971-5), and the Pole Witold Lutoslawski. There were of course noted British composers whose work was distinctive, most obviously Britten (1913-76) and Tippett (1905-98), both of whom produced important operas.

English popular music was far less affected by the Continent. It was greatly influenced by American popular music in the 1950s. Rock 'n' Roll arrived with the playing of Bill Haley and the Comets on the soundtrack of the film *Blackboard Jungle*, which was released in Britain in 1956. Later films, such as Haley's *Rock Around the Clock* and Elvis Presley's *Jailhouse Rock* and *King Creole*, had a big impact on youth audiences.

English Culture

English singers, both male and female, modelled their performance on Americans and sang their songs, as they had done from the 1920s, although they also drew on British light entertainment. Thus, Marion Ryan, one of the most successful singers in 1956-62, recorded versions of Perry Como's *Hot Diggity* and Peggy Lee's *Mr Wonderful*. American culture affected British youth through film stars, especially James Dean and Marlon Brando, and films such as *Rebel Without a Cause* and *The Wild One*. Bebop – improvised jazz with complex rhythms that was developed in America – was played in London by Ronnie Scott and John Dankworth, and in 1959 Scott opened the jazz club named after him.

Jazz, however, became far less popular as dance music in the 1960s; part of a wider rejection of American musical styles. From the early 1960s, English groups developed their own sound and became the most popular of all on the Continent. The Beatles were to lead a musical invasion whose sounds were to be heard across the Atlantic. The Beatles became a global as well as a national product. Their broadcast of 'All You Need Is Love' in 1967, transmitted to 26 countries, was seen by about 400 million people. Thanks largely to the Beatles, popular music became a British industry. It was to become a major export.

In many cases, Continental groups had to produce their material in English, not primarily in the hopes of reaching a world market, which none did (save ABBA, who essentially became English by adoption), but because if they did not they appeared parochial and out of date, even in their own countries. With the pop explosion of the 1960s and English leadership in such areas as fashion, design and photography, London displaced Paris as the cultural capital of Europe.

One of the most important sources of Continental influence had been the large number of refugees who fled the traumas of

1900 to the Present: 'National, American, Europe, or What?'

Continental politics. Large-scale immigration from European Russia, especially Poland, in the late nineteenth century, was followed in the 1930s by refugees, mostly Jewish, from the Nazis, not only from Germany, but also from Austria and other countries threatened or occupied by the Germans: Freud came from Vienna to Hampstead in 1938. In addition, Communist takeovers led to immigration, both after 1917 and in the late 1940s. Although London was not as cosmopolitan as Beirut or Constantinople at the beginning of the century, it was more so than it had been in the past.

Immigrants brought different interests and new methods. In some spheres, they were particularly important. Many found university posts and greatly influenced the intellectual life of the country. Foreign economists, such as Thomas Balogh and Nicholas Kaldor, had an impact on the economic policies of the Labour governments of 1964-70. F. A. von Hayek wrote his highly influential text _The Road to Serfdom_ in 1944 while he was Professor of Economic Science and Statistics at London University. His views on the evils of collectivism influenced the Conservative Party during the 1945 election and, more powerfully, in the 1980s, and he was made a Companion of Honour in 1984 for his achievements in economic thought.

The arts were also enriched. This was especially true of the performance of music. Soloists such as Alfred Brendel strengthened the musical life of the country. Architecture was also greatly affected. The leading English architect of mid-century, Berthold Lubetkin (1901-90), was born in Tbilisi, the son of a Georgian mother and a Russian Jewish father. Trained in Moscow, Berlin, Warsaw and Paris, he was influenced by Marxist method, and by the German art philosopher Wilhelm Worringer, and proclaimed his affiliations with his responsibility for the short-lived Lenin Memorial in Finsbury.

English Culture

By the early 1990s, however, most of these notable immigrants had died or retired, and there was no new wave from the Continent to replace them: in the late 2000s and early 2010s, when large numbers of immigrants from the EU arrived, mostly from Eastern Europe, they were not generally intellectual refugees, although there were some important exceptions. The influence of the earlier immigrants had been considerable, and it did not entail sympathy for political developments there. As with many immigrants to America, those who took refuge in England had no reason to feel much warmth towards Continental political cultures.

Tourism has been crucial to the relationship between Britain and the outer world, for it obliges people to be aware that there is an 'other': other places, other peoples, and other ways of organising life. The impact of such experience can be lessened by many of the aspects of 'package holidays', specifically going abroad to cocoons, environments in which the foreign is tamed or simply ignored.

In the first half of the twentieth century, tourism was limited by war and the cost of foreign travel; and for those in the middle class who could afford it, fashion and habit limited the lure of abroad. Thus, the working class was apt to go to the seaside resorts developed in the Victorian period, such as Blackpool, Skegness, and Southend, while the middle classes went to more 'select' coastal resorts, such as Torquay and Sidmouth. Only the more affluent were familiar with the Alps or the Riviera, and, even then, many preferred the British countryside.

Far greater numbers travelled for pleasure from the late 1950s. This was a consequence of greater disposable wealth among the working class, especially skilled artisans, the development of the package holiday, the use of jet aircraft, and the spread of car ownership. As a consequence, although a large number never

1900 to the Present: 'National, American, Europe, or What?'

went abroad, far more than ever before visited the Continent. And far more than ever before made a regular habit of doing so, some went several times a year. If many visited 'little Englands' in nondescript resorts, such as Benidorm, others did not. A growing percentage of the population chose to live abroad, especially in retirement, or had second homes there. This became particularly the case in France and Spain in the 1980s and 1990s, and was a consequence of membership of the European Union and of the liberalisation of financial controls under Thatcher. It became easier to transfer funds abroad and to own foreign bank accounts.

Such links were an important aspect of a reconceptualisation of relations with the Continent in which the latter became more familiar. For many in England, this was the key element of globalisation. This was related to a shift in the notion of patriotism. Patriotic sentiment was less frequently expressed from the 1960s, and attitudes towards abroad became less adversarial. The expression of hostile views was frowned on. Sensitivity to criticism of the Continent was shown, for example, during the 1996 European football championships. England was drawn against Germany in the semi-final, and much of the popular press employed martial images or language. The *Sun* declared 'Let's Blitz Fritz', while the *Daily Mirror* of 24 June carried headlines such as 'Mirror Declares Football War on Germany' and 'Achtung! Surrender. For you Fritz, ze Europe 96 Championship is over.' In the face of complaints to the paper, the editor was severely reprimanded and had to apologise. The Germans won of course, and then won the final.

Notions of identity and habits of expressing identity were both in flux in the closing decades of the century. It would be mistaken to pretend that they had ever been constant, but the last half century was one of particular fluidity. The loss of empire, alliance

English Culture

with America, and membership of the European Union were far more than simply political issues.

Cosmopolitanism and Nationalism

The tension between cosmopolitanism and xenophobia became more acute with time, although there was also a marked reduction in the acceptability of racism. This was partly a matter of legislation, but far more was involved. Individual artistic forms were greatly affected. Racism had clearly been to the fore in Blackface minstrelsy. Developed in the nineteenth century, this form of music hall translated to television in *The Black and White Minstrel Show* (1957-63).[9] Racism can also be seen in the more complex, but still often critical, account of the Irish.[10] The forms of the tension between cosmopolitanism and xenophobia varied. In some respects there was not so much tension as a positive synergy.

Food

This was most clearly the case with food. The impact of foreign cuisine was linked to the deficiencies of English food culture, as there was no level below which British food could not drop. For many, food that actually tasted of something was a new experience. English cuisine was totally reconceptualised as a result of the popularity and, to a degree, Anglicisation of foreign foods. Initially this was a matter of Italian restaurants, which, as with Italian ice-cream, spread after 1945, in part as many Italian prisoners-of-war stayed in Britain. The end of food rationing was also important.

Particular dishes entered the English diet and vocabulary. Thus, from Italy, 'spag bog,' or Spaghetti Bolognese, became an English staple, as did lasagne, veal escalope and tiramisu. Some of these dishes, notably 'spag bog', could become convenience

1900 to the Present: 'National, American, Europe, or What?'

foods, and were tinned and sold accordingly. Chilli con carne was Spaghetti Bolognese's Mexican counterpart. There was singularly little resistance on the part of the defenders of more traditional food like mutton, sheep's cheeks, eel pies, and offal. The eating of kidneys, liver and tongue declined markedly, let alone hearts, although the cooked 'English breakfast' of bacon and egg continued to hold sway at the start of the day. Most of the bacon came from Denmark.

From the 1960s, the Anglicisation of foreign food began to affect Chinese and Indian cuisine, ironic as each civilisation had had a far more varied and long-lasting impact on English culture.[11] Particular adaptations served the English market, and some elements of Chinese and Indian cuisine did not translate: a more meat-based choice was offered to British consumers, and less in the form of vegetarian food. It took a while for the more delicate South Indian dishes to join the North Indian and often Bangladeshi tandoori dishes and strong curries that British restaurant-goers favoured.

Chinese and Indian restaurants were and are not just common in areas with concentrations of immigrants, but found across the country. Their cuisines are also extensively stocked in supermarkets. The National Catering Inquiry published in 1966 indicated that 11 per cent of Londoners had visited an Indian restaurant at some point. The percentage subsequently increased sharply, with newly affluent young males playing a key role, drinking a lot of lager and eating strong curries, notably vindaloo, which accordingly entered the vocabulary. This was very much an Anglicisation of Indian food, indeed a translation to Britain of developments in India under British rule. Afro-Caribbean cuisine brought jerk chicken, chickpeas and sweet potatoes.

Other national cuisines broke into the English restaurant world and into supermarket cuisine. This was true of Thai and Mexican

English Culture

food. Like Chinese food, these cuisines did not have the former imperial link seen with the British popularity of Indian food and the Dutch and French popularity of Indonesian and Vietnamese food respectively. Japanese and then Korean food entered the British restaurant world, although with less of a penetration than Thai or Mexican. By the 2000s, London had replaced New York as the restaurant capital of the world, in part due to the cosmopolitan nature of the city (whether permanent residents or transients), which included large numbers of American, Arab, French, Japanese, Portuguese, and Russian residents.

The international tendency was less pronounced in other cities. For example, Itsu, the profitable and expanding English-owned Asian fast-food chain, had 69 stores by July 2016, of which 58 were in London. Nevertheless, across the country, Thai green curry or lasagne became commonplace pub dishes alongside fish and chips. In Exeter where I live, a city of about 134,000 people, there are Chinese, French, Indian, Italian, Lebanese, Japanese, Moroccan, Nepalese, Palestinian, Spanish, Thai, Turkish and Vietnamese restaurants or cafés. The situation was very different when I arrived in 1996.

TV Cookery programmes were increasingly devoted to producing foreign dishes. For example, *The Great British Bake-Off,* a highly popular competition BBC television programme that was launched in 2010, saw contestants asked to produce foreign cakes and pastries, as well as British. In 2015, Nadiya Hussein, a Muslim woman, won the competition using baking that brilliantly reflected her heritage, a result applauded by David Cameron, the Prime Minister, whose wife went on to win a related celebrity competition in 2016. That year, the launch episode of series seven drew a record audience of ten million, nearly half the total viewing public that night. There was controversy when the series was sold to Channel Four. *Strictly Come Dancing* on BBC1's

1900 to the Present: 'National, American, Europe, or What?'

prime Saturday night slot, naturally included foreign dances like the tango. Salsa classes became common.

In cookery books, the French staples were challenged first by Italian cooking. In 1979, Marks and Spencer published the all-colour *Italian Cooking*. In the introduction to *Jamie's Italy* (2005), a book based on a television series, Jamie Oliver regretted not being Italian: 'Why, oh why, was I born in Southend-on-Sea?'[12] Subsequently, the geographical repertoire widened greatly. First published in 1948, and selling over two million copies by 2014, the *Good Housekeeping Cookery Book* in the new edition published that year included recipes for Béarnaise Sauce, Beurre Blanc, Borscht, Prawns fried in garlic, Mixed Italian Bruschetta, Fritto Misto di Mare, Poussins with Pancetta, Artichoke and Potato Salad, Risotto Milanese, and Spanish Omelette.

The issue of 'cultural appropriation' came to play a contentious role even in the case of food. In August 2018, a tweet from Dawn Butler, Shadow Secretary of State for Women and Equalities, attacked cultural 'appropriation' by Oliver. In turn, the *Sun* on 21 August published a comment piece by Brendan O'Neill, in which he attacked the 'miserabilist, divisive PC worldview'. His theme, instead, was liberation, with the argument that 'the global intermingling of food and art has enriched human life.'

Constrained by the climate, gardening programmes were far more 'national' in their tone and content. There was attention to introducing foreign plants, as there had been for centuries, but the centre of attention was on the already-established range of what were assumed to be British plants. 'Gardeners' Question Time' on the radio enjoyed significant listening and viewing figures. Their presenters, for example Alan Titchmarsh and Monty Don, became celebrities, as did media chefs. Whereas Fanny Cradock, the most prominent early television chef, had focused on helping housewives to cook more adventurously in the years after

English Culture

rationing, her successors in the 2010s, such as Rick Stein, took off with the television cameras around the world, in his case to India.

Tourism

The great growth in English tourism to foreign countries from the 1960s proved particularly significant in encouraging interest in foreign lifestyles, not least in the form of food and drink, for example Spanish tapas, which became increasingly available in restaurants from the 2000s. The numbers taking holidays abroad rose. Jet aircraft, package holidays, television advertising, and the search for the sun, all encouraged foreign tourism, and, while many did not travel abroad, domestic tourism still suffered a drop. Domestic routes were abandoned, for example the ferries taking South Wales workers across the Bristol Channel to resorts in the West Country, notably Ilfracombe and Minehead. Opened in 1994, the Channel Tunnel ended the need to go by ferry if taking a car abroad, and was part of a more general diminution in sea travel. In this context, it was ironic, but also symbolic of the potency of long-lasting national images, that in 2005 Radio 4 listeners voted Turner's *Fighting Temeraire* (1838) the nation's favourite painting. It was a nostalgic self-image of past grandeur, and was featured thus in the James Bond film *Skyfall* (2012). It was also ironic in that it depicted a heroic ship now decommissioned being towed to be broken up for scrap.

In the 2000s and 2010s, the expansion of inexpensive flights, including from more regional airports, and the development of direct train services to the Continent via Eurotunnel increased numbers. Booking online made the process easier. Entrepreneurial companies like EasyJet, RyanAir and Flybe played a key role in creating, defining and satisfying demand; they also provoked a swell of grievances about their terms and conditions thus creating a national conversation. Travel companies, a feature of the late

1900 to the Present: 'National, American, Europe, or What?'

twentieth century, both those that provided holidays and the travel agencies that sold them, were hit badly.

Trends were affected by more immediate circumstances, notably so in 2016 as sterling fell significantly after the Brexit vote. This suggested that more British tourists would stay at home, and, in 2016 PM Theresa May in fact pressed the case for 'staycations' and announced a £40 million fighting fund to assist tourism within Britain. In the summer of 2016, the Edinburgh Fringe and other festivals saw higher attendances than ever before.

A trend for more holidays at home had actually already developed prior to Brexit. In 2015, as a result of tourism from abroad and at home, 43.7 million overnight stops were taken in England, costing £10.7 billion. Both figures were up seven per cent. Although London topped the list, coastal towns, essentially catering for British tourists, also did well, notably Scarborough, Blackpool, Skegness, Torbay, Whitley Bay, Brighton, Margate and Llandudno in Wales. The affluent, and also Londoners, proved much keener to go abroad than other British travellers.

Conclusions

In this period there were vogues for particular genres that were made available in translation, for example Scandinavian crime stories in the 2000s and, even more, in the 2010s. A greater openness to foreign influence was increasingly apparent. The key foreign influence was America, most obviously through cinema, popular music and, from the 1950s, the increasingly ubiquitous television. At the same time, mainstream culture could display hostility toward Americans, as in the critical treatment of a visiting President by a British Prime Minister in the romantic film *Love Actually* (2003).

Immigrant writers were highly significant. 'Bookworm' commented in *Private Eye* on 2 May 2013 on the choice of Best

English Culture

Young British Novelists in the magazine *Granta*, which included four with Asian links, four with African or Caribbean ones, two born in North America and one in Australia. There was 'no sign of any reaching out to small non-metropolitan publishers in a search for undiscovered talent'.

Immigration was a key way in which Englishness appeared fluid – to the immigrants themselves, the other English whatever their origins, and to foreign commentators and tourists. On a longstanding pattern, there was an assimilation that in practice affected existing practices, a maintenance of difference, and the development of a distinctive context, content and tone, as in 'Black British Culture'.[13]

The concept of multiculturalism became widely applied, both in the sense of institutional policy and with reference to the activity (agency) of immigrants. The results ranged from successful cross-fertilisation and redefinition of Englishness, to irritation, exclusion and unfairness.[14] In the 2010s, London adopted Chicago's drill music but gave it a particular slant, with the use of Multicultural London English (MLE), a London dialect that incorporates street language, notably Jamaican patois. MLE then went round the world. In the 2000s, grime music had spread from East London. More will definitely follow.

ENVOI

In his essay 'The Lion and the Unicorn' (1941), which he reworked as *The English People* (1947), George Orwell wrote:

> There is something distinctive and recognisable in English civilisation. It is a culture as individual as that of Spain. It is somehow bound up with solid breakfasts and gloomy Sundays, smoking towns and winding roads, green fields and red pillar-boxes. It has a flavour of its own. Moreover, it is continuous, it stretches into the future and the past, there is something in it that persists, as in a living creature... The suet puddings and the red pillar-boxes have entered into your soul.

In 2024, none of these definitions resonate in the same way, and even talking about 'the English people' would be seen as non-inclusive and inappropriate in many quarters. Diet has become lighter, with muesli replacing bacon and eggs (though obesity continues to rise). Sundays have become less gloomy because changes in law and custom mean

English Culture

that Sunday observance is far less common. The television broadcasts of professional sport – cricket from the late 1960s and football from the 1980s to now – make Sunday much like any other day. Towns have become less smoky as a result of the Clean Air Acts of 1956 and 1968 and the creation of smokeless zones.

Winding roads have been largely superseded. If motorways are now less commonly driven straight through the countryside with scant allowance for its topography than was the case a generation ago, and are more sensitive to the landscape, they are certainly not Orwell's winding roads. Instead, they represent the triumph of town over country, a theme in this book. Furthermore, as another aspect of change, traditional crops and green fields have been replaced by oilseed rape or maize, or housing. The post is practically an anachronism in the age of the internet and many post offices have been closed. The issues of a multiracial society, integration versus multiculturalism, have now been pushed to the fore in an instance of shifting 'values' that would have surprised Orwell.

At the same time, rural themes continued to be popular, as in the bestselling 'Aga-sagas' of Joanna Trollope, notably *The Best of Friends* (1995) and *Marrying the Mistress* (2000). The countryside as a positive setting was captured in the television series *All Creatures Great and Small* (1978-80, 1988-90, 2020-), which were based on the novels published from 1970 by James Wright under his pen-name James Herriot (1916-95). A more urban (albeit small-town) account of the Pennines was seen in another television series, *Last of the Summer Wine* (1973-2010), which was set and filmed in and around Holmfirth. This celebration of Northernness and the Pennine environment was presented in terms of a comedy of character that played on another aspect of the national self-image, tolerance of eccentricity: the disreputable, grubby, poorly dressed, ferret-keeping Compo was presented positively.

Envoi

There was a romance for many in these series of a supposedly kinder past. This was a form of 'heritage industry'. Nostalgia was powerfully presented on television but also proved adaptable, as in *Strictly Come Dancing* and *The Great British Bake Off*.

The alternative form to the works cleaving to fashionable critical movements such as post-modernism, deconstruction, and post-structuralism, was the popular fusion of alternative reality, the occult, the surreal and children's works found in J. R. R. Tolkein, Roald Dahl, Philip Pullman, Terry Pratchett, J. K. Rowling and *Game of Thrones*. The literary recognition given Pullman's novels was not the only example of the closing gap between children's literature and the established canon. Some religious groups criticised these authors for depicting a universe without God.

Orwell's piece serves as a pointed reminder of the porosity and changeability of manifestations of national civilisation. So also is the contradiction noted by Wilkie Collins, in his novel *No Name* (1862), when discussing the inhabitants of the then poor London area of Vauxhall Walk:

> Here, the loud self-assertion of Modern Progress – which has reformed so much in manners, and altered so little in men – meets the flat contradiction that scatters its pretensions to the winds.

The differences, distinctions, that wealth could bring were matched along the range of possible criteria, including gender, place and age. This is a central aspect of cultural history. Style and form are not simply imposed. They are also a matter of preference, by individuals and all sorts of groups, from the family to the community. At the same time, there are moods, many of them encoded in language. Thus, in recent decades, emotion and feeling have become more significant in the justification of attitudes, preferences, ideas and policies. Clearly, emotions are far

English Culture

from new. Nevertheless, they vary in their application and their importance.

In *Martin Chuzzlewit*, Dickens describes a Salisbury bookshop: 'In the window were the spick-and-span new works from London, with the title-pages, and sometimes even the first page of the first chapter, laid wide open.' The excitement and enticement of novelty keeps existing forms and practices vibrant and also poses a possible challenge to audience responses.

There is every likelihood that this process will become more pronounced over the coming years. Commentators repeat many of the anxieties of the past. The expansion of the press in the late nineteenth century appeared to threaten order and propriety, as individuals could use the personal advertisements to construct identities and create illicit links, not to mention for pranks and fraud. A free market in identity also offered plots for detective writers such as Arthur Conan Doyle. This situation looked toward the recent social-media explosion, which again has posed problems in terms of the accuracy of self-representation and of exploitation by and of users.

AI-generated books are already an issue on Amazon, as is the cloning of musicians' voices. Indeed, the monopoly of human creativity in the arts may be on the way out, with much of culture looted/incorporated in order to train AI systems, while cultural choices by algorithms may become more pronounced. The means of cultural production have always affected content. Technical issues were and are significant to input. Some means were more time-consuming and expensive, for example steel engraving as opposed to wood engraving.[1] This will remain the case.

At the international level, it is unclear if the English role in the Anglosphere will actually remain to the fore, and if not, what the consequences may be. The likeliest consequence will be the circulation of foreign models and content, a process encouraged by the extent to which the English language permits such porosity.

Envoi

It is notable that the Booker Prize is frequently won by non-British works.

The diversity of the artistic marketplace is most notable. The element that tends to be underrated is that of regional and local diversity, which is likely to become more significant as devolved authorities within England, for example elected mayors or (in the future) regional assemblies, seek to sponsor particular cultural contexts and contents, a process of identification on the pattern of what occurred in Scotland and Wales from 1998. The institutional background is relatively new, the Arts Council only establishing its first regional boards in 1960. Bodies such as Northern Arts, one of the boards, sought to support and energise distinctive cultural consciousness, but this in the end could prove to be simply a matter of buying into established local themes, so the the culture of the North-East is urban working-class culture,[2] an approach that underrated other approaches, notably those focused on rural and small-town cultures.

Meanwhile, national culture became more diverse with minority media, the minorities of sexuality and ethnicity to the fore. This variety is not one that is readily open to any critical judgment. Furthermore, democratisation is not new. Ordinary members of the public wrote for anonymous readers in eighteenth-century newspapers, as they do in modern social media. Community publishing and the teaching of creative writing are now part of the process.[3]

There is scant consensus about quality, significance and relevance, and no sign that this will change. Indeed, it is likely that a book of this type will become more difficult to write and more contentious. This is not inherently a problem, but one that is part of a contemporary cultural situation that slips easily into an opaque history. English culture is not so discernibly English or at least distinctive as would have been the case as late as the 1950s, but rather a jumble of all sorts of influences, the jumble agitated more rapidly than in the past.

FURTHER READING

It is best of course to read, look at, listen to, and watch works of the period. A sample of the literature on the relevant period can be found the footnotes and in the following.

Aldrich, M. *Gothic Revival* (1994).

Alexander, M. *A History of English Literature* (2000).

Armes, R. *A Critical History of British Cinema* (1978).

Atkinson, H. *The Festival of Britain: A Land and Its People* (2012).

Barr, C. *Ealing Studios* (1993).

Black, J. *Defoe's Britain* (2024).

Booth, M. *Theatre in the Victorian Age* (1991).

Chapman, J. *Licence to Thrill: A Cultural History of the James Bond Films* (1999).

Dentith, S. *Society and Cultural Forms in Nineteenth-century England* (1998).

Further Reading

Frith, S. et al. *The History of Live Music in Britain I: 1950-1967* (2013).

Groes, S. *British Fictions of the Sixties. The Making of the Swinging Decade* (2016).

Harris, T. (ed.) *Popular Culture in England, c.1500-1850* (1995).

Hewison, R. *Culture and Consensus: England, Art and Politics since 1940* (1995).

Hoock, H. *The King's Artists: The Royal Academy of Arts and the Politics of British Culture, 1760-1840* (2003).

Horejsi, N. *Novel Cleopatras: Romance Historiography and the Dido Tradition in English Fiction, 1688-1785* (2019).

McKinney, D. *Magic Circles: The Beatles in Dream and History* (2003).

McLeod, J. *Art and the Victorian Middle Class* (1996).

Morley, P. *The Age of Bowie: How David Bowie Made a World of Difference* (2016).

Ortolano, G. *The Two Cultures Controversy: Science, Literature and Cultural Politics in Postwar Britain* (2009).

Richards, J. *Films and British National Identity: From Dickens to Dad's Army* (1997).

Rose, J. *The Intellectual Life of the British Working Classes* (2001).

Seidel, K. *Rethinking the Secular Origins of the Novel: The Bible in English Fiction* (2021).

Shellard, D. *British Theatre since the War* (1999).

Snodin, M. and Styles, J. (eds) *Design and the Decorative Arts: Georgian Britain, 1714-1837* (2004).

Sall, D. (ed.) *A Concise Companion to the Restoration and Eighteenth Century* (2005).

Whyte, I.B. (ed.) *Man-Made Future: Planning, Education and Design in Mid-twentieth-century Britain* (2007).

Willis, P. *Charles Bridgeman and the English Landscape Garden* (2002).

ENDNOTES

Preface: The Importance of Culture

1. N. Humphreys, *Lost Women* (London, 2023), p. 68.
2. O. C. Jensen, *Napoleon and British Song, 1797-1822* (Basingstoke, 2015).
3. F. P. Lock, 'Drama from Etherege to Fielding,' *Southern Review*, 11, 2 (1978), p. 204.
4. P. Trolander and Z. Tenger, *Sociable Criticism in England, 1625-1725* (Newark, Del., 2007).
5. P. Leary, *The Punch Brotherhood: Table Talk and Print Culture in Mid-Victorian London* (London, 2010).
6. D. Fowler, *Youth Culture in Modern Britain, c.1920-c.1970* (Basingstoke, 2008); M. Worley, *No Future: Punk, Politics and British Youth Culture, 1976-1985* (Cambridge, 2017); Special issue of *Britain and the World*, 11 (2018).
7. Hare to Newcastle, 18 Aug. 1733, London, British Library, Department of Manuscripts, Additional Manuscripts, volume (hereafter BL. Add.) 32688 fol. 136.

Endnotes

8. J. A. Downie, 'How Useful to Eighteenth-Century English Studies is the Paradigm of the "Bourgeois Public Sphere"?' *Literature Compass*, 1 (2003), pp. 1-18, and 'Public and Private: The Myth of the Bourgeois Public Sphere,' in C. Wall (ed.), *A Concise Companion to the Restoration and Eighteenth Century* (Oxford, 2005), pp. 58-79.

9. C. Williams (ed.), *Sophie in London 1786* (London, 1933), pp. 94-5.

10. For a similar decision, N. J. G. Pounds, *The Culture of the English People: Iron Age to the Industrial Revolution* (Cambridge, 1994).

11. The play has been attributed to Samuel Foote but more probably the transplanted Irish writer Arthur Murphy, S. Trefman, 'Arthur Murphy's Long Lost *Englishman From Paris*: A Manuscript Discovered,' *Theatre Notebook*, 20 (1966), pp. 137-8.

12. J. Austen, *Emma* (London, 1815), I, 12.

13. *Ibid.*, III, 6.

14. D. Hume, *The History of England from the Invasion of Julius Caesar to the Revolution in 1688* (originally published 1754-62; 8 vols, London, 1813 edn), VIII, 316.

1 Background: 1500-1700

1. D. Gray, *Simple Forms: Essays on Medieval Popular Literature* (Oxford, 2015).

2. J. Good, *The Cult of St George in Medieval England* (Woodbridge, 2009).

3. R. Brackmann, *The Elizabethan Invention of Anglo-Saxon England: Laurence Nowell, William Lambarde and the Study of Old English* (Cambridge, 2012).

4. J. Bate, *Shakespeare and Ovid* (Oxford, 1993); A. Taylor, ed., *Shakespeare's Ovid: The 'Metamorphoses' in the Plays and Poems* (Cambridge, 2000).

English Culture

5. L. Oakley-Brown, *Ovid and the Cultural Politics of Translation in Early Modern England* (Aldershot, 2006); R. S. Miola, *Shakespeare and Classical Tragedy: The Influence of Seneca* (Oxford, 1992). For the broader context, K. Newman and J. Tylus, eds, *Early Modern Cultures of Translation* (Philadelphia, Penn., 2015).

6. G. Rosser, *The Art of Solidarity in the Middle Ages: Guilds in England, 1250-1550* (Oxford, 2015); N. R. Rice and M. A. Pappano, *The Civic Cycles: Artisan Drama and Intensity in Premodern England* (Notre Dame, Ind., 2015).

7. D. George, ed., *Records of Early English Drama: Lancashire* (Toronto, 1991).

8. Anne Lancashire, *London Civic Theatre: City Drama and Pageantry from Roman Times to 1558* (Cambridge, 2002) and, ed., *Records of Early English Drama: Civic London to 1558* (3 vols, Cambridge, 2015); Anon., *History of the City of Chester* (Chester, 1815): 282, 284-85.

9. H. Cooper, *Shakespeare and the Medieval World* (London, 2010); K. A. Schreyer, *Shakespeare's Medieval Craft: Remnants of the Mysteries on the London Stage* (Ithaca, New York, 2014).

10. J. Willis, *Church Music and Protestantism in Post-Reformation England: Discourses, Sites and Identities* (Farnham, 2010).

11. C. Davies, 'The Woolfes of Wine Street: Middling Culture and Community in Bristol, 1600-1620,' *English Historical Review*, 137 (2022), pp. 386-415.

12. D. Bruster, *Drama and the Market in the Age of Shakespeare* (Cambridge, 1992).

13. A. Gurr, *Playgoing in Shakespeare's London* (Cambridge, 1987).

14. S. Gossett, ed., *Thomas Middleton in Context* (Cambridge, 2011).

Endnotes

15. B. Groves, *Texts and Traditions: Religion in Shakespeare, 1592-1604* (Oxford, 2007).

16. J. E. Curran, *Hamlet, Protestantism, and the Mourning of Contingency: Not to Be* (Aldershot, 2006).

17. A. F. Kinney, ed., *Hamlet: New Critical Essays* (London, 2002).

18. S. Amussen and D. Underdown, *Gender, Culture, and Politics in England 1560-1640: Turning the World Upside Down* (London, 2017).

19. Flyer for production at Exeter Northcott Theatre, 9-13 May 2017.

20. T. Freeman, 'Fate, faction and fiction in Foxe's *Book of Martyrs*,' *Historical Journal*, 43 (2000): 601-23.

21. N. Millstone, *Manuscript Circulation and the Invention of Politics in Early Modern England* (Cambridge, 2016).

22. I. Archer, 'Social networks from Restoration London: the evidence from Samuel Pepys's diary,' in A. Shepard and P. Withington (eds), *Communities in early modern England. Networks, place, rhetoric* (Manchester, 1997), p. 90.

23. A. McRae, *Literature, Satire and the Early Stuart State* (Cambridge, 2004).

24. E. Holberton, *Poetry and the Cromwellian Protectorate: Culture, Politics, and Institutions* (Oxford, 2008).

25. W. Gibson, 'Music at the British Court, 1685-1715. The Discord of Politics and Religion,' *Mélanges de l'École française de Rome*, 133, 2 (2001), https:/doi.org/10.4000/mefrim.11045

2 Eighteenth Century: Spheres of Patronage

1. John Ley to his mother, 19 October 1793, Exeter, Devon Record Office, 63/2/11/6.

2. *Sense and Sensibility* II, 14.

English Culture

3. D. Le Faye, 'Three Missing Jane Austen Songs,' *Notes and Queries*, 244, 4 (1999): 454-55; R. Leppert, *Music and Image. Domesticity, Ideology and Socio-Cultural Formation in Eighteenth-Century England* (Cambridge, 1988).

4. *Pride and Prejudice* I, 8.

5. S. Rosenfeld, *The Georgian Theatre of Richmond Yorkshire and its Circuit* (London, 1984).

6. James Raven, 'The Publication of Fiction in Britain and Ireland, 1750-70,' *Publishing History*, 24 (1988): 32-35.

7. Published on 4 April.

8. Wellcome Library, London, Wilkes diary, September 1741, p. 118.

9. Jacque Carré, 'Burlington's Literary Patronage,' *British Journal for Eighteenth-Century Studies*, 5 (1982): 26-27.

10. K.J. H. Berland, 'Satire and the *Via Media*: Anglican Dialogue in *Joseph Andrews*,' in J. D. Browning (ed.), *Satire in the 18th Century* (New York: Garland, 1983): 83-99.

11. *Mansfield Park* II, 7.

12. D. Selwyn, *Jane Austen and Leisure* (London, 1999).

13. S. E. Whyman, *The Pen and the People: English Letter Writers 1660-1800* (Oxford, 2009). See also, on provincial culture, her *The Useful Knowledge of William Hutton: Culture and Eighteenth-Century Birmingham* (Oxford, 2018).

14. *The Rivals* I, 2.

15. B. Darby, *Frances Burney, Dramatist: Gender, Performance and the Late-Eighteenth-Century Stage* (Lexington, KY, 1997).

16. B. McCrea, *Frances Burney and Narrative Prior to Ideology* (Newark, DL, 2013).

17. R. Porter, *Enlightenment: Britain and the Creation of the Modern World* (London, 2000); K. Sloan, ed., *Enlightenment. Discovering the World in the Eighteenth Century* (London,

2003); R. G. W. Anderson, M. L. Caygill, A. G. MacGregory and L. Syson, eds, *Enlightening the British: Knowledge, Discovery and the Museum in the Eighteenth Century* (London, 2004).

18. *Emma* I, 18.

19. J. Golinski, *British Weather and the Climate of Enlightenment* (Chicago, 2007); J. Kington, *The Weather of the 1780s over Europe* (Cambridge, 1988).

20. *Pride and Prejudice* I, 11.

21. *Emma* III, 6.

22. *Sanditon* 1.

3 Eighteenth Century: Sites and Styles

1. S. Dickie, *Cruelty and Laughter: Forgotten Comic Literature and the Unsentimental Eighteenth Century* (Chicago, Ill., 2011); A. Marshall, *The Practice of Satire in England, 1658-1770* (Baltimore, Md., 2013).

2. M. Craske, *The Silent Rhetoric of the Body: A History of Monumental Sculpture and Commemorative Art in England, 1720-1770* (New Haven, Conn., 2007).

3. T. Fawcett, *Music in Eighteenth-Century Norwich and Norfolk* (Norwich, 1979).

4. S. Hague, *The Gentleman's House in the British Atlantic World, 1680-1780* (Basingstoke, 2015).

5. J. Sparrow, 'An Oxford Altar-Piece', *Burlington Magazine*, 102 (1960), pp. 4-9.

6. E. R. Delderfield, *Cavalcade by Candlelight: The Story of Exeter's Five Theatres* (Exmouth, 1950), p. 25.

7. R. Wendorf, *The Elements of Life: Biography and Portrait Painting in Stuart and Georgian England* (Oxford, 1990).

8. F. H. Ellis, *Sentimental Comedy: Theory and Practice* (Cambridge, 1991).

English Culture

9. Samuel Johnson to Elizabeth, 9 March 1774, 6 February 1775, to his father, 23 February 1775, Exeter, Devon Record Office, 5521 M/F4/1.

10. Reynolds to Lord Grantham, 2 May 1774, Bedford, Bedfordshire Record Office, Lucas papers, 30/14/32b/3.

11. J. M. Levine, *The Battle of the Books: History and Literature in the Augustan Age* (Ithaca, New York, 1991); D. Spadafora, *The Idea of Progress in Eighteenth-Century Britain* (New Haven, 1990).

12. *Morning Post and Daily Advertiser*, 17 March 1786.

13. D. Jacobson, *Chinoiserie* (London, 1993).

14. M. Butler, *Romantics, Rebels and Reactionaries: English Literature and its Background, 1760-1830* (Oxford, 1981).

15. A. Janowitz, *England's Ruins: Poetic Purpose and the National Landscape* (Oxford, 1990).

16. T. Whately, *Observations on Modern Gardening* (London, 1770), p. 155.

17. F. P. Lock, *Edmund Burke I, 1730-1784* (Oxford, 1998), pp. 91-124.

18. E. J. Clery, *The Rise of Supernatural Fiction, 1762-1800* (Cambridge, 1995).

19. B. Sutcliffe (ed.), *Plays by George Colman the Younger and Thomas Morton* (Cambridge, 1983), p. 10.

20. N. Penny, 'An Ambitious Man: The Career and Achievement of Sir Joshua Reynolds', from N. Penny (ed.), *Reynolds* (London, 1986), p. 39.

21. Frances Crewe, journal, BL, Add. MS 37926, fol. 107.

22. Pitt to James Oswald, 19 September 1751, Hockworthy, autograph volume no. 6, printed in *Memorials of the Public Life and Character of the Right Hon. James Oswald of Dunnikier* (Edinburgh, 1825), pp. 112-14.

Endnotes

Public Life and Character of the Right Hon. James Oswald of Dunnikier (Edinburgh, 1825), pp. 112-14.

4 Eighteenth Century: Xenophobia versus Cosmopolitanism

1. M. Riley and A. D. Smith, eds, *Nation and Classical Music from Handel to Copland* (Woodbridge, 2016).
2. Echard, *History*, II, 1.
3. *Ibid.*, II, 910.
4. G. Lyttelton, *Letters from a Persian in England* (4th edn, London, 1735), pp. 179-98.
5. J. Black, *A Subject for Taste: Culture in Eighteenth-Century England* (London, 2005).
6. G. Quilley, 'Missing the Boat: the place of the maritime in the history of British visual culture,' *Visual Culture in Britain*, 1, 2 (2000), pp. 79-92, and *Empire to Nation: Art, History, and the Visualization of Maritime Britain, 1768-1829* (New Haven, Conn., 2011).

5 Nineteenth Century: Spheres of Patronage

1. T. Hardy, 'Candour in English Fiction,' *New Review*, 2 (1890), pp. 15-21.
2. J. Conlin, *The Nation's Mantelpiece: A History of the National Gallery* (London, 2006); C.S. Smith, 'The Institutionalisation of Art in Early Victorian England,' *Transactions of the Royal Historical Society*, 20 (2010), pp. 113-25.
3. H. Hoock, *Empires of the Imagination: Politics, War, and the Arts in the British World, 1750-1850* (London, 2010).
4. T. C. W. Blanning and H. Schulze (eds), *Unity and Diversity in European Culture c.1800* (Oxford, 2006).
5. L. Howsam, *Past into Print: The Publishing of History in Britain, 1850-1950* (London, 2009).

English Culture

6. C. Steedman, *An Everyday Life of the English Working Class: Work, Self and Sociability in the Early Nineteenth Century* (Cambridge, 2013); A. Briggs, *Victorian People* (London, 1954).

7. P. Borsay, 'A Room with a View: Visualising the Seaside, *c.*1750-1914,' *Transactions of the Royal Historical Society*, 23 (2013), pp. 175-201.

8. B. Assael, *The London Restaurant, 1840-1914* (Oxford, 2018).

9. J. R. McCulloch, *A Dictionary; Geographical, Statistical, and Historical* (1851, new edn, London, 1859), II, p. 6, 268, 274.

10. S. Bilston, *The Promise of the Suburbs: A Victorian History in Literature and Culture* (New Haven, Conn., 2019).

11. I. Hesketh, *Victorian Jesus: J. R. Seeley, Religion, and the Cultural Significance of Anonymity* (Toronto, 2017).

12. F. Knight, *Victorian Christianity at the Fin de Siècle: The Culture of English Religion in a Decadent Age* (London, 2016).

13. M. W. Turner, *Trollope and the Magazines: gendered issues in mid-Victorian Britain* (Basingstoke, 2000).

14. J. Hall-Wit, *Fashionable Acts: Opera and Elite Culture in London 1780-1880* (NH, 2006).

15. S. Allan, *The Cumberland Bard: Robert Anderson of Carlisle 1770-1833* (Carlisle, 2020).

6 Nineteenth Century: Sites and Styles

1. F. Dillane, *Before George Eliot: Marian Evans and the Periodical Press* (Cambridge, 2013).

2. C. Bolton, *Writing the Empire: Robert Southey and Romantic Colonialism* (London, 2007); D.M. Craig, *Robert Southey and Romantic Apostasy: Political Argument in Britain, 1780-1840* (Woodbridge, 2007).

Endnotes

3. Jeffrey Cox (ed.), *Seven Gothic Dramas, 1789-1825* (Athens, Ohio, 1992).

4. Thomas Chrochunis (ed.), *Joanna Baillie, Romantic Dramatist* (London, 2004); Diane Hoeveler, 'Joanna Baillie and the Gothic Body: Reading Extremities in *Orra* and *De Montfort*,' *Gothic Studies*, 3, 2 (2001), pp. 117-33.

5. Julie Murray, 'At the Surface of Romantic Interiority: Joanna Baillie's *Orra*,' *Romanticism and Victorianism on the Net*, 56 (2009).

6. A. Briggs, *The Age of Improvement* (London, 1959) and *Victorian Cities* (London, 1963).

7. P. Dubois, 'Porous Places: Music in the (Late) Pleasure Gardens and Social Ambiguity,' *Revue d'Études Anglo-américaines* *XVII-XVIII*, 72 (2015), p. 126.

7 Nineteenth Century: The Culture of Empire?

1. P. Readman, *Storied Ground: Landscape and the Shaping of English National Identity* (Cambridge, 2018) and 'Landscape, National Identity and the Medieval Past in England, *c*.1840-1914,' *English Historical Review*, 137 (2022), pp. 1174-1208.

2. P. Gurney, *Wanting and Having: Popular Politics and Liberal Consumerism in England, 1830-70* (Manchester, 2015).

3. J. Neuheiser, *Crown, Church and Constitution: Popular Conservatism in England, 1815-1867* (New York, 2016).

4. T. Barringer, G. Quilley and D. Fordham (eds), *Art and the British Empire* (Manchester, 2007).

5. C. Payne, *John Brett, Pre-Raphaelite Landscape Painter* (New Haven, Conn., 2010).

6. M.R. Kingsford, *The Life, Work and Influence of W.H.G. Kingston* (Toronto, 1947).

7. B. Beaver, *Visions of Empire: Patriotism, Popular Culture and the City, 1870-1939* (Manchester, 2012).

English Culture

8. C. Jones, 'French Crossings: I. Tales of Two Cities,' *Transactions of the Royal Historical Society*, 6th ser., 20 (2010, pp. 1-26.

9. R. Parker and S. Rutherford (eds), *London Voices, 1820-1840: Vocal Performers, Practices, Histories* (Chicago, Ill., 2019).

10. M. O'Neill and M. Hatt (eds), *The Edwardian Sense: Art, Design, and Performance in Britain, 1901-1910* (New Haven, Conn., 2010).

11. J. Hobson, *The Psychology of Jingoism* (London, 1901), p. 8.

8 *1900 to the Present: Spheres of Patronage*

1. F. W. Croft, *The End of Andrew Harrison* (London, 1938), p. 77.

2. S. Marriott, 'The BBC, ITN and the Funeral of Princess Diana,' *Media History*, 13 (2007), pp. 93-110.

3. J. I. M. Stewart, writing as Michael Innes, *Death at the President's Lodging* (London, 1936), p. 4.

4. A. Taylor, *London's Burning: Pulp Fiction, The Politics of Terrorism and the Destruction of the Capital in British Popular Culture, 1840-2005* (London, 2012).

5. J. Williams, *Entertaining the Nation: A Social History of British Television* (Stroud, 2004).

6. T. Mo, *Sour Sweet* (London, 1983), p. 3.

7. P. Catterall, ed., 'The Origins of Channel 4,' witness seminar, *Contemporary British History*, 12 (1998): 91.

8. G. Ortolano, *The Two Cultures Controversy: Science, Literature, and Cultural Politics in Postwar Britain* (Cambridge, 2009).

9. N. Thompson, *Social Opulence and Private Restraint: The Consumer in British Socialist Thought since 1800* (Oxford, 2015).

Endnotes

10. D. O'Neill, 'No Cause for Celebration: The Rise of Celebrity News Values in the British Quality Press,' *Journalism Education*, 1, 2 (2012), pp. 26-44.
11. *Sunday Times*, 19 August 2018.
12. S. Dawson, *Holiday Camps in Twentieth-Century Britain: Packaging Pleasure* (Manchester, 2011).

9 *1900 to the Present: Sites and Styles*

1. F. W. Crofts, *Sudden Death* (London, 1932), p. 218.
2. A. Higgott, *Mediating Modernism: Architectural Cultures in Britain* (London, 2007).
3. D. Ryan, *Ideal Homes, 1918-39: Domestic Design and Suburban Modernism* (Manchester, 2018).
4. K. Reynolds, *Left Out: The Forgotten Tradition of Radical Publishing for Children in Britain, 1910-1949* (Oxford, 2016).
5. B. Foss, *War Paint: Art, War, State and Identity in Britain, 1939-1945* (New Haven, Conn., 2007).
6. P. Stansky and W. Abrahams, *London's Burning: Life, Death and Art in the Second World War* (London, 1995).
7. *Landscape in Britain 1850-1950*, Hayward Gallery, London, 1983, exhibition.
8. J. Black, *Winston Churchill in British Art, 1900 to the Present Day: The Titan with Many Faces* (London, 2017).
9. H. Atkinson, *The Festival of Britain: A Land and its People* (London, 2012).
10. I. B. Whyte (ed.), *Man-Made Future: Planning, Education and Design in Mid-twentieth-century Britain* (London, 2007).
11. S. Frith, M. Brennan, M. Cloonan and E. Webster, *The History of Live Music in Britain. I: 1950-1967: From Dance Hall to the 100 Club* (Farnham, 2013).

English Culture

12. C. Macinnes, *Absolute Beginners* in *The Colin Macinnes Omnibus* (London, 1985): 139.

13. A. Campsie, 'Mass-Observation Left Intellectuals and the Politics of Everyday Life,' *English Historical Review*, 131 (2016): 120.

14. G. Ortolano, *The Two Cultures Controversy: Science, Literature and Cultural Politics in Postwar Britain* (Cambridge, 2009).

15. D. McKinney, *Magic Circles: The Beatles in Dream and History* (Cambridge, Mass., 2003); K. Gildart, *Images of England Through Popular Music* (Basingstoke, 2013).

16. A. Turner, *Goldfinger* (London, 1998): 89.

17. S. Groes, *British Fictions of the Sixties. The Making of the Swinging Decade* (London, 2016).

18. Or, with a different tone, J. Mortimer, *Dunster* (London, 1992).

19. M. Bradbury, *The History Man* (London, 1975): 227.

20. P. Morley, *The Age of Bowie. How David Bowie Made a World of Difference* (London, 2016).

21. W. Whyte, *Redbrick: A Social and Architectural History of Britain's Civic Universities* (Oxford, 2015).

22. P. Shapely, *The Politics of Housing: Power, Consumers and Urban Culture* (Manchester, 2007).

23. E. Steafel, 'Life of Riley,' *Telegraph Magazine*, 18 Aug. 2018, p. 17.

24. *David Hockney. Fleurs fraîches. Drawings on IPhone and iPad*, Paris exhibition at Fondation Pierre Bergé-Yves Saint Laurent, 2010-11, exhibition brochure: 1.

25. M. Drabble, 'The Spirit of Place: A Certain Road to Happiness,' in *David Hockney. A Bigger Picture*, exhibition catalogue (London, 2012): 38, 41.

26. S. Brett, *The Body on the Beach* (London, 2000): 58.

10 *1900 To the Present: National, American, Europe, or what?*

1. *The Times*, 13 March 2021.
2. J. Sedgwick, *Popular Filmgoing in 1930s Britain. A choice of pleasures* (Exeter, 2000).
3. M. Glancy, *When Hollywood Loved Britain. The Hollywood 'British' film 1939-1945* (Manchester, 1999).
4. A. Heinonem, 'A Tonic to the Empire? The 1951 Festival of Britain and the Empire-Commonwealth,' *Britain and the World*, 8 (2015), pp. 76-99.
5. S. Haggerty, A. Webster and N. White (eds), *The Empire in One City? Liverpool's Inconvenient Imperial Past* (Manchester, 2008).
6. A. Bartie and others, 'Historical Pageants and the Medieval Past in Twentieth-Century England,' *English Historical Review*, 133 (2018), pp. 866-902.
7. J. Walkowitz, *Nights Out. Life in Cosmopolitan London* (New Haven, Conn., 2012).
8. L. Mazdon and C. Wheatley, *French Film in Britain: Sex, Art, and Cinephilia* (Oxford, 2013).
9. M. Pickering, *Blackface Minstrelsy in Britain* (Aldershot, 2008).
10. M. de Nie, *The Eternal Paddy: Irish Identity and the British press, 1798-1882* (Madison, Wisc., 2004).
11. A. K. Chatterjee, *Indians in London: From the Birth of the East India Company to Independent India* (New Delhi, 2021).
12. J. Oliver, *Jamie's Italy* (London, 2005): x.
13. R. Waters, *Thinking Black: Britain, 1904-1985* (Oakland, Calif., 2019).
14. A. Bidnall, *The West Indian Generation. Remaking British Culture in London, 1945-1965* (Liverpool, 2017).

English Culture

Envoi

1. H. Miller, *Politics Personified: Portraiture, Caricature and Visual Culture in Britain, c.1830-1880* (Manchester, 2015).
2. N. Vall, *Cultural Region: North East England, 1945-2000* (Manchester, 2011).
3. For the 1920s to 1960s, C. Hillard, *To Exercise Our Talents: The Democratisation of Writing in Britain* (Cambridge, Mass., 2006).